Security 2020

Security 2020

Reduce Security Risks This Decade

Doug Howard
Kevin Prince

WILEY

Wiley Publishing, Inc.

Security 2020: Reduce Security Risks This Decade

Published by
Wiley Publishing, Inc.
10475 Crosspoint Boulevard
Indianapolis, IN 46256
www.wiley.com

Copyright © 2011 by Doug Howard and Kevin Prince
Published by Wiley Publishing, Inc., Indianapolis, Indiana
Published simultaneously in Canada

ISBN: 978-0-470-63955-9
ISBN: 978-1-118-00831-7 (ebk)
ISBN: 978-1-118-00832-4 (ebk)
ISBN: 978-1-118-00833-1 (ebk)

10 9 8 7 6 5 4 3 2 1

For general information on our other products and services please contact our Customer Care Department within the United States at (877) 762-2974, outside the United States at (317) 572-3993 or fax (317) 572-4002.

Wiley also publishes its books in a variety of electronic formats. Some content that appears in print may not be available in electronic books.

Library of Congress Control Number: 2010932423

I have been fortunate to work with many professionals in the world. Some were business experts, others contributed through capital investments, and many were technology leaders. Equally important were those that I worked alongside of and had the pleasure of supporting in the day-to-day activity of protecting our clients. You know who you are, and to each of you I say THANKS. Special thanks to Bruce Schneier, who was the CTO and founder of Counterpane and who I worked with for over four years. He graciously offered to write the forward to Security 2020 and provide some thoughts throughout. Thanks also to Toby Weir-Jones who contributed his expert review. In good conscience I must recognize my family, for without their support, and the continuous encouragement and consideration of my loving wife, I would not have had the energy to complete this time-consuming goal.

— Doug Howard

To my mom, a single mother with five children, who allowed me as a young boy to max out her only credit card with the purchase of my first computer, which I had to work to pay off with one full year of paper route money. Opportunity often comes when others believe in us and our dreams. That single act by my mother has led to more opportunity, fortune, travel, and other experiences than I could have ever possibly imagined. Thanks for believing in me, mom.

— Kevin Prince

About the Authors

Doug Howard, the CEO of VBrick Systems, leads a team of professionals that has a stated goal of being the world leader within the streaming video industry. In 2010, after over 20 years in the IT security industry, Doug decided to put his historic criticisms to work and try to build security within an IT product. He admits it's a challenging career change, but one he hopes he can look back on when he returns to the IT security industry and say "security can truly be built within the core of a product," as well as bring back to the security industry more experience on how non-security product and application providers can improve their products and services.

When he took his sabbatical from the IT security industry in 2010 to join VBrick, Doug was the chief strategy officer of Perimeter, responsible for the mergers and acquisitions and the service strategy for the company. In addition to his position with Perimeter, he was the president of USA.NET, a company focused on delivering secure unified communications and which was a wholly owned subsidiary of Perimeter.

Prior to joining Perimeter, Doug served as COO of BT Counterpane where he was responsible for the business's ongoing operations. He led the teams responsible for the development, implementation, operations, and marketing of BT Counterpane's product and service line. Earlier he served as vice president of security and business continuity for AT&T Corp. There, he formed an organization that developed and launched new security services for each of the company's business lines of service—commercial, government, wholesale—as well as provided direction for the business continuity practice that delivered solutions for AT&T and its clients.

Doug started his career in the U.S. Air Force, where he worked for the Joint Chiefs of Staff at the Pentagon and had a temporary duty assignment to Cheyenne

Mountain. After the military, he moved into the private sector and held positions in sales, operations, engineering, product management, and business development for companies such as Sprint, FLAG Telecom, Telenet, and Computer Sciences Corporation (CSC). He founded Technology Research International, Inc. in 1989, which was purchased by NBC Broadcasting in 1991.

Doug attended K–12 in eastern North Carolina where he grew up. Like the coauthor of this book, Kevin Prince, Doug came from a humble beginning, and while his family lived in a trailer park (not even a doublewide), his divorced parents never left him wanting for technology. In high school he received his first computer for Christmas, a Radio Shack TRS80 Color. Basic programming was all it did, and he was able to save his work on an attached cassette tape. Looking back, it's hard to believe it all began with a Christmas gift from his parents.

You can find a complete copy of his resume at:

```
http://www.linkedin.com/in/doughoward
```

The most valuable information I convey in this book is based on my interactions with some of the leading experts in the security field. My career strategy has always been simply to work with the smartest people I could find. If I can't be the smartest guy in an area of focus, then I'll befriend the smartest guy. I have been very fortunate to work with some real legends, befriend some of the most impressive intellects, and to have countless meetings and dinners with the most knowledgeable CISOs, CSOs, CIOs, and business people in the world.

I originally conceived this book in such a way that I could leverage this network of experts and create a knowledge base that was a consolidation of a lot of different people's views, the authors acting as moderators to guide the subject areas and focus the discussions. Well, remember that speech about setting a goal and creating a plan? I failed on that when it came to writing a book. So, I again got creative and engaged Kevin Prince, who I work with at Perimeter and who always produced consistent, high-quality content, articles, whitepapers, and the like, and suggested we write a book together and use my original concept. What follows is just that. I hope you enjoy!

Kevin Prince is the Chief Technology officer at Compushare, a SMART Technology Management Solutions provider for the Financial Services Industry. Prior to Compushare Kevin worked as Chief Technology Officer for Perimeter E-Security, a leading managed security service provider.

Kevin is a frequent speaker at various industry conferences, trade shows, and so on. He has written many whitepapers, articles, blog posts, and bylines on information security topics. He has spent considerable time training federal examiners on information security methodologies, technology solutions, and auditing practices. Many people recognize his end of year summaries on information security as well as his threat predictions for the coming year.

Kevin has more than 22 years of information technology experience, 14 of which have been focused specifically on information security. When he was a junior in high school, he began working in the computer labs at Salt Lake Community College (SLCC), where he fixed computers and tutored and helped students. He had a copy of Windows 1.0 on 5 ¼ floppy disks. He later became the Computer Lab Coordinator at SLCC when he was a senior in high school, and began building networks and even taught basic computer use labs to students.

Later Kevin went to work for a company called Intellitrends where he learned how to build computers. He then got a job at National Computer Systems where he did basic PC support. He worked for NCS for 5 years and went from PC support to Network Project Lead, with responsibility for the team that designed and built the network operation center, and supported the wide area network and server farm. That is also when he was introduced to the Internet, and soon after he was responsible for the corporate firewall. He was one of the first Microsoft Certified System Engineers (MCSE) when Microsoft released their training program. He went through a variety of courses, including Cisco certification and many others.

Kevin then had the opportunity to work for a "dot com" startup called Intellispan. He was one of the key individuals tasked with the design and implementation of a PKI-based nationwide secure dial-up network using unheard of "virtual private network" technology. The company raised over 30 million dollars and brought in a new CEO who decided to move the company from Arizona to Georgia. Kevin decided not to move with the company, but they wanted him to stay on so he transitioned into a sales engineering role where he had his first interaction with customers and got to see firsthand what organizations needed. This is where he learned that what they had asked them to build was not exactly what customers wanted. Kevin recommended that they modify the product to give customers what they needed, but the company refused.

Along with a friend, Kevin left Intellispan and started a company called Red Cliff Solutions. They were essentially integrators for a basic suite of information security solutions. The first year of any boot-strap startup is rough, and theirs was no different. After the first year, Kevin's partner decided he needed to get a "real job" and Kevin bought him out. Kevin established relationships with the credit union national association and began offering a managed security solution specifically designed for financial institutions. Later he was asked to train the federal examiners on information security practices and audit procedures. This led to a many speaking engagements each year as well as other partnerships, primarily in the financial space. After 5 years, he had successfully built Red Cliff Solutions into a very successful business that included about 500 financial institution customers. Red Cliff offers solutions such as firewall, intrusion detection and prevention, web content filtering, anti-virus, virtual private networks, and vulnerability assessments, all with 24/7 management and monitoring. In early 2006 Kevin sold Red Cliff Solutions to Perimeter E-Security, the leader in managed security services to financial institutions in the United States.

These experiences have given Kevin a unique blend of technical, sales, compliance, and business expertise. He is able to take real-world needs and understand the business drivers around them. He can help an organization meet regulatory compliance objectives without overselling them things that won't offer appropriate risk mitigation value. His experience lends itself to a high level view of the evolution of information security and where it is headed, so writing *Security 2020* feels very natural. Using 20/20 vision of the history of information security we can look ahead towards the year 2020 and predict the future of information security.

For can view a complete copy of my resume at:

```
http://www.linkedin.com/pub/kevin-prince/3/70a/501
```

Credits

Executive Editor
Carol Long

Project Editor
Tom Dinse

Technical Editors
David A. Chapa
Toby Weir-Jones

Production Editor
Kathleen Wisor

Copy Editor
Foxxe Editorial Services

Editorial Director
Robyn B. Siesky

Editorial Manager
Mary Beth Wakefield

Freelance Editorial Manager
Rosemarie Graham

Marketing Manager
Ashley Zurcher

Production Manager
Tim Tate

**Vice President and Executive
Group Publisher**
Richard Swadley

**Vice President and
Executive Publisher**
Barry Pruett

Associate Publisher
Jim Minatel

Project Coordinator, Cover
Lynsey Stanford

Proofreader
Beth Prouty,
Word One New York

Indexer
Johnna VanHoose Dinse

Cover Image
©Thomas Northcut/Digital Vision/
Getty Images

Cover Designer
Ryan Sneed

Contents at a Glance

Contents

Foreword

There's really no such thing as security in the abstract. Security can only be defined in relation to something else. You're secure from something or against something. In the next 10 years, the traditional definition of IT security—that it protects you from hackers, criminals, and other bad guys—will undergo a radical shift. Instead of protecting you from the bad guys, it will increasingly protect businesses and their business models from you.

Ten years ago, the big conceptual change in IT security was *deperimeterization*. A wordlike grouping of 18 letters with both a prefix and a suffix, it has to be the ugliest word our industry invented. The concept, though—the dissolution of the strict boundaries between the internal and external network—was both real and important.

There's more deperimeterization today than there ever was. Customer and partner access, guest access, outsourced email, VPNs; to the extent there is an organizational network boundary, it's so full of holes that it's sometimes easier to pretend it isn't there. The most important change, though, is conceptual. We used to think of a network as a fortress, with the good guys on the inside and the bad guys on the outside, and walls and gates and guards to ensure that only the good guys got inside. Modern networks are more like cities, dynamic and complex entities with many different boundaries within them. The access, authorization, and trust relationships are even more complicated.

Today, two other conceptual changes matter. The first is *consumerization*. Another ponderous invented word, it's the idea that consumers get the cool new gadgets first, and demand to do their work on them. Employees already have their laptops configured just the way they like them, and they don't want another one just for getting through the corporate VPN. They're already reading their mail on their BlackBerrys or iPads. They already have a home computer, and it's cooler than the standard issue IT department machine. Network administrators are increasingly losing control over clients.

This trend will only increase. Consumer devices will become trendier, cheaper, and more integrated; and younger people are already used to using their own stuff on their school networks. It's a recapitulation of the PC revolution. The centralized computer center concept was shaken by people buying PCs to run VisiCalc; now it's iPads and Android smart phones.

The second conceptual change comes from cloud computing: our increasing tendency to store our data elsewhere. Call it *decentralization*: our email, photos, books, music, and documents are stored somewhere, and accessible to us through our consumer devices. The younger you are, the more you expect to get your digital stuff on the closest screen available. This is an important trend, because it signals the end of the hardware and operating system battles we've all lived with. Windows vs. Mac doesn't matter when all you need is a web browser. Computers become temporary; user backup becomes irrelevant. It's all out there somewhere—and users are increasingly losing control over their data.

During the next 10 years, three new conceptual changes will emerge, two of which we can already see the beginnings of. The first I'll call *deconcentration*. The general-purpose computer is dying and being replaced by special-purpose devices. Some of them, like the iPhone, seem general purpose but are strictly controlled by their providers. Others, like Internet-enabled game machines or digital cameras, are truly special purpose. In 10 years, most computers will be small, specialized, and ubiquitous.

Even on what are ostensibly general-purpose devices, we're seeing more special-purpose applications. Sure, you could use the iPhone's web browser to access the *New York Times* website, but it's much easier to use the NYT's special iPhone app. As computers become smaller and cheaper, this trend will only continue. It'll be easier to use special-purpose hardware and software. And companies, wanting more control over their users' experience, will push this trend.

The second is *decustomerization*—now I get to invent the really ugly words—the idea that we get more of our IT functionality without any business relationship. We're all part of this trend: every search engine gives away its services in exchange for the ability to advertise. It's not just Google and Bing; most webmail and social networking sites offer free basic service in exchange for advertising, possibly with premium services for money. Most websites, even useful ones that take the place of client software, are free; they are either run altruistically or to facilitate advertising.

Soon it will be hardware. In 1999, Internet startup FreePC tried to make money by giving away computers in exchange for the ability to monitor users' surfing and purchasing habits. The company failed, but computers have only gotten cheaper since then. It won't be long before giving away netbooks in exchange for advertising will be a viable business. Or giving away digital cameras. Already there are companies that give away long-distance minutes in exchange for advertising. Free cell phones aren't far off. Of course, not all IT hardware will be free. Some of the new cool hardware will cost too much to be free, and there will always be a need for concentrated computing power close to the user—game systems are an obvious example—but those will be the exception. Where the hardware costs too much to just give away, however, we'll see free or highly subsidized hardware in exchange for locked-in service; that's already the way cell phones are sold.

This is important because it destroys what's left of the normal business relationship between IT companies and their users. We're not Google's customers; we're Google's product that they sell to their customers. It's a three-way relationship: us, the IT service provider, and the advertiser or data buyer. And as these noncustomer IT relationships proliferate, we'll see more IT companies treating us as products. If I buy a Dell computer, then I'm obviously a Dell customer; but if I get a Dell computer for free in exchange for access to my life, it's much less obvious whom I'm entering a business relationship with. Facebook's continual ratcheting down of user privacy in order to satisfy its actual customers—the advertisers—and enhance its revenue is just a hint of what's to come.

The third conceptual change I've termed *depersonization:* computing that removes the user, either partially or entirely. Expect to see more software agents: programs that do things on your behalf, such as prioritize your email based on your observed preferences or send you personalized sales announcements based on your past behavior. The "people who liked this also liked" feature on many retail websites is just the beginning. A website that alerts you if a plane ticket to your favorite destination drops below a certain price is simplistic but useful, and some sites already offer this functionality. Ten years won't be enough time to solve the serious artificial intelligence problems required to fully realize intelligent agents, but the agents of that time will be both sophisticated and commonplace, and they'll need less direct input from you.

Similarly, connecting objects to the Internet will soon be cheap enough to be viable. There's already considerable research into Internet-enabled medical devices, smart power grids that communicate with smart phones, and networked automobiles. Nike sneakers can already communicate with your iPhone. Your phone already tells the network where you are. Internet-enabled appliances are already in limited use, but soon they will be the norm. Businesses will acquire smart HVAC units, smart elevators, and smart inventory systems. And, as short-range communications—like RFID and Bluetooth—become cheaper, everything becomes smart.

The "Internet of things" won't need you to communicate. The smart appliances in your smart home will talk directly to the power company. Your smart car will talk to road sensors and, eventually, other cars. Your clothes will talk to your dry cleaner. Your phone will talk to vending machines; they already do in some countries. The ramifications of this are hard to imagine; it's likely to be weirder and less orderly than the contemporary press describes it. But certainly smart objects will be talking about you, and you probably won't have much control over what they're saying.

One old trend: deperimeterization. Two current trends: consumerization and decentralization. Three future trends: deconcentration, decustomerization, and depersonization. That's IT in 2020—it's not under your control, it's doing things without your knowledge and consent, and it's not necessarily acting in your best interests. And this is how things will be when they're working as they're intended to work; I haven't even started talking about the bad guys yet.

That's because IT security in 2020 will be less about protecting you from traditional bad guys, and more about protecting corporate business models from you. Deperimeterization assumes everyone is untrusted until proven otherwise. Consumerization requires networks to assume all user devices are untrustworthy until proven otherwise. Decentralization and deconcentration won't work if you're able to hack the devices to run unauthorized software or access unauthorized data. Deconsumerization won't be viable unless you're unable to bypass the ads, or whatever the vendor uses to monetize you. And depersonization requires the autonomous devices to be, well, autonomous.

In 2020—10 years from now—Moore's Law predicts that computers will be 100 times more powerful. That'll change things in ways we can't know, but we do know that human nature never changes. Cory Doctorow rightly pointed out that all complex ecosystems have parasites. Society's traditional parasites are criminals, but a broader definition makes more sense here. As we users lose control of those systems and IT providers gain control for their own purposes, the definition of "parasite" will shift. Whether they're criminals trying to drain your bank account, movie watchers trying to bypass whatever copy protection studios are using to protect their profits, or Facebook users trying to use the service without giving up their privacy or being forced to watch ads, parasites will continue to try to take advantage of IT systems. They'll exist, just as they always have existed, and—like today—security is going to have a hard time keeping up with them.

Welcome to the future. Companies will use technical security measures, backed up by legal security measures, to protect their business models. And unless you're a model user, the parasite will be you.

— Bruce Schneier

Introduction

The future is a result of the thoughts, dreams, and actions we take each day. Much like a butterfly's wings resulting in a hurricane across the world, the seemingly small actions we take within our daily roles in IT security can result in something as gentle as the wind, or as destructive as a hurricane.

—Doug Howard

Allow us to start with the obvious: the world around us is extremely fragile—the Earth's environment is fragile, the human psyche is fragile, and the technology on which we daily depend is fragile. To maintain the balance between Mother Nature, humanity, and technology, we must plan, execute, and adapt our activities. Regardless of how inconsequential each of us may feel at times relative to broader world events, each of us has a role in maintaining this balance. There should be no doubt that if each of us takes responsibility and contributes in small, simple ways, we can help maintain this extraordinary equilibrium in the world. This may seem an overly optimistic, maybe even a flowery statement, but we have all seen what big impacts small actions can have on an individual, an organization, and on the world as a whole. A small number of people in the world make headlines, but millions make an impact each and every day. Our goal in this book is simply to provide you with knowledge that can be used to perform your role as a user, an administrator, or as an executive to make the world of the future a little more secure than it is today. We accomplish this by providing you with a foundation of information for today's activities, but more broadly, with a view of the changes that are predictable through 2020 and beyond. This glimpse of the future will allow you to create and adapt your unique plan to worldly realities, threats, and demands as they evolve. Within these pages you will find content that will support your functions as an information technology (IT) security expert within this evolving and complex technology ecosystem.

These predictions, forecasts, and stories will be valuable assets for planning your strategies, tactics, and activities and have a small (or, it is our hope, a profound) impact on your organization and the world.

When establishing a goal or objective, you must understand the building blocks that will make up a plan to reach that goal. Not all plans will include the same building blocks, but the core components are the same within most organizations when it comes to IT security. When creating an effective security program for an enterprise, you must understand not only the technology capabilities and limitations, but also the future technology, industry, regulatory, and business opportunities and challenges that will impact your future strategies and tactical actions, as well as your capital and operational investments. This book provides you with the information you need to understand how these core components influence and are influenced by the future.

As authors, we feel that not only must our predictions for the future be based on a realistic assessment of where IT security has been, but we must also consider how periods of rapid technological change and unexpected technology revolutions have and will affect the future. All this must also be balanced with the recognition that rapid change in business will be matched equally with new and evolving complexity, threats, and risk.

The Authors

While both of us believe we have a good grip on the marketplace, we also recognize that there are many right answers to every question in the security industry. We also recognize the value of having perspectives from business leaders, users, and investors, as well as from technology leaders. Therefore, we've written the book in a format that allows us to easily introduce the thoughts and observations of many contributors into various sections. In some cases, they simply reinforce what we have stated, while at other times they completely disagree with us or provide a completely different perspective from ours. In all cases, they add richness of content and experience to the book.

Now let's take a step back and set some context. One of the key considerations each of us noodles on when we pick up any book is what credibility, experiences, and perspectives do the authors bring to the subject area or the story? More specifically, what real-world experience does the author bring that will help me better understand the subject? Since this is our first book, it was recommended that we provide you some background on our experience and perspective so as to better establish our credibility on the subjects of security, business continuity, and governance. If you're like us, you have a unique set of skills and experiences that many of your peers could learn from. We are no different. Sure we've probably spoken at more venues, been quoted in the press often, and even shown up on radio and television shows representing the security industry, but those are simply footnotes in one's career. What's important is if we convey our knowledge and experience in an entertaining and professional manner. Maybe even more important are the experiences and opinions of our peers that we have brought to bear throughout.

The Variables of 2020

In order to understand our experiences, we welcome you into our minds, the minds of IT security professionals who have lived the life of fun, intrigue, risk, stress, and many sleepless nights . . . rarely does boredom find its way into our lives. Unlike many professionals in the IT security industry, we have spent the majority of our lives in IT security services companies. This may not seem to be an important differentiation; however, it allows us to provide you with a significant insight into the context of our vantage point. While most enterprise IT security professionals will have a few interesting experiences in their professional lives, those of you, as we have, who work as service providers see many more security incidents because of the number of customers they support. In addition to protecting hundreds, sometimes thousands of customer networks simultaneously, you also must protect one of the largest, most valuable targets there is . . . your own service provider network. It's often said that working for an IT security service provider exposes you to the world, threats, and not so obvious risks like no other role in the industry. It certainly will age you a little faster, too.

Leveraging these real-world experiences, our network of contributing authors, and industry information, we first provide a historical review and then a look into the future of IT security. Thus, the book provides those with little IT expertise an overview and historical perspective of IT security; it is also a good refresher for experts. History, or 20-20 views of the past, provide each of us a great base of knowledge from which to grow. No matter how vast or limited your experience is, you are always forced to start with what you know. When we began the journey of writing this book, we knew far less than when we completed it; often this was because of input from others, sometimes because of research, and surprisingly frequently because of our just taking the time to think through a subject. A series of projections based on what we know today and how various factors will influence those projections is the resulting content. Our journey into the future attempts to connect your emotions and imagination with the evolutions and revolutions in the IT security industry through 2020 and beyond. While many of the subjects are technical in nature, this is meant to be a book to awaken the concerns associated with reality and actual risk, while debunking media hype and unnecessary concerns. It stays high-level due to the breadth of subjects, but hopefully it's deep enough to provide value for each reader. We also outline future risk scenarios that may surprise you and some that you may have already considered. The book further prepares you with knowledge that can be used to anticipate and prepare for the threats in the upcoming years.

The future is defined by many variables, and many of them are in constant flux. Is that a statement to hedge our bets? No, simply a disclaimer to say neither of us claims to be futurist, rather intelligent players within the industry. Most of the projections we make are logical extensions of the trends and technologies already in play today. We chose the title *Security 2020* for two reasons: first, because 20-20 reflects that vision in hindsight that is often so valuable, and secondly, that 2020 is only 10 years from now and making projections with reasonable accuracy is an achievable goal.

As we mentioned earlier in this introduction, our goal is simply to provide you with knowledge that can be used to perform your role as a user, an administrator, or as an executive to make the world of the future a little more secure than it is today. We hope when you finish this book you will feel that you have a few more building blocks in your plan, some considerations to adjust based on future predictions, and an appreciation for the job security that the IT security industry can provide in the foreseeable future.

Security 2020

What Has History Shown Us?

*The good news is that we can predict the future
by knowing we are bound to repeat the past.*

—Kevin Prince

Hindsight is clearly not 20/20!

Most people believe that, with the passing of time, an accurate history is documented and we may rely on that record as a true witness of the past. The truth is that the history that we are taught is often very different from the realities of the past.

Often, histories are not accurately documented because of the biases of those doing the recording. Sometimes story elements are handed down many times, with each repetition bringing about a slight change. Sometimes history is rewritten to hide shame, some horrific act, or an action that is no longer politically acceptable. Still other times, storytellers exaggerate the story each time they tell it to keep the listeners engaged. Whether it be one Egyptian ruler having the carvings, names, manuscripts, and sculptures of the previous pharaoh destroyed and his own likeness put in their place, or a short, overweight, and sexually confused European prince having all the paintings of him show him as a tall, strong man with a beautiful woman beside him, we have a habit of changing our recorded histories based on the history we want, not the realities that occurred.

Pick up any history book in any school in America and you can read the story of the midnight ride of Paul Revere. This experience got little attention during his life and for another 40 years after his death, when Henry Wadsworth Longfellow wrote the famous poem "Paul Revere's Ride," later memorized by generations of schoolchildren and which included the famous lines: "Listen, my children, and you shall hear / of the midnight ride of Paul Revere." Longfellow took many liberties with the events of that evening, most especially giving sole credit to Paul Revere, when in reality there were several riders. Revere and the others didn't shout "The British are coming," but rather "The Regulars are coming out."

So, why is it that we remember this important night as the sole work of one man? Was Paul Revere selected for the poem as a result of his role, or because his last name rhymes with "hear"? Would one of the other riders have received all the credit if it had been written "Listen, my children for there is cause that led to the ride of William Dawes"?

Now that you've seen how an inaccurate historical record can gain currency, this chapter will show you, through a review of information security history—including the milestones and millstones—how, with an accurate view of history, we are better able to predict future events. By knowing what is likely to come, we are better equipped to make changes now so that we can achieve the future that we desire rather than repeating the mistakes of the past. There is now enough water under the information security bridge to analyze, and even predict, what we might see in the future.

The History of Data Breach Disclosure

Changing the historical record is a behavior companies have exhibited in the past and still exhibit today. Since the early days of computers, there have been data breaches. However, companies often chose to sweep them under the rug. Because of that practice, it wasn't until the first data breach disclosure law (SB 1386) went into effect in California on July 1, 2003 that we began to get some sense of the frequency and impact of these breaches, and of the methodology used by criminals to compromise networks. Prior to that time, we had little information regarding data breaches because companies rarely disclosed them. The only breaches we became aware of were those that were made public as a result of insider information leakage, the occasional whistle blower, or when fraud or other crimes were committed as a result of the breach.

Of course, data security breaches happened quite frequently prior to 2003, but organizations would attempt to hide or downplay them to limit financial loss, to avoid a negative impact on their reputations and brands, and to avoid public ridicule. They would do just about everything they could to rewrite their histories of data compromise, but the information that was stolen or compromised by cyber-criminals would be used to commit fraud and identity theft. Horror stories were seen on the news about how people's lives had been turned upside down and their credit ruined as a result of cyber-theft. Consumers began to become very concerned. Enough cases came to light that lawmakers began to take notice.

California led the way for state data breach disclosure laws. Now 45 states, the District of Columbia, Puerto Rico, and the U.S. Virgin Islands (at the time of this writing) have similar laws. South Dakota, New Mexico, Kentucky, Alabama, and Mississippi are the only states who do not yet have similar legislation. Additionally, a number of bills that would establish a national standard for data security breach notification have been introduced in the U.S. Congress, but none has passed Congress as of this writing.

As a result of these laws, the past several years have seen thousands of data breaches disclosed, giving us a significant data set to analyze for trends, sources, motivations, targets, methods, and more. Data breaches come from a variety of sources including hackers, malicious insiders, careless and untrained employees, thieves, improper document and equipment disposal, and third parties, to name just a few.

One result of the increased knowledge about data breaches has been an increase in the terminology used to describe information security threats. However, information security experts classify, label, and discuss information security threats to the point where the average person does not even understand what they are talking about. Most Americans could not tell you the difference between a virus and a worm unless you are talking about something that makes you sick and something that wiggles. What about all those words that begin with "ph" like phishing, pharming, phreaking, and the like? It might help to know that every bad thing that happens in information security can be put into one of two basic categories: *vulnerability exploits* (discussed next) and *insiders* (discussed at length later in the book). In the late 1990s and in the first several years of the twenty-first century, cyber-attacks primarily resulted from vulnerability exploits.

The History of Vulnerability Exploits

A vulnerability is simply a flaw in the way software is written, configured, or implemented. In other words, a vulnerability is an aspect of a program that can be manipulated to do something that it was not designed or intended to do. This software could be an application like Microsoft Word, Adobe Acrobat, or Oracle, or an operating system (OS) like Windows 7, Macintosh, or Linux. It could even be an Internet browser such as Internet Explorer, Opera, or Firefox. Hackers exploit these software vulnerabilities to force systems to grant them access to unauthorized data, run malicious code, gain remote control, or infect the system further.

In the early days of computers, we referred to problems in software as "bugs." The term came from moths that would get caught in the vacuum tubes of the first computers. These bugs would cause the circuit to short and need to be cleaned or replaced. Modern day "bugs" or software programming flaws—which we call vulnerabilities—exist in nearly all computer software. These vulnerabilities can be detected and exploited, which can lead to a criminal's ability to fully compromise and completely control the system under attack.

Cyber-criminals use these vulnerabilities to compromise systems such as personal computers, workstations, databases, print servers, and file servers. Systems that are accessible directly from the Internet such as email servers, web servers, and firewalls are often targeted to find and exploit any discovered vulnerabilities. These systems can be attacked from any other system on the Internet, wherever it is in the world, because there are no borders and no universal laws governing the Internet.

Software developers with malicious intent began writing software that would programmatically exploit these system vulnerabilities and spread to other systems with similar vulnerabilities. The first of these systematic exploits were called *computer viruses*. Some computer viruses exploit software glitches and bugs, while others simply need a human to perform an action (which is often as easy as "double-clicking") to infect systems and spread to others.

The History of Viruses and Worms

Computer viruses, Trojans, and computer worms were often used to perpetrate attacks in the early days of computers. Viruses with self-propagation techniques have been around for quite some time. For example, the Christmas Tree EXEC virus brought down a number of the world's mainframes over two decades ago, in 1987.

Virus outbreaks on personal computers at a significant scale began in the 1980s with viruses that were passed primarily on floppy disk. However, as soon as personal computers began to be connected to each other (more specifically these networks began to be connected together over the Internet), viruses on personal computers for the first time could do global damage.

The ILOVEYOU virus hit personal computers beginning on May 4, 2000 with the subject line of "ILOVEYOU" and an attachment. Upon opening the attachment, the virus would infect the system, send a copy of itself to everyone in the user's address list (appearing to come from the user), and perform malicious acts such as overwriting important files. It spread to 10 percent of the computers connected to the Internet in a single day, and within nine days had infected 50 million systems. This was one of those eye-opening moments for IT and security persons, as we saw just how destructive malicious code like this could be and how quickly it could spread.

Then, in July of 2001, we saw the Code Red worm, which attacked Microsoft's IIS web servers. On the 19th of that month, 359,000 servers were infected. While the patch that would make systems impervious to this exploit had existed for over a year, many IT administrators weren't as yet taking timely patching seriously. In fact, the vulnerability that Code Red exploited first came to light in June of 1999. Additionally, this attack performed a "buffer overflow," which manipulates the memory of a system when the developer has not properly restricted utilization.

January 25, 2003 was the day that the SQL Slammer worm infected 75,000 victims within 10 minutes, which accounted for 90 percent of all vulnerable systems. This was another time when a patch had been available long before the worm was unleashed. In this case, the patch had been released six months earlier. Sometimes I wonder if the greater damage was caused by the way SQL Slammer exploited a vulnerability and self-propagated to other vulnerable systems, or by the IT administrators who left their systems unpatched for months or years. Incidents like this highlight the fact that all cyber-crimes are the result of a vulnerability exploit, carelessness, or both.

The History of Edge-Based Security

Vulnerability exploits, whether by direct attack, virus, worm, or something else, were the most common method used by cyber-criminals for several years. One of the reasons they were so successful was that operating systems used at the time (primarily Microsoft Windows) had a nearly unlimited number of these vulnerabilities that could be exploited. The first major mistake we made was not developing operating systems and software applications with security in mind. This is a lesson that, even now, many developers haven't learned or don't practice effectively. This lack of discipline created a very lucrative and powerful cyber-crime underworld that we will spend the next several decades combating. While there is no way to write software that is vulnerability free, the expertise and difficulty level required to exploit systems should be much higher.

The second major mistake we made was thinking that we could create a fortified barrier between our networks and the attackers on the Internet to keep our systems secure. We call this *edge-*, or *perimeter-based security*, which is roughly equivalent to the use of a moat and defensive walls during medieval times to protect a castle. While these limited or slowed some attack types, invaders resorted to other methods such as catapulting diseased body parts over the walls or loosing fiery arrows to burn the inhabitants out.

On August 12, 2004 most computer users had a very bad day. Their computer systems simply stopped working. That is the day when Windows XP Service Pack 2 was released. For the first time, Microsoft enabled by default a security software firewall. Many applications were written to take advantage of the native insecurity of the Windows platform. When the security features were enabled, many applications stopped working.

What most people do not realize is that this fundamental change by Microsoft packed a huge blow to hackers. Until that time, most cyber-criminals considered hacking into systems relatively easy, especially if they were accessible directly from the Internet. Now the systems that were the most highly prized by hackers were protected with some basic security software. The hackers had to develop alternative methods to compromise systems.

Firewall appliances are used by just about every organization that has a high-speed connection to the Internet. Firewalls are quite effective devices to stop inbound traffic. What I mean is that, if you do not want to allow any traffic from the Internet into your network, you can simply turn off all inbound access, and your firewall, regardless of make, model, and age, will do a fair job of keeping this traffic out. That works for businesses, however, that do not want any traffic to enter their network. Today, this is not a viable option for most companies. Organizations need to receive email. They want to have their customers access their website. The Internet is an amazingly diverse platform on which an unlimited number of applications can reside. Any time one of these applications (or *services* as they are called) needs to allow inbound traffic from the Internet, a *port* or *access point* needs to be opened on the firewall to allow traffic in. Most businesses now have many ports open on their firewall to conduct business. Each port acts as a door through which they can access systems on the network. All cyber-criminals need to do is see if they have a *key* (in the form of a vulnerability exploit) to enter. While firewalls still have value, they can no longer be looked at as the single defensive measure that needs to be taken.

We all knew the limitations of firewalls, and with the expanding use of the Internet, their security efficacy became less and less. The result was that intrusion detection systems (IDS) and intrusion prevention systems (IPS) that did more than just simple port filtering and monitoring were used. These devices analyzed the traffic and compared the contents with known hacker scripts and attacks. In other words, a firewall is like a toll booth where there are rules that say yellow buses and all minivans can pass, but nothing else. An IDS/IPS will look at the vehicle *and* what is inside. It attempts to determine what the payload of the car is. Does any of the cargo match explosives? Do any of the passengers match terror suspects?

Both firewalls and IDS/IPS devices were used by most organizations that had systems and networks they needed to protect. Companies felt that as long as they had both a firewall and an IDS/IPS, they were safe from hackers. This created a society-wide sense of security that continues to this day. The truth is that, while firewalls and IDS/IPS systems are usually necessary for good network and system security, they are only a small part of what a total package needs to include. Some organizations, I am sad to say, get very little protection from these solutions because of improper deployment, misconfiguration, and lack of resources to analyze the events that are generated.

The History of Patching

Many security experts believe that the false sense of security that organizations got from their firewalls led to poor execution of patching systems. Patching a system effectively makes it no longer vulnerable to the specific exploit the patch is designed to mitigate. A vulnerability is similar to finding out that the manufacturer of the lock on your door at home made a mistake and millions of keys are available that can open your door. Rather than going out and buying a new lock, or rekeying it, you decide to put up a fence to keep criminals out of your yard. Then, you add a camera to view the yard 24/7, combined with adding a guard to respond to someone coming through the fence. Surely, you can see how absurd this would be; yet this is the approach IT administrators have taken for many years in regard to their system security. If we should have learned anything from these worms, viruses, and other attack methods, it is that nothing equals the value of patching a system.

In July 2007, Verizon acquired CyberTrust, one of the leaders in data security. Verizon's business risk management team released a report[1] at the end of 2008 that analyzed more than 500 data breach incidents that they had been involved in, for forensic investigation. One of the aspects they looked at was the availability of patches at the time an information security breach occurred where a vulnerability exploit was used. In other words, they asked: "If a vulnerability was exploited as part of the data breach, was there a patch available but not applied? If there was, how long had it been available? How negligent had the IT administrators been?" Figure 1-1 shows a pie chart illustrating the length of time between when a vulnerability was reported and when a patch addressing it was available.

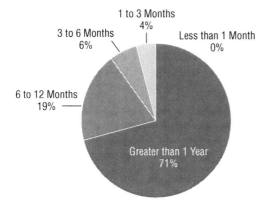

Figure 1-1

Verizon's findings showed that 90 percent of vulnerabilities exploited had patches available for longer than six months. The remaining 10 percent of cases had patches available for between one and six months. There were no incidents in their caseload where patches weren't available or a 0-Day exploit was used (where an exploit occurs using a vulnerability where no patch exists).

It was only a few years ago that software programmers began to be trained in and conscious of information security development practices. This has helped significantly; however, more and more code is built on code from the past. You have to try to imagine the billions of lines of code that are currently in use today, and only a small fraction has ever been analyzed or written within a security framework or by someone with application security training. This means that, for many years to come, we will continue to be plagued with a tremendous number of vulnerabilities and their associated exploits.

According to the open source vulnerability database (OSVDB), on average, there are 20 new vulnerabilities found on a daily basis. The current database of vulnerabilities and exploits is larger than 40,000. Looking deeper into the study by Verizon cited earlier in this section, it shows that, most of the time, hackers use well-known (older) vulnerabilities more frequently than more recently discovered ones. One may conclude that it is simply easier to use the tried-and-true exploits, especially when the number of vulnerable targets is so plentiful.

Maybe trying to tackle the problem of vulnerability exploits is just too difficult. Maybe we have to attack the problem from the other side; going after the hackers themselves.

Hacker Methodologies

I am often asked why we can't just track down these "hackers" and throw them into prison. This is very difficult to do for a variety of reasons. First, hackers usually don't exploit other systems from the computer they are sitting in front of. Usually their system has access to another system that has remote control of yet another system and so forth. Sometimes each computer that is controlled and subsequently sending commands to another computer is a referred to as a *hop*. The distance between the attacker's computer and the system they are trying to exploit can be as many as 10 or more hops.

Furthermore, these various exploited computers might reside in nations that are not on good terms with each other. For example, if I wanted to attack a system in the United States, using a compromised system in China to do that has a lot of advantages. Obviously, the U.S. government, when attempting to perform any type of forensic investigation, will have a difficult time getting China to cooperate, but I would control the system in China from one in the U.K. and I would control that one from India. Using various systems in nations that are not friendly with each other makes the attack virtually impossible to track down. World politics provides a great level of protection to cyber-criminals. Spain, for instance, has few laws concerning many aspects of information security. It is not unusual to see various types of cyber-attacks launched from Spain as a result.

Most security professionals will tell you that if a talented hacker wants to break into your organization, they can and they will. Some organizations believe that because they haven't been compromised, their security posture must be adequate. I often ask them, "How do you know you aren't compromised? How do you know that a hacker hasn't infiltrated your network and right now has access to whatever systems and data you have on your network?" At the same time, many organizations have successfully maintained the integrity of their networks up to now. One of the main reasons that this is the case is simply that there are so many available systems and networks to compromise. Hackers simply haven't gotten to those systems yet. Hackers' motives are not terribly complicated. If there is something they want from you, they will get it. If not, it is a game of attacking the lowest-hanging fruit. They will simply compromise those systems and networks that are the easiest to exploit.

While we have been feeling safe and secure behind our firewalls and network intrusion detection systems, cyber-criminals have developed more sinister ways of compromising networks. Using these methods, cyber-criminals can bypass firewalls and subvert intrusion detection and prevention systems.

There are two classifications of attacks. One is *inbound attacks*. The other is *malware*. Inbound attacks require a greater degree of technical sophistication. Malware usually involves some kind of social engineering or an insider mistake. Inbound attack methods are used when a cyber-criminal has a specific target. Malware can be used more broadly but is also often used in specific attacks.

Inbound Attacks

One method for a direct inbound attack is to scramble the sequence that the data packets are usually sent in. Because some IDSs rely on packets coming through the network sequentially to properly identify a hacker "signature," scrambling the order of these packets prevents detection by the IDS, which sits between the source and destination systems. The destination device reassembles the packets in their proper order as part of its standard session-building process.

Encoding is another method that can trick an IDS. Encoding is a method of changing elements of the packet in a way that does not change the message on the receiving side but is sufficient to evade an IDS. For example, the Unicode equivalent of a space (when you press the space bar) is "%20". So all spaces can be replaced with %20 in a message. If the IDS signature is not designed to "normalize" the traffic by replacing all %20s with a space, it may miss the attack.

While methods such as these are employed by cyber-criminals to carry out direct attacks against specific targets, most hackers have moved to the use of malware for easier, quicker exploitation of systems.

The History of Malware

Less sophisticated tactics were developed and quickly became the primary methods employed by hackers to compromise networks and systems. Malware, which is short for *malicious software*, is software specifically written to infect a system, usually opening up "back doors" for remote control. Malicious software is often written for a specific purpose. *Malware* describes any software that the user or administrator of a system did not authorize or want on their computer. It goes by many names, including spyware, grayware, adware, Trojan horses, keystroke loggers, back doors, rootkits, and more. Each of those has its own specific characteristics. The industry has seemed to move toward a more simplified approach, calling any and all of this bad software "malware."

Because the technical skill requirement for inbound attacks was increasing, less sophisticated hackers turned to malware to accomplish the same thing. Once installed (so the machine is then infected), the software is nearly invisible and the firewall, IDS/IPS, and other traditional edge- or network-based security solutions cannot detect or stop the traffic this software enables. The trick for criminals is to get the malware installed on the systems sitting behind the security measures. They have developed many ways to accomplish this, including sending the malware directly to users, for example, in a phishing email. They also lure unsuspecting victims to websites that are compromised or hosted by the attackers, where simply accessing the website could compromise the end user's system with malware. This method has been termed *drive-by downloads*. Criminals lure users out to these sites with any of several methods, including phishing emails, pharming attacks, search engine manipulation (also known as search engine poisoning), and a variety of others.

PHARMING

Pharming attacks include several methods that allow attackers to capture data or compromise systems without any fault by the user. A domain name system (DNS) poisoning attack might be used to change an IP address and effectively redirect traffic to a compromised or malicious site. Website defacement might be used to inject a script that redirects users to an alternate site. "Hosts" file manipulation, iFrame use, man-in-the-middle attacks, or other methods that capture data or compromise systems are commonly known as pharming attacks.

Once malware is successfully loaded on an internal machine, nearly all edge-based security solutions are useless. Firewalls are not normally configured to block egress (outbound) traffic. Even when egress filtering is used, certain ports are required to be open for normal use—such as port 80 for web browsing. The malware uses these common ports to "phone home" to the command and control (C&C) systems to get software updates and new instructions. It can also use these ports to transmit captured sensitive information from the malware, including login and system credentials obtained from keyloggers and screen captures, and other network traffic from sniffers. The malware often uses encryption so that an IDS/IPS cannot decrypt or analyze the traffic. The command and control, as well as any extracted data, is virtually invisible to all traditional security solutions.

The outbound connections are made in such a way that a hacker or command and control system can take remote control of the compromised PC. Additional malicious software can be loaded, with the result that the system is effectively under the control of the hacker. Command and control instructions can be issued in myriad ways. The system can call home to a website or other Internet-accessible system; use peer-to-peer (P2P) protocols; or use a knock technique, whereby a series of specific packets in a specific order sent at particular times can invoke action, as well as many other methods. Each method has its pros and cons. For example, the call home to a website method is very simple for hackers to use but also easy to detect and block. Open source communities research, track, and report these sites. This detection can also lead to the shutdown of the malicious site. The knock method is more limited in its use because it only works well for Internet-accessible devices, but it can stay completely under the radar from a detection perspective.

However, relying on individual users to make mistakes, or taking an action that compromises their systems without their knowledge, is not the only method hackers employ. Once any system is infected by malware, there are several other methods the software can use to compromise additional systems. Scanning for and exploiting vulnerabilities now becomes quite effective, because the software is operating from the inside of the network and is not being blocked by a firewall. Internal systems often don't have the same level of security applied to them that Internet-accessible ones do. They often are not patched and maintained with the same frequency that Internet-accessible systems are. Much malware even uses portable media such as USB thumb drives to infect systems and spread. This makes it relatively easy to compromise and spread to other internal systems.

The impact of compromised internal systems cannot be overstated. These are the same computers that employees use to perform work each day. These are the servers that house the intellectual property of a company. These are the systems that process orders, credit cards, billing, and payment information. These are the internal computers that maintain healthcare, insurance, employment, and other information. With internal computers under the control of someone else, "the game is over," as they say.

Automated Attacks

Performing vulnerability exploits directly from systems on the Internet is still a common practice today. However, this process is very often automated. A system under the command and control of a hacker can go system by system, IP address by IP address, and scan for vulnerabilities on any other Internet system. Once a vulnerable system is found, it can exploit that system, install back-door software and Trojan horses, and almost immediately start using the new system to scan, compromise, spread, and infect other systems. These automated applications are freely available on the Internet with point-and-click graphical user interfaces (GUIs) that nearly anyone can use.

An individual computer is capable of making hundreds or thousands of these requests every second. When you look at the number of compromised systems being used for automated vulnerability exploits, you will quickly see that there is so much of this behavior happening on the Internet that most systems are subjected to many scans every day. A few years ago, the University of Maryland did a study in an attempt to see just how often these scans actually occur. The result? On average, they saw an automated network or vulnerability scan every 38 seconds.

When less technically sophisticated persons hear this, they usually freak out, and it is easy to see why. Imagine if every few minutes you had a burglar rattling your front door knob or checking to see if your windows were unlocked. You would be calling the police every few minutes. Many companies expect their security staff or third-party security providers to react each time this happens. The problem is that it happens so frequently that it has become all but "background noise" to security experts. The reality is that, for many years now, we have had to ignore this activity and actually focus on when attackers get inside the network, rather than simply "prowling around outside."

The History of Hacker Motivation

While all of this was going on, hackers were getting smarter in terms of economics, not just technology. At the end of the 1990s and early in the following decade, we would often see defaced websites, where a hacker would compromise the site, changing it to show a picture or some innocuous message. Pictures of themselves holding up signs or political messages were commonly seen. For a time, there were even contests held where various hacker groups would see who could compromise the most sites in a weekend. There were websites dedicated to the standings and achievements of these individuals and groups. I was always amazed that cyber-criminals had fully compromised these sites and had complete access, but all they did was put their picture up. Well, this practice quickly ended when they learned that good money could be made through compromising systems.

The economics of cyber-crime are quite compelling. When 0-day exploit code can be sold for three times the American annual median household income, you can probably see why some people do this. Money is made on the compromise, capture, extraction, selling, reselling, and use of the information. There is a clear and unmistakable relationship between the money a cyber-criminal can make, and their creative use of the latest technology and exploitation methods. In 2008, Bruce Schneier, one of the industry's foremost experts, said:

> *Modern worms are stealthier and they are professionally written. The criminals have gone upmarket, and they're organized and international because there is real money to be made.*

> *Bruce Schneier (John Markoff, "Thieves Winning Online War, Maybe Even in Your Computer," New York Times, December 5, 2008.)*

Previously, I said that because of Windows XP Service Pack 2, "the systems that were the most highly prized" were now protected. Service Pack 2 is a software update or "patch" that helps protect the individual system. Pirated versions of software do not receive updates and are, therefore, more susceptible to compromise. In many parts of the world, especially developing nations, pirated software continues to be a major problem. This means trouble for all of us because the number of these systems that fall under the control of cyber-crime organizations and malicious individuals is staggering.

The History of Botnets

When a system gets infected with malware and falls under the command and control of another, the system is then referred to as a *zombie*. When many zombies are under the command and control of an individual or group, the collective zombies are known as a *botnet* (roBOT NETwork).

Vint Cerf—who is most often called "the father of the Internet"—at the January 2007 World Economic Forum in Davos, Switzerland said that up to 25 percent of PCs were compromised and part of a botnet. At the time, there were 600 million computers with Internet access. Today there are estimated to be 1.2 billion computers on the Internet and a higher percentage of infections than ever before. We're sure even Al Gore would agree with this.

In February 2000, a high school student who went by the moniker Mafiaboy took down several prominent websites, including Dell, CNN, Amazon.com, eBay, E*Trade, and the second most popular website at the time, Yahoo.com. He did this through a vulnerability exploit of systems on about 200 university networks in the United States, to which he then launched a series of distributed denial of service attacks (DDOS). These systems simultaneously would flood a website with requests to establish a session. With hundreds or thousands of systems sending thousands of requests each second, the websites were not able to respond to legitimate requests. This marks one of the first highly publicized instances of botnets.

In the subsequent years, the sophistication, stealthiness, methods of transmission, and infection rates of malware increased to mind-blowing levels. For example, modern botnet software can infect other systems through email, direct network access, malware websites, and portable media. While corporate workstations are not immune to malware infection, the greatest numbers of zombies come from home computers and those using pirated operating system software.

Today's botnets are controlling on average 250,000 computers each, with some appearing to control 10 million systems or more. The force of a single computer is amazing, but when thousands or millions of systems (zombies) work collectively and simultaneously, the power they wield is unimaginable. So while pirating software seems to be a harmless act, it has escalated into one of the greatest threats to us today.

The History of Search Engine Hacking

Another weapon in the hacker's ever-growing arsenal is Internet search engines. *Google hacking* is a term applied to using search engines to find targets. Search engines have done an absolutely amazing job of indexing sites on the Internet. This happens automatically and fairly frequently. The advanced searching capabilities give attackers several methods of finding vulnerable systems. For example, web servers that are new often have default web pages that get indexed. If you search for these pages, you will get a list of brand-new systems that haven't been configured or protected. Web pages that have scripting language or other code that can be compromised are indexed, and searching on the file names or other criteria will give you an exact list of vulnerable sites. For example, a vulnerable operating system might have a file named "remotex.scr" that can be exploited. As Google indexes the site, it would capture that file name. This allows hackers to type "remotex.scr" into Google and find all the websites that have this file and are, therefore, vulnerable. This type of attack works well if the hackers aren't targeting any particular organization, but there are other methods that can target specific companies. Sometimes source code for web pages and applications is indexed in search engines. This can be analyzed by attackers and then exploits can be run, specifically designed for companies that use those programs.

The History of Data Loss

While there are many scenarios where data loss takes place, search engines exacerbate the problem. There are many data breach incidents where an untrained or careless employee inadvertently posts a database, Excel spreadsheet, Word document, or other file with sensitive information to a location that can be indexed by a search engine. In fact, between 2000 and 2009, this was the number one cause of data security breaches. Cyber-criminals can search on common extensions such as `.xls` or `.doc` and find file after file of information that often an organization had no intention of posting online. Also, often it isn't enough to simply remove the files or information from the Web. Once information is posted, indexed, and cached on the Web, it is often very difficult to have it not be out in cyberspace in one form or another. The Internet never forgets.

As a result of these and other methods of exploitation, many data breaches have occurred in the past several years. Thousands of data breaches are known, primarily as a result of the data breach disclosure laws now in effect in most states. According to some research, most organizations still sweep these incidents under the carpet. According to one survey[2] taken at an RSA conference, only 11 percent of data breaches are actually disclosed. In the other 89 percent of cases, companies would rather deal with potential fines from noncompliance rather than the backlash and other negative repercussions from public disclosure. Sometimes they are just rolling the dice to see if they will get caught or not. With the average cost of a data breach reaching $6.6 million at an average of about $200/record compromised, it is easy to see why some organizations take this approach. This doesn't take into account the cost of lawsuits that almost always follow publicly disclosed breaches. Even with publicly disclosed data breaches, in 25 percent of cases the number of records compromised is not disclosed. Perhaps the company doesn't know how many records were involved in the incident; others likely just don't disclose the number to help reduce negative exposure.

A common approach taken by cyber-criminals can be discerned from an examination of some of the largest publicly disclosed security breaches, as the following list shows.

Cardsystems (May 2005): CardSystems said their data security breach of 40 million records happened because intruders were able to exploit software security vulnerabilities to install a rogue program on the network. The malware captured credit card information and sent it to the attackers.

TJX (December 2006): TJX stores, which include 2500 stores, among them TJMaxx and Marshalls, experienced a data breach where the perpetrator's access and software were embedded in their network for 18 months prior to discovery. What started as an exploit of a wireless network at one of the stores led to malicious software being installed that could capture credit card transactions. The number of records compromised is somewhat debated but is between 45.7 million and 94 million. Some banks have reported fraudulent purchases tied to this breach as far away as Sweden and Hong Kong.

Hannaford (March 2008): Hannaford Brothers had a data security breach of 4.2 million records. They became aware of the breach when authorities informed them of over 1800 fraud cases that were all linked to Hannaford. Upon investigation, malware was discovered on servers where credit cards were processed and information was securely transmitted to the perpetrators. There doesn't seem to be any evidence as to how the malware came to be on the servers; however, it is believed to have happened in conjunction with a vulnerability exploit.

Heartland (January 2009): Likely the largest data security breach to date, Heartland Payment Systems became aware of malware that was installed on their servers that captured credit card information as the credit cards were being processed. The software had access to the systems that process over 100 million credit card transactions each month and appeared to have been in place for many months. One hundred thirty million records are reported to have been breached, while some claim the number was closer to 60 million. The numbers reported are likely to be of unique records compromised, while the total number is much larger. In other words, the same person's credit card could have been compromised dozens of times, but that would only count as one record. It is either not known, or has not been disclosed, how the malware got installed.

Some lessons can be learned from how Heartland decided to disclose their data breach. They decided to announce it simultaneously with the inauguration of President Barack Obama on January 20, 2009. The CEO of Heartland is under investigation relating to the sale of a large amount of stock at the end of 2008. More than 650 banks have come forward saying they have had cases of fraud that are tied to the Heartland breach.

Once attackers have gained entry and access, they install malware that can be used to allow future access for themselves exclusively. Criminals then install rootkits and other malicious software that can be used to capture and send sensitive data back to themselves. (Rootkits are software packages that increase the privileges of hackers to those of administrators or above and create "back doors" for them to remotely control the system with little chance of detection.)

The History of Security Solutions

Gartner, the market analysis firm, releases annually what they call their Hype Cycle. It is a graph that plots various security technologies with their relative maturity, visibility, proliferation, and years to mainstream adoption. Figure 1-2[3] shows the Information Security Hype Cycle chart they released in September 2001.

The 2001 chart looks significantly different from the Information Security Hype Cycle chart Gartner published in September 2007, which is shown in Figure 1-3. Notice the number of technologies charted has more than tripled.

Some technologies did not even make it onto the later chart. Each of these technologies represents a solution to a very real information security problem. Each addresses and reduces the risk associated with a different aspect of information security.

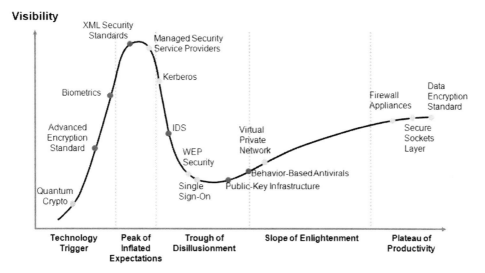

Figure 1-2

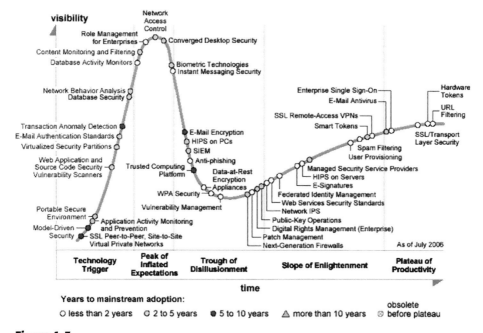

Figure 1-3

Security professionals and security technology companies have done a relatively good job understanding and developing solutions to fight the various threats from cyber-criminals. The problem is that companies are not usually timely enough in the way they deploy these valuable security solutions. Also, organizations do not budget and spend enough on the right security technologies to properly mitigate their risk. So while the bad guys aren't any smarter than the good guys, the bad guys are winning because of the apathy, naivety, and detrimental prudence of companies.

Organizations all too often don't spend their budgets on the right solutions. They do not perform an up-to-date risk analysis or a proper gap analysis. According to the Gartner chart shown in Figure 1-3, the need for the service begins at the far left side. The time to mainstream adoption is usually two to five years. Those years are the time when you need the solution most. In other words, companies do not deploy the needed solutions when they will do them the most good. Most organizations are always behind the proverbial 8 ball.

As with most statistics, there is a wide variance in what organizations report about their IT security spending. Most companies 2007 Security Budgets Increase: The Transition To Information Risk Management Begins report that between three and five percent of their IT budgets are spent on information security. Industry experts projected[4] that 2008 would be the peak in this spending at around seven and a half to nine percent, which does not appear to have happened. Others[5] have found that the number for the last few years is likely between one and two percent, which is quite low.

The Making of a Cyber-Super-Villain

Imagine, if you will, that you are an evil mastermind. You plan to take over the world and bring it under your ultimate and complete control. To do this, you plan to build the ultimate super-villain. You begin by listing the following attributes that you want this ultimate evil being to possess.

- Persuasiveness
- Power/strength
- Malice/destructiveness
- Ability to replicate himself
- Fast . . . I mean really FAST!
- Invisibility/cloaking ability
- Be anywhere and everywhere at once
- A super-genius

- Large/massive
- Unlimited resources

A super-villain like this could literally destroy our society. This is what we are dealing with today with what hackers have created. Sophisticated and powerful software have all of these "cyber-super-villain" attributes:

- Code that utilizes social engineering techniques (the power of persuasion)
- Systems that can make millions of requests a second
- Software that can corrupt, destroy, or take down systems and networks
- Malware that self-replicates and spreads from system to system in a variety of methods
- Worms and virus type code that can spread to thousands or millions of machines in a matter of minutes
- Code that is virtually undetectable and executes without anyone knowing
- Software that spreads to systems literally in every part of the globe
- Systems that utilize the infinite data that resides on the Internet and is indexed for simple searching
- Infected systems that number in the tens of millions worldwide
- Software that is designed for monetary gain as its primary function

We have done relatively little to combat this comprehensive threat. For each attribute or threat I listed above, various technologies, processes, and solutions have been created in an attempt to mitigate the risk. For the characteristics of stealth and propagation, we deploy systems to monitor and attempt to detect and stop this behavior. For DDOS attacks we develop redundancy, load balancing, routing methodologies, and so forth. But the good guys have no single product, solution, process, or methodology to combat this cyber-super-villain as a whole.

The difference between an inexperienced chess player and a pro is the ability to use the pieces on the board in combinations and look several moves ahead to dominate the board and ultimately put the other player in checkmate. The inexperienced player doesn't think ahead and is always responding defensively with individual pieces and moves. The inexperienced player quickly gets maneuvered into a position where few moves are left but doesn't realize just how bad the situation is. Cyber-criminals may very well have us near checkmate at this time, while we all still feel we have lots of moves left.

As of this writing, they have done little (relatively speaking) with their harnessed power. Botnet owners primarily have used these networks of compromised computers for the purpose of sending spam. While this is lucrative for them, much of the strength and ability of the botnet has yet to be truly tapped, but this is quickly changing.

The Botnet in Action

In late 2007, the country of Estonia was attacked by a coordinated DDOS attack largely directed at government systems. Most believe that the Russian government was behind this attack as retribution for the removal of a Soviet-era memorial in the center of the country's capital. Over a period of a month, there were more than 125 DDOS attacks. Several of the attacks measured in at 90 mbps and lasted more than 10 hours each, completely crippling their targets.

On November 12, 2008, the Internet connectivity to McColo Corp was cut by both its connectivity providers, effectively disconnecting McColo from the Internet. McColo had been identified as the number one source of spam sent from the United States. After disconnection, overall worldwide spam levels dropped significantly and China took the lead as the main generator of these annoying and sometimes malicious emails. Unfortunately, this reduction didn't last long as overall spam levels returned to their previous highs within a few months.

In 2009, spam levels reached between 90 and 95 percent of all email sent on the Internet. While the future and evolution of botnets will be discussed later, they will certainly remain a problem primarily because of the never-ending supply of vulnerable hosts available for compromise.

Hindsight is NOT 20/20

The human mind has limited retention for fear. Fear is often employed by the government, advertising, and others to spur individuals into action. As a result of the fear from September 11, 2001, laws were changed, new departments of the government were created, and freedoms were willingly sacrificed. Events such as this generate fear; however, that feeling is short-lived. The coping mechanisms of the mind deal with and suppress this fear.

Our reaction to threats from the Internet is no different. The emotional toll of having your identity stolen, or dealing with a hacker breach, can be overwhelming. When we hear about these events happening to other individuals and companies, that fear can often engage us in actively pursuing methods to mitigate our risk of a similar fate. Then, time passes and all too quickly we forget about the lessons of the past and what we have learned from others. For a short time, we evaluated and implemented solutions to help address the risk, but because security practices are not part of our DNA, we chose to put band-aids on problems rather than curing the disease.

It's said that hindsight is 20/20, implying that because we have seen or lived through an experience, we have perfect vision or a complete and perfect perspective of those events. This phrase is often used when talking about regrets.

We have probably all said "If I had only known, I would have acted differently; but hindsight is 20/20." This phrase also implies that we should learn from the past because, if it is true that history repeats itself, our previous experiences can be used to make better decisions in the future. Unfortunately, our culture and collective mindset is such that we will likely continue to make the same mistakes again and again until some big catastrophe occurs, creating fear, uncertainty, and doubt. We will give up more freedoms in the false hope of becoming safer and more secure. In the end, we will likely be worse off than we are now.

But it doesn't have to be this way. We can use the lessons of the past and build and deploy real solutions to combat these ever-growing threats. To do this, we have to change the way we look at these problems and be willing to invest in the solutions. We need to modify our cultural DNA to be more security conscious. We need to work together to prepare for what will certainly be an onslaught of attacks from cyber-criminals in the future.

FROM OUR CONTRIBUTORS

Paul Stich, Chief Executive Officer, Dasient

The world within IT security is an interesting and dynamic place. There are no borders, there are no islands, and there are no universal laws. We are all vulnerable and the attackers have too many places to hide. Enterprises, security companies, government agencies, and countries have to cooperate, trust, and work together if we are going to make a dent in the success of cyber-crime. Over the past few years we've watched the attacks dramatically change: the attackers are more sophisticated with huge research and development budgets, and they are making hundreds of millions of dollars.

Having the benefit of a career that has spanned both large companies like AT&T, British Telecom, IBM, KPMG, and McAfee, as well as innovative security startups Counterpane and Dasient, I've had hundreds of meetings with executives, technical experts, law enforcement agencies, and armed forces and government officials on how best to defend against cyber attacks. Almost all agree they need help, and that the only way to win this battle is better communication and sharing of data between the private and public sectors. History has shown us that we don't share information very well in this industry and we must learn from this mistake.

I love the challenge of IT security, it is an exciting, global, team-oriented chess match with very high stakes. Unfortunately, we won't be able to win until we are able to successfully arrest and prosecute the attackers. History has shown us that waiting for changes outside of our control to correct our current problems rarely is an effective strategy. Safe havens have to be minimized and we know this won't happen soon. So we continue the fight, defending our clients and customers with the best technology and processes we can develop to deter the attackers and send them to less protected targets.

Continued

FROM OUR CONTRIBUTORS   *(continued)*

Suzi Connor, Director Information Technology Infrastructure and Operations, United States Department of Health and Human Services

The information security arena is a dynamic space in which to operate. The challenges of defending the infrastructure and data constantly evolve. Over the years, I have witnessed cyber security attacks evolve from small groups to organized and sophisticated targeted attacks against our nation's federal and commercial information systems. You must understand the tactics and techniques of your opponent: rest assured he knows your weaknesses and plans to exploit them.

   As an IT professional spanning both the private and public sector for large IT companies as well as cutting edge security startups, I am continuously focused on aligning our technologies to meet the ever-changing demands of our infrastructure and to safeguard their data from any further exploitation. If there is but one lesson to learn, historically speaking, anything that can be used for good can equally be used for bad.

Notes

1. 2008 Data Breach Investigations Report (`http://www.verizonbusiness.com`/resources/security/databreachreport.pdf)

2. Survey: 90% of Security Incidents Went Unreported Last Year (`http://www.darkreading.com`/document.asp?doc_id=160591&f_src=drdaily)

3. The Hype Cycle is copyrighted 2001 and 2007 by Gartner, Inc. and its affiliates and is reused with permission. Hype Cycles are graphical representations of the relative maturity of technologies, IT methodologies, and management disciplines. They are intended solely as a research tool, and not as a specific guide to action. Gartner disclaims all warranties, express or implied, with respect to this research, including any warranties of merchantability or fitness for a particular purpose. For the purpose of this book, the charts are displayed for historical reference and do not represent Gartner's current view of the marketplace.

4. 2007 Security Budgets Increase: The Transition To Information Risk Management Begins (`http://www.forrester.com`/Research/Document/Excerpt/0,7211,41247,00.html)

5. David Lacey's IT Security Blog (`http://www.computerweekly.com`/blogs/david_lacey/2007/03/how_much_do_we_really_spend_on.html)

External Influences on Security

*If you don't have stress in your life, you're probably
not reaching your full potential.*

—Kevin Prince

With the history of information security in our rear view mirror, let's now look forward. What follows is a collection of our thoughts as well as comments from our peers in the industry providing their own insights. We have done our best in this chapter to provide ideas from some of the brightest minds in the security industry.

Information Security Drivers

It is widely believed that monetary loss is the catalyst for most invention, new development, and progress in the information security industry. However, while that is often a factor, there are also deeper and more compelling reasons for innovation in information security. Quite frequently decisions around the development and deployment of information security solutions are made in an emotional frame of mind based on our basic need for security rather than a more logical, risk-based approach. The impact that a wide variety of events have on our emotions is often the primary driver for information security advancements. Feeling safe and secure is a basic human need.

Abraham Maslow discussed the need for safety and security in his 1954 book *Motivation and Personality* in what is now dubbed "Maslow's Hierarchy of Needs." In his theory, people require five levels or categories of basic needs to be met.

The first level is physiological, which includes basic needs such as breathing, food, water, and the like. Without most of these, a person would simply cease to live. Once the first level is met, our psyches require the next level of need to be addressed. Figure 2-1 illustrates these basic needs in the form of a pyramid.

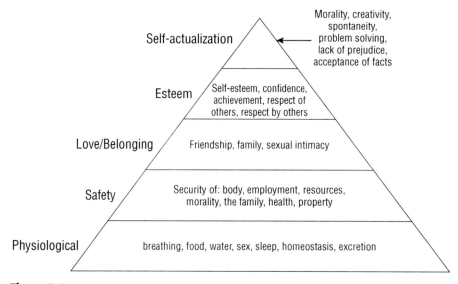

Figure 2-1

Once these physiological needs are met, level two of his hierarchy is "Safety," which includes security of body, employment, resources, family, health, and property. It is at this basic emotional level that cyber-attacks and information security threats impact us.

There are many emotions surrounding our need for safety that impact the information security landscape, including fear, uncertainty, and doubt, followed by greed, anxiety, anger, confusion, guilt, and panic, just to name a few. The tragic events of September 11, 2001 serve as an example of how far we are willing to go to ensure a safe environment. The Patriot Act would never have made it through Congress unless there had been an event such as 9/11. That legislation has had large-scale ramifications on information security and privacy.

What caused Americans to accept such a controversial piece of legislation as the Patriot Act? Was it the physical damage and monetary loss caused by terrorists plunging two airplanes into the World Trade Center buildings and one into the Pentagon, resulting in a stock market drop, short-term recession, and new laws that stripped Americans of many of their basic freedoms? Perhaps in part. Was acceptance of the Patriot Act driven more by the loss of 2,976 lives?

Again, perhaps in part, although many times that number of lives has been lost in other catastrophic events and wars, and through natural disasters and other events, without nearly the same emotional impact. Was it the simplicity of the attack that few had imagined? The shock of the unexpected? Was it the fact that millions of people around the world watched on TV, in real time, as the attack took place, and how quickly the events unfolded? Was it because the media and pundits often tell us how we should feel about the events they are reporting to us? (They all displayed obvious shock, fear, uncertainty, and certainly a lot of doubt.) While these are all factors, it is how we felt about all of them combined that led us, often willingly, to give up many freedoms. We did this in the hope of a continued safe and secure environment, one of the fundamental needs that all of us have, and the fulfillment of which Americans have enjoyed for decades like citizens of few other nations in the world.

Why do we react this way when serious events such as 9/11 occur? Many nations and their citizens are wealthy today. That wealth has led to a very comfortable lifestyle. That comfort has led to many governments and their citizens becoming complacent. That complacency now leads to insecurity around the fear our lifestyle can be taken away . . . especially when an unexpected event like 9/11 occurs. Insecurity rapidly leads to paranoia as we see, learn, and realize that the comfortable lifestyle we enjoy is at risk—that we personally don't have within our power or control the ability to continue to meet this basic need and that it can be taken away from us. We notice that our society, economy, and very way of life are quite fragile, then we start taking notice of the world around us, and those events that seemed so distant before now threaten our way of life. Thus, we react (often inappropriately and rashly) in an effort to maintain that lifestyle and meet those basic human needs.

Emotional events lead to emotional decisions that are not always in our long-term best interest. We have seen in years past that emotions around events such as virus outbreaks, worms, and hacker incidents drive information security spending, but that spending might not be the best use of those dollars if risk mitigation is the goal.

FROM OUR CONTRIBUTORS

Tom Dunbar, CISO of XL Capital

The bottom line is that the primary motivator for many people in our culture is money, and this will probably never change. However, there are many enterprises and leaders that are able to balance doing right with achieving the financial goals of an organization. In fact, I would argue that many organizations fit this description.

Continued

> **FROM OUR CONTRIBUTORS** *(continued)*
>
> Companies also need a competitive edge to succeed in our world and ensuring that their customers and prospective customers feel safe is a significant competitive edge, especially in the financial services industry. From making sure that business transactions are secured to protecting company and individual specific information, customers must feel that their information is always being protected and that this is a given if they do business with your company. As we move into the next decade, this requirement will become more of a competitive differentiator and one that will separate winners from losers.

The Emotions

In order to predict the security landscape even a decade from now, we need to understand what events may occur and the emotional impact they will carry. Historically, emotional impacts have been challenging to measure after an event has occurred. Predicting emotional impact prior to an event is extremely difficult.

> *I was living near Los Angeles in 1992 when a jury acquitted four police officers of beating Rodney King. I don't believe that there were many people that predicted the emotional impact that would have including the riots that followed where 55 people died, 2,300 were injured and 1,100 buildings were destroyed.*
>
> — *Kevin Prince*

Thus begins the natural security life cycle: first a threat is identified, then a solution is developed, then the solution is deployed to mitigate the threat. On the other hand, if no new threats are developed, new mitigation technologies are unneeded. If fraud and identity theft are eliminated, the fear of individuals that perform these crimes no longer exists. If monetary losses subside, there is no need for strict regulatory requirements.

To predict the future of information security, we must imagine what events could impact this industry combined with the likelihood that they might occur as well as the likely emotional impact they will have. History, common sense, and the evolution of information technology says that risk will increase and threats will continue.

So, let's walk through some reasonable, high-risk scenarios and their impact on information security and the emotions that will likely drive this industry up to and through the year 2020.

FROM OUR CONTRIBUTORS

Zachary Scott, Chief Executive Officer (CEO), Ironlike Security Consulting

During the last century, many social theorists have concerned themselves with not only the government's responsibilities to the people of our society, but also with people's civic responsibility to the society to which they belong. Today, the formal study of "civics" is largely thought of as an examination of people's rights and responsibilities under a democratic government, or more simply put, how to be a responsible citizen. Why all the talk of responsibilities? From the senate floor of ancient Rome to the early meetings of the American Revolution, leaders have known that with the new power that every individual possessed in a democratic society, came a new onus of individual responsibility.

The revolution of today has been one of technology. And like prior revolutions, technology has brought great new powers and new responsibility. As we find ourselves staring down the barrels of a national identity management program, cyber-terrorism, and ever-increasing economic damage due to online fraud, the need for a civic-education approach to security becomes clear.

When looking at the end goals of organizations such as the National Security Telecommunications Advisory Committee, Biometrics Identity Management Agency, or even the Department of Homeland Security, we can see that a citizen-level end-user security awareness training not only aligns lockstep with these organizations' overall aim — it is perhaps the most critical piece. In the near future, it is easy to imagine a scenario where, if even an average citizen's identity was compromised, perhaps due to ignorance of basic best practices, that identity could be used for such things as fraudulent online voting, accessing restricted information, buying restricted items, funding of terrorist groups, and countless other nefarious activities. So it follows that if one were to steal multiple citizens' identities, the thieves would in a sense be amassing power.

If we are to mitigate risk at the national level, then it is only security education — early and often — that will ensure that as the interaction with our democracy becomes less ballot box and more broadband, our citizens will have the security-savvy to keep our society vibrant and safe. For years schools have taught children the Dewey Decimal System in order for them to access the holdings of our great public libraries. Likewise, driver's education programs teach teenagers the knowledge and skills needed to be safe when accessing the vast intertwining of our nation's many roads and highways. Additional courses for these citizens to learn how to be safe when

Continued

FROM OUR CONTRIBUTORS   *(continued)*

accessing our information superhighways would not only help make them productive members of a democracy (if only from an information gathering perspective) once they hit adulthood, but it would also help to keep them safe from the new wave of cyber-predators and cyber-bullies.

Our society has outgrown the standard public service announcement urging us "to never talk to strangers." The PSAs of today need to hit on things like looking for "https" in a browser's address bar and how to create strong passwords. Due to the dramatic increase in Internet security threats, it is now logical that before accessing public works websites, users should be expected to complete a quick online training module that "certifies" them for access. Public school courses must be updated and parental conversations must be expanded. Talks about the birds and the bees must now also include the viruses and the worms. Should all of this new responsibility really be shouldered by each individual citizen? Yes. As sure as the dawn of the Internet age has been the tide that has lifted all ships, as Benjamin Frankly reminded us, "A small leak will sink a great ship." Every citizen now has a new responsibility to not be the small data leak that adversely affects the society as a whole.

World Events

One such event is another terrorist attack. While that sounds obvious, it is the specific elements of another terrorist attack that could strongly impact the future of information security. For example, a terrorist attack on U.S. soil is going to have a far greater impact than one somewhere else in the world, even if U.S. citizens or assets are targeted. If the terrorists bypass border security to enter the U.S. or subvert security protocols or technologies, it will have a greater impact than otherwise. The emotional impact is greater when it is on our homeland. One must consider the financial, political, and emotional impact of a wide variety of terrorist activities to lead to any picture of what information security will be like in 2020.

Broadly, a terrorist attack on U.S. soil occurring in the next 10 years is considered a high probability by most people.

Given my military background and the fact that I live just outside Washington DC, I network with a lot of government personnel, especially those in security. Not one believes that some additional event will not happen on US soil within the next 10 years. In addition, most believe that a major, life-impacting cyber-event, with a high risk to public infrastructure such as transportation or utilities, will happen in conjunction with or at a different time to a physical attack as well.

— Doug Howard

Although another type of event, the fear of pandemic, was widespread in 2009, little came of it. The H1N1 flu virus was not nearly as severe as some had imagined. The government, although with some delay and a bit disorganized, did a fair job of manufacturing and distributing vaccines, especially to those with the greatest exposure. So, while temporary fears of a pandemic have subsided, a worldwide pandemic is considered a high probability in the next decade.

A pandemic would have considerable impact on information security because a pandemic requires people work from home. The negative consequences are intensified for organizations that aren't prepared to send a large workforce home prior to the pandemic. A large remote user population accessing resources and sensitive data from a central network can lead to an information security breach. Theft of laptops and other portable devices is a common reason for this. Remote users are often the culprits in infecting networks with viruses and worms collected while being "remote." Hackers can use remote user systems as bridges to gain entry to corporate networks. User and system policies are much more difficult to enforce with a remote workforce. Remote employees are not subject to the same information security technologies that exist when a user is physically on the corporate network.

A number of other factors will have an impact on how the information security market will evolve in the coming years. Continuation of existing, and possibly new, wars need to be factored in. The beginnings of an energy crisis (or at least the end of inexpensive energy) is another factor. The political motivations of both major parties in the United States will have some impact. Immigration policies, the fear of global warming, cyber-terrorism, emerging operating systems and applications, technologies (such as encryption techniques), recessions and/or depression, market bubbles, the value of the dollar, market stability, and much, much more will all play their part in forging the information security landscape for 2020 and beyond.

The result of these events and threats will drive us to relinquish certain liberties and quite possibly basic human rights in order to reduce our risk from another large, unexpected event impacting our way of life. Each has a major impact on the way information security risk is perceived and, therefore, on the solutions that are developed and deployed. Now, let's explore some of the ongoing trends that we anticipate having an impact by the year 2020.

FROM OUR CONTRIBUTORS

Rick Howard, Director of Intelligence, iDefense (a Verisign company)

The security community is transitioning. The center of gravity for cyber-security thought leadership, spending, and professional development, is moving away from the traditional commercial entities that have dominated the space for the past decade. It is quickly moving toward government entities who have publicly, for the fist time, just realized that threats like cyber-crime, cyber-warfare, cyber-espionage (Advanced Persistent Threat), cyber-mercenaries, and "cyber-activism" are a real and present danger. It seems that most of the world has either transitioned or is in the process of transitioning into the third wave of developing nations made popular by Alvin Toffler in 1980 (first wave: agricultural, second wave: industrial, third wave: informational).

After a series of humiliating breaches in corporate and governmental networks since 2008, governments from around the world have begun to understand that counter-tactics alone will not solve the problem. Many geo-strategically powerful governments have taken steps to implement or refine official cyber-warfare policies and capabilities. They have begun forming the nexus for strategic thinking and dedicating large sums of money to the problem. This is a shift. Heretofore, financial institutions, information technology (IT) departments and global security companies provided thought leadership for the security industry and the impetus to spend money. As more and more governments wade into the fray, the center of gravity for these activities is shifting away from private enterprise and into the government sector. Between 2009 and 2010, this is just a small list of what governments from around the world are doing:

- In the U.S., the U.S. Department of Defense officially established the U.S. Cyber Command (CYBERCOM), which will control the military's primary cyber defense and warfare capabilities.

- In Europe, politicians from the EU Commission and the UK government are calling for a cyber czar and a central cyber-security agency.

- In Asia, Japan has initiated an intensive increase in dialogue and institutional cooperation among information security personnel across all government ministries. South Korea is building a program to train 3,000 cyber-security specialists in 2010 and 2011. China continues to fund the development of cyber-militia units. Singapore created the Infocomm Technology Security Authority (SITSA) to handle technology-related threats to the city-state's national security.

- In the Middle East, Iran created its first cyber-police force.

This shift does not imply that cyber-space will be safer, at least in the short term. As government entities grapple with the problem, they will throw large sums of money and pass sweeping legislation in an effort to improve the situation. In practice, their efforts will be muddled as entities within the same country compete for resources and for who is in charge of the space. International cooperation is incipient and will most likely not become coherent by 2020. But that does not matter. Governments are moving forward.

This center of gravity shift does not mean that commercial entities will abandon the space. It just means that their efforts will be dwarfed by the volumes of money governments will spend in comparison. It also means that commercial entities will be reacting to new legislation that the governments from around the world put into play.

The Impact of Politics

We are deep into Obama's presidency as we write this book, and he is the first president to ever use the words IT and security in the same sentence. In contrast to Al Gore, who during an interview with Wolf Blitzer on March 9, 1999 claimed to have invented the Internet, Obama seems to clearly understand the importance that IT plays within the government and how it can provide a foundation to cost reduction and efficiency gains.

It took President Obama nearly a year to put in place a cyber-czar. Howard Schmidt, a former eBay and Microsoft executive, became the government's cybersecurity coordinator in December of 2009. Many have questioned the value of such a position based on historical precedents. In the past, this was largely a powerless role with little more duties than being a scapegoat. That may be why it was such a difficult process to find someone to take the position. The process dragged on for months as several people turned down the job.

A cyber-czar properly empowered could offer our country some amazing benefits. A top-down approach to the thought, strategy, and effort related to information security is the proper approach, but there are several troubling questions to be answered. Can the administration take IT threats seriously? Will this position be empowered to cut through all the bureaucracy and red tape required to make real change across many departments and organizations? Most experts say that is unlikely.

The two-party system in the United States creates an environment that gridlocks any real change or progress. While there are, of course, more than two parties, none other than the Republicans and Democrats has generated enough of a movement to adequately take a position of leadership and political power to force change. As a result, Republicans and Democrats spend the majority of their time attempting to hold onto the power they have and politically maneuver to get more. In the meantime, little is done to solve the problems that face America, including problems related to IT security. In Chapter 9, we will discuss specific threats and scenarios that are likely to arise, many of which are because our political environment is so poisoned we gridlock the process to make meaningful change. The lack of change fosters an environment that terrorists, cyber-criminals, and other malicious people can and will exploit.

FROM OUR CONTRIBUTORS

Frank J. Ricotta Jr., Chief Technology Officer, Enterprise Information Management, Inc.

The financial damage due just to identify theft is staggering. As many as 10 million Americans a year will be impacted by this crime, averaging, for each victim, $15,000 and as much as 5,000 hours to rectify. This crime also affects businesses. The Aberdeen Group estimates that identify theft cost businesses $221 billion per year worldwide. These activities have gone well beyond those of individual basement hackers. They are backed by organized crime — cyber-crime is big business. Additionally, the cyber-world is a haven for state-sponsored terrorist activities, referred to as "cyber-terrorism." cyber-terrorists use the Internet to coordinate activities, recruit new members, and disrupt government and commerce activities.

Over the last few months, a saga involving Google has played out both in public and in private. The company faced a significant amount of criticism for collecting and geo-locating WiFi hotspots for commercial purposes. While doing so, the company gained access to personal information. Privately the company has been struggling with how much they should leverage and profit from personal information gathered from Gmail, chat, and web surfing activities. Facebook, a growing competitive force in this arena, has faced many of the same criticisms by setting "default" privacy settings to "Everyone."

Finally, there are all forms of content available to anyone on the net. For many parents, protecting their children from cyber-predators and accessing age appropriate content is extremely important.

There is a fine line between the government protecting its citizens and censorship. Governments have a role to play by passing and enforcing tough cyber-crime legislation, fighting cyber-terrorism, protecting individual freedoms and privacy, and providing guidelines for "rating" content. With that said, the government should not be in the business of censorship. Free speech is a fundamental tenant of our society and a foundational building block to liberty.

The Impact on Journalism

Around the turn of the century, the Internet was still very young, and frankly was not taken very seriously by most. Little did they know this medium would become a power like no other for news and information.

High-quality journalism is sourced from various news organizations that rely on advertising to survive. Early in this century, newspaper publishers decided that they would not charge Internet-based distribution media (such as search engines and websites) for the articles and stories they generated. Rather they decided the Internet's "limited" value should be used to gain awareness for their print publications, which they thought would drive up subscriptions and advertising dollars. This gave rise to search engines, such as Yahoo!, Google, Craigslist, and many others, to capture and offer news to those that use their services at no cost. Content was, and is, king, but the content was free to help get these new businesses off the ground. This allowed websites, email distribution lists, and many other electronic distribution methods for news to use the high-quality journalism performed by these reputable sources at little or no cost. The newspaper industry did not realize at the time that they had planted a time bomb that was set to go off about 10 years later. The decision to not charge for online content has been dubbed publishers' "Original Sin."

Today, as a result of this decision combined with the recession that began at the end of 2007, newspaper agencies and other print mediums are going out of business or scaling back at an alarming pace. The only people that are surprised at this are some publishers themselves. This certainly doesn't surprise the generations of people (nearly everyone 40 and younger) that use the Internet or television as their news sources. Obviously, the vast majority of revenue collected by newspaper companies are from advertising and subscriptions. As people can now get all of the information for free, in an easier format, delivered straight to their computer or mobile phone, it isn't hard to see why these companies are having serious problems.

There is a very significant impact we will all feel as a result of the bomb that has devastated newspaper publishing companies, that is, a significant reduction in the quality of journalism on which we all rely as well as the speed and ease in which false information can spread on the Internet, as the following paragraphs illustrate.

While traditional journalism is not perfect, by and large it has done a good job getting the major facts and figures correct most of the time. However, we live in a world where many people believe without question what they read or hear from their news sources. Now, imagine a world where this news is being disseminated without being proofed, fact checked, or edited. This is a world where entertainment is more important than fact. The slow but steady decay of quality journalism is the era we are entering.

On June 25, 2009, Michael Jackson, the pop singer and icon, died at age 50. It happened to be on the same day that '70s superstar and actress Farrah Fawcett died and the same week Ed McMahon (sidekick of Johnny Carson on the *Tonight Show* for many years) passed away as well. Within days there was a swarm of false reports of other famous individuals passing away. One of the more interesting of these were the reports that the actor Jeff Goldblum had died. A news agency in New Zealand reported that police had confirmed that Jeff Goldblum had fallen to his death on the set of his latest movie. Because a local television station had announced the news, it spread like wildfire and was believed to be true by many until Jeff showed up on the Comedy Central show *The Colbert Report* where he confirmed his own death (as a joke of course) live before a studio audience. The same day Britney Spears's Twitter account was hacked and someone posted "Britney has passed today. It is a sad day for everyone. More news to come."

For cyber-criminals, manipulating the facts on a large, global scale can be a powerful weapon. Perhaps you remember the events of September 8, 2008 when the stock of United Airlines plummeted and the SEC halted trading for that company. The *Sun-Sentinel*, a south Florida newspaper, had an archive of old online articles. In that archive was an article originally posted by the *Chicago Tribune* on Dec. 10, 2002, entitled "United Airlines files for Ch. 11 to cut costs." While this was a 6-year-old story, it was difficult to tell because it had no posted date on the article itself. The article did make the home page of the *Sun-Sentinel* website six years later apparently because of a glitch in their system. When enough people access archived articles on the *Sun-Sentinel* website, those articles are put in a special section on the home page featuring most read or interesting articles. Google's search spiders, which often index news sites, including the *Sun-Sentinel's*, picked up the article and posted it as if it were current news. (There is a bit of finger pointing as to why this happened and who is to blame.) Because the original article didn't have a date within the article content, Google captured the headline and (because it was on the home page) assigned it a current date.

A contracted Florida investment advisor saw the news announcement on Google with the current date. Without fact checking, he posted it to the Bloomberg subscription service, so it immediately popped up on the monitors of stock brokers, investment advisors, and other Wall Street investors around the world. At 11:00 a.m. the airline's stock began to tank. With a stock price of $12.17 the day before, there were 15 million shares traded and at 11:30 a.m. the SEC halted trading, which ended at $3.00 per share—over a 75 percent drop in a matter of minutes! The next day (after the truth was discovered) the stock rebounded to $10.92. Through this series of unfortunate cyber-events, resulting from poor journalism, a lack of checks and balances, and our reliance upon automated systems for news aggregation, hundreds of millions of dollars were lost in a matter of minutes.

Some speculate that perhaps this wasn't an accident at all. If a cyber-criminal had observed that "featured" articles on the *Sun-Sentinel* website had the capability of ending up on Google's "current news," and all it takes to become a featured article is to be clicked on many times . . . how difficult would it be to propel an article to the front page? How difficult would it be to find an old, undated article and short the stock of a major U.S. corporation? Did perhaps a criminal make millions of dollars that day?

So, let's call hacking using the media *macking* (media-hacking). Or take a different angle and call it *mishing* to go along with phishing and vishing and all the other "ishings." Regardless of what you may call it, imagine the types of mass media attacks that will likely plague us in the future. Imagine the sophisticated manipulation of media, news, and search engines that will create unimaginable monetary opportunities for criminals. Imagine what could be done with injecting false information into the Internet. Anything that can impact the share price of a public company's stock or impact their reputation will be used. The Internet obviously can be used to ruin individuals as well. Remember, the Internet never forgets . . . even when the information is completely false.

FROM OUR CONTRIBUTORS

Christopher Hart, CISSP, Chief Information Security Officer (CISO) for Life Technologies

The Internet has almost driven the media to commodity. It has made it very easy for users to become a media outlet and even a news outlet (for example, look at WikiLeaks). Anyone can post anything about whatever they want. The accuracy and level of journalistic diligence is entirely up to the author. Once published, a story is given a minor degree of credibility by Google by simply popping up as a search result. These works are also sometimes given significant credibility when they are used as a source or information data point by more traditional media.

This impacts information security in a couple of ways. As security leaders, we need to be part marketer and evangelist. Applying rational business thought to media hype is a significant part of our responsibility. We must also understand that data which is leaked, lost, or stolen can become very public, very quickly. There is also no assumption the data will be accurately represented. In many of the media outlets of the blogosphere, information is very slanted to the agenda or opinion of the author.

Rob Bolton, Senior Director, 1901 Group, and Author, "Lose the Pressure . . . Win the Deals"

The Internet is becoming the de facto standard media outlet, and there is clearly a learning curve for end users. There is an, "if I read it, it must be true" mentality with often little or no thought given to who is the source, their credibility or motivation, or any potential risks involved with accepting the veracity of the information. Moreover, technology advancements are making it easier for end users to access the Internet anytime and anywhere. Multi-purpose

Continued

The Social Engineer

Social engineering is the practice of exploiting humans through methods of manipulation. In other words, if computer hacking is exploiting computer systems, social engineering is hacking people. Social engineering has been part of popular culture for many years. There are many books that have been written by famous social engineers. Blockbuster movies have even been made based on the lives of well-known criminals that were masters of social engineering, such as *Catch Me If You Can* starring Leonardo DiCaprio and Tom Hanks, sensationalizing the life of Frank Abagnale Jr. One of my favorite old movies that illustrates the power of social engineering is *Sneakers*, starring Robert Redford. There are even more modern movies that glorify this behavior, including the *Oceans 11, 12*, and *13* trilogy.

   While it does happen, social engineering as a lone method used to compromise companies is quite rare. Looking back at information security with 20/20 hindsight, one sees that there is a very interesting relationship between social engineering and hacking. The availability and usability of discovered vulnerabilities and tools have a cycle or pattern. At times when there are lots of easy to exploit vulnerabilities we see that social engineering is used less. When using technical exploits requires a greater measure of skill, you find that social engineering techniques are often used to make up the difference. Figure 2-2 illustrates the relationship between social engineering and traditional hacking, including when social engineering is most used.

   While the ease of exploitation doesn't follow quite such a predictable pattern, there is an increased use of social engineering techniques when fewer tools are available and more skill is required to exploit systems. New vulnerabilities that are easy to exploit will continue to be discovered. However, by and large, exploits require great skill to execute. As a result, tools that can decrease the technical skill required to exploit these vulnerabilities are continually being developed.

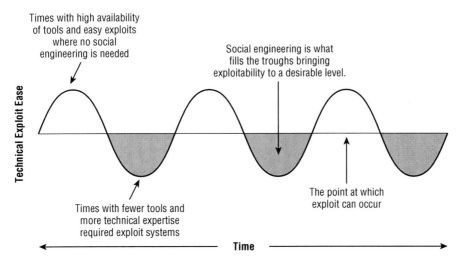

Figure 2-2

Automated systems and tools will make up for some of the human technical deficiency in the exploit systems, but through 2020 and beyond we will continue to see criminals use social engineering techniques. This is simply because that approach is easier than many technical exploits. Let's be honest; is it easier to use a brute force software package attempting each and every possible user-name and password combination until the system gets it correct or simply to trick the user into giving it to you? So, while hackers would of course prefer to do everything without ever involving another human or requiring an insider to be tricked into helping with the exploit, social engineering is easy to do and very effective.

Social engineering is widely used today, although many not in the information security industry know about these methods by the name of specific attacks rather than as "social engineering." Phishing is a type of social engineering attack that many are aware of. Phishing is a social engineering attack in which criminals send an email that appears to be legitimate to an unsuspecting user. The criminals hope the recipient will follow the instructions and either com-promise their system or be led to a website or phone system that can capture their sensitive information. In other words, for the attack to be successful, the insider must be tricked into doing something that leads to the exploit of the system. Phishing attacks simply do not work without someone on the inside making a mistake.

Social engineering is considered to be one of the most effective methods for committing crimes. Through social engineering techniques, criminals can acquire sensitive information, can gain access to otherwise unauthorized systems, and may even be granted physical access to computers and networks. Most IT personnel will tell you that if a skilled criminal can gain physical access to a system, there is little you can do to keep that system protected.

How difficult would it be for a criminal to get a job with the cleaning company that cleans your office? The criminal could then access systems, install Trojan horse programs on available systems, and so forth. Most employees will hold a security door open for someone else . . . especially if they are holding something difficult to carry. We as human beings are naturally trusting. We naturally want to help others. We inherently do not want to cause disruptions or issues.

For years, we have offered social engineering engagements as one of the services our customers can utilize. In these engagements, a social engineering expert (with the written permission of the company of course) will call employees and trick them into giving them their usernames and passwords. Historically speaking, our experts are successful more than 75 percent of the time. Often IT administrators and other executives do not believe they or their employees could fall prey to such attacks. I use a recording of one of these social engineering engagements in some of my presentations to illustrate how willing some users are to give up their credentials. It involves one of our social engineering experts, Mike, calling into a community bank in the Midwest. You will see that Mike refers to "Lynn," who is their IT person. Lynn's name was derived from the domain name registration on the Internet. Mike also learned what core processing software (the main software package used by financial institutions to run the bank) they were using from their website's list of "partners." Here is the transcript of that real social engineering call.

Nicole: "This is Nicole."

Mike: "Hi Nicole, this is Mike Ballard from [core processing software]."

Nicole: "Uh-huh."

Mike: "I just got a call from Lynn and she did an upgrade on the core processor, and the computer you're on is not accepting the upgrade. And I want to run a real quick test for Lynn and then I need to get back to Lynn."

Nicole: "Okay."

Mike: "I'm sorry. Are you with a customer right now?"

Nicole: "No . . . no."

Mike: "I'll make this very quick."

Nicole: "That's fine."

Mike: "If a customer shows up I can call back. It's not a big deal."

Nicole: "Okay."

Mike: "Okay. In the lower-left-hand corner of your screen right-click on the Start button. This will be your only right-click. Another screen will open."

Nicole: "Okay."

Mike: "Click on 'Explore,' not 'Explore all users,' just 'Explore.'"

Nicole: "Okay. Now I have another screen open."

Mike: "Look at the top, where it says File, Edit, View all that."

Nicole: "Yep."

Mike: "Over to the far right you will have 'help.'"

Nicole: "Yep."

Mike: "Click on Help and 'About Windows 'should pop down. Click on that."

Nicole: "Okay."

Mike: "We have three versions that are affected from this on your operating system. It is 5.0, 5.1, and 5.2. Is there one of those there?"

Nicole: "5.2."

Mike: "5.2. That is what I thought. Okay. That's what the other ones were, too. I'm going to patch this really quick and then can you transfer me back to Lynn or do I need to call back in?"

Nicole: "No, I think you'll probably have to . . ."

Mike: "That's okay. I've got to call her next anyway no matter what the result is here."

Nicole: "Okay."

Mike: "When you sign into our system in the morning, what username you sign in with?"

Nicole: "Into [software name]?"

Mike: "Yes."

Nicole: "nicole . . . just n-i-c-o-l-e. But I'm not signed into this computer today."

Mike: "That's okay. And the password? And this is very case sensitive, so it has to be exactly as you type it into the system in terms of upper and lower case. What's that?"

Nicole: "It's nicole16 . . . not very creative." (Nicole laughs)

Mike: "Upper case or lower case?"

Nicole: "Lower."

Mike: "Okay. Thank you. That's all I need. If Lynn has a problem with this, she'll probably call you back now. Okay, thank you."

Nicole: "THANK YOU! Bye."

You probably noticed how Mike used Lynn's name no less than five times during the call to establish legitimacy. He also referenced the software manufacturer's name and application name throughout the call. He references an upgrade that didn't work right. All of this is done in an effort to create a sense of legitimacy and urgency. Companies seem to be always amazed at just how easily their employees will fall prey to something like this.

Criminals have found success pretending to be an authority figure such as a fire marshal. Other times, they disguise themselves as a pest control person or someone who needs to have access to all areas of a building. But in-person social engineering is just one method and frankly not used nearly as often as other methods.

Social engineering experts have been known to leave infected CDs, DVDs, USB thumb drives, and the like with malware in parking lots, near elevators, or other places where employees will see and pick them up. If some media is found and has a label that says "Employee Compensation Spreadsheet – CONFIDENTIAL," or something equally enticing, one of two things will happen. The person that finds it will take it to the HR manager. The HR manager will plug it into their system, which will infect it with a Trojan horse program or other malware. Employees who do not take it to HR will likely plug it into their computer and be similarly infected. Either way, the perpetrator gets his or her way by exploiting the good nature or curiosity of people.

Social engineering attacks using telephony are rapidly increasing. This is especially true with the availability of open source voice over IP telephone systems. VoIP systems can be programmed to show false information on a recipient's caller ID making it look legitimate. These systems can be programmed, so an automated attendant will ask for personal information that can be typed into the phone, which often feels more legitimate to an end user than an email.

Social engineering will continue to flourish into 2020 and beyond. This will be exacerbated by the expanded use of smart phones where voice, texting, Internet access, and social networking have all converged onto a single device that exists in everyone's pocket. At this point, smart phones with unlimited voice and data are a fairly small percentage of all mobile phones used. Mobile phone voice and data companies continue to move toward relatively low-cost unlimited plans, which will then open up users to greater communication options as well as methods criminals will use to compromise them.

Social engineering is only limited by the creativity of fraudsters and criminals. The techniques and methods they employ today, and will use in the future, will likely amaze us. More often than not, they will use these techniques in combination with other types of attacks to achieve their goals. The IT security professional today and in the future needs to prepare his or her organization for such methods of attack.

Of course, what we will continue to see most often with social engineering attacks is fraudsters taking advantage of what I consider to be the lowest-hanging fruit: social engineering techniques used in conjunction with politics, world events, disasters, or anything else that makes the news. People have a natural curiosity, and when big news events happen, criminals very opportunistically take advantage of these situations.

Right after Hurricane Katrina made landfall in 2005, many "Katrina Relief" websites came online, many of which were fraudulent attempts to take advantage of people who were trying to help the victims through donations or other relief efforts. The official Super Bowl website has been compromised several years in a row in the recent past. Political elections are always used by criminals to generate social engineering content and lures. The bottom line is criminals have always been, and will always be, opportunistic. Criminal activity through the use of social engineering will likely continue to be very profitable in 2020 and beyond.

Mike Svihra, Deputy Director, Information Systems, U.S. Department of Health and Human Services

Social engineering is a clear and present danger for both government and commercial organizations and will continue to be a key area of focus for some compromises far into the future. Unlike many computer threats, the physical presence risk is often avoided by most people attempting to hack systems. This is especially true with government facilities where the legal implications can be severe. Unfortunately, social engineering can involve gathering information through other means such as email, false links, telephone calls, and so forth. These attempts to steal information from end users, which then can be used for remote penetration, are prevalent across any organization. Often within businesses and government, end users are not IT literate, and certainly not IT security literate. This leads to the human element being a major weakness within IT.

Organizations around the world continue to focus on end user awareness and training to reduce this threat. This will not only continue into the future, but through improved training content, testing, and automated tracking to make sure users complete and are tested on what they have been tasked to learn, this will increase the overall effectiveness as well. Equally important are the layered security technologies we have and will apply which will allow us to protect users from common mistakes such as visiting compromised websites or those they attempt to reach through phishing exploits, blocking of certain known IPs and telephony origination points, and mobile device protection, to name a few. Anything that can be done though automation to protect users will only strengthen and improve end users' awareness of the risks and associated ways to protect themselves and their organization.

Christopher Hart, CISSP, Chief Information Security Officer (CISO) for Life Technologies

The risks of social engineering grow as the user understands less about the technology and processes around that technology. The more removed people are from that understanding, the easier it is for baddies to exploit that lack of understanding. This is that ever-tough-to-control insider human vector. Since it is largely impractical for everyone to have a deep understanding of the technology and processes around a given technology, those who gain "enough understanding to be dangerous" can cause other risks and threats by overstating (or understating) risks to the public. We see this in the media. The multifunction copier exposure which was recently aired on CNBC is an example; It contained much more hype than substance. While there is some risk associated with the multifunction printer devices, it is perhaps overstated,

Continued

and can be made manageable through good lease return processes and solid physical security control of the printers.

This same lack of understanding around the technology leads to a significant portion of the insider threat as well. People need to be given the opportunity to do the right thing. If you don't give them that opportunity, they are essentially prisoners. This is not to say that controls should not be in place; controls are essential. However, in many situations, the better value is to instill greater understanding and awareness of a technology. This understanding will reduce many of the accidental risks and, in many cases, negligent risks as well. You can educate your way out of most insider risk (except for the maliciousness), and if you do so, you have achieved a good thing. There are other mechanisms to deal with maliciousness and ill-intent.

GRC

Governance, risk analysis, and compliance/regulatory management have historically been managed as three separate and mostly disparate disciplines. Governance, risk, and compliance, or GRC, is an integrated approach to address these three areas holistically, across the entire enterprise. The definition beyond the conceptual meaning, however, is highly debated. A proposed short definition derived from an extensive GRC literature review and validated through a survey among GRC professionals reads:

> GRC is an integrated, holistic approach to organisation-wide governance, risk and compliance ensuring that an organisation acts ethically correct and in accordance with its risk appetite, internal policies and external regulations through the alignment of strategy, processes, technology and people, thereby improving efficiency and effectiveness.[1]

GRC is often a difficult concept to comprehend, even for those of us who have been around security, governance, and regulatory compliance for a lifetime. The common mistake is to consolidate each of the independent disciplines under one manager, find a corporate sponsor, and consider the project to be complete. GRC is about finding the common elements between governance, risk, and compliance and leveraging them into a program that creates a sustainable culture in which the organization is constantly evolving practices and procedures to improve the overall integrity of the organization: integrity to do right by the employees, the partners, the customers, the shareholders, and the industry in which the company operates.

The future of GRC is very much dependent on consensus on a common definition, a common approach, and establishing metrics (potentially at a vertical industry level). Much like IT security, where adoption was slow because of the inability to measure return on investment (ROI), GRC will have a struggle for acceptance. Like IT security, GRC will develop some following simply because of the fact that it includes the umbrella elements of compliance, security, and governance, all of which are seen as mandatory functions within most enterprises. Companies such as Corporate Integrity (www.corp-integrity.com) are attempting to formalize elements of GRC, which should lead to wide-scale adoption. Figure 2-3 identifies the Enterprise GRC Reference Architecture as proposed by Corporate Integrity.

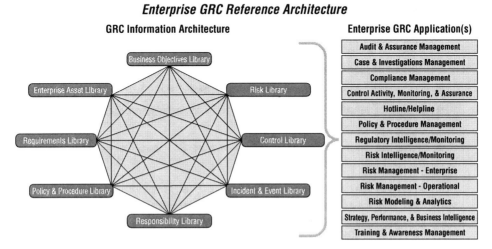

Figure 2-3

http://corp-integrity.blogspot.com/2009/11/grc-reference-architecture-grc.html

Regardless of the successes to date, we would propose that the slow rate of adoption will continue through the next five years while standards and definitions are established to further define actionable items for GRC programs. In 5+ years, the adoption rate and adoption will be less missionary sales and have a higher pull rate from enterprises attempting to mature their approach to GRC.

FROM OUR CONTRIBUTORS

Michael Rasmussen, CEO, Corporate Integrity

GRC is more than a catchy acronym used by technology providers and consultants to market their solutions — it is a philosophy of business. This philosophy permeates the organization: its oversight, its processes, and its culture.

Continued

FROM OUR CONTRIBUTORS   *(continued)*

The challenge of GRC is that each individual ingredient — governance, risk, and compliance — has varied meanings across the organization. For "governance," there is corporate governance, IT governance, financial risk, strategic risk, operational risk, IT risk, corporate compliance, Sarbanes-Oxley (SOX) compliance, employment and labor compliance, and privacy compliance. The list of mandates and initiatives goes on and on.

In fact, it is easier to define what GRC is not:

- GRC is *not* about silos of risk and compliance operating independently of each other.

- GRC is *not* solely about technology — though technology plays a critical role.

- GRC is *not* just a label for the services consultants provide.

- GRC is *not* just about Sarbanes-Oxley compliance.

- GRC is *not* another label for enterprise risk management (ERM), although GRC encompasses ERM.

- GRC is *not* about a single individual owning all aspects of governance, risk, and compliance.

GRC is an approach to business that harmonizes governance, risk, and compliance efforts across the business. It is about individual GRC roles across the organization working cooperatively to provide a complete and integrated view of GRC. It is about collaboration and sharing of information, assessments, metrics, risks, investigations, and losses across roles. GRC's purpose is to show an enterprise view of risk and compliance to identify interrelationships in today's complex, dynamic, and distributed business environment. GRC is a federation of professional roles — the corporate secretary, legal, risk, audit, compliance, IT, ethics, finance, line of business, and others — working together in a common framework, collaboration, and architecture to achieve sustainability, consistency, efficiency, accountability, and transparency.

GRC is a three-legged stool: Each of its three elements must be managed successfully to support the others; for example, good governance can only be achieved through diligent risk and compliance management. Ignoring a federated view of GRC means processes, partners, employees, and systems behave like leaves blowing in the wind. Successfully implemented GRC means inefficiencies, errors, and potential risks are identified, averted, or contained, reducing exposure and ultimately creating better business performance. Organizations that attempt to build a GRC strategy with home-grown solutions, spreadsheets, or islands of technology not built to meet a range of needs are left in the dark, boxed into a view of the world that has become limiting.

Good GRC requires a common framework, integrated processes, and technology architecture that span the organization and its individual risk and compliance issues. This ensures a GRC strategy that is ready to tackle issues at their roots, through core processes leveraged across the organization.

GRC success starts with a simple five-step plan:

1. **Identify the interrelated processes, problems, and issues:** An understanding of the scope of GRC issues, processes, technology, and requirements is the first step. Organizations should start with a survey assessment to identify and catalog the number of processes, technologies, methodologies, and frameworks used for risk and compliance across all business operations. This assessment is best aligned with the OCEG GRC Capability Model.

2. **Establish GRC goals and objectives:** Once the organization identifies the scope of GRC along with a vision and mission statement, it can establish goals and objectives. These goals can determine GRC program structure — centralized, federated, or some form of deliberate but ad hoc collaboration. It also determines consistent and relevant use of technology.

3. **Develop short-term strategy for fulfilling GRC requirements:** With goals in mind, identify quick wins that demonstrate GRC success and improvement. Tackle items that show a fast return. This builds greater buy-in to the GRC strategy across business operations. The short-term plan should not exceed 12 months.

4. **Conduct a comprehensive organizational risk assessment:** Part of the short-term plan should be a detailed risk assessment that provides a common framework and catalog of corporate risks across GRC management silos. This risk assessment can further identify and feed into a long-term comprehensive GRC strategy. This helps the organization better understand, manage, and monitor risk exposure.

5. **Provide a comprehensive action plan:** With the short-term plan in place, the organization can begin working on the long-term: a strategic plan to develop a comprehensive GRC strategy focused on process improvement. The more challenging GRC components should be brought into this plan. This plan is optimal when it covers a three- to five-year period.

Prioritization of risk and compliance activities must be decided at an enterprise level. This can be difficult, as silos of risk and compliance can be buried within different functions. To facilitate a top-down approach, executive buy-in and support is essential. This endorses the effort, and supersedes resistance from silos that want to keep working independently. It has taken more years than expected to get to the current level of maturity within GRC, and will probably take 10 more years to have GRC widely adopted.

Continued

Andy Greenawalt, Founder and CEO, Continuity Control

I'll start with making my biases clear. Much of the debate around GRC is one of the industry's creation. With consultants often playing a central role, the drive to brevity, clarity, and actionability can be weak. Having spent years trying to interpret complicated models for holistic (bla, bla, bla), I needed a "see spot run" model for my own use.

At the core of the issue is "bad stuff," negative outcomes or risks. In broad terms, a list of things you'd prefer to avoid. These bad things emerge and go from possible, to probable, to likely. They can take the form of fraud, technology faults, natural disasters, or a combination of these things. As the awareness of these risks matures, and the impact of them becomes better understood, the government (or some other broadly concerned body such as VISA with PCI) will pass a law or requirement making the reasonable control of a given risk mandatory.

So the realm of compliance is actually quite simple. As an organization, you need to have an understanding of the risks that you encounter in the course of your business and be able to demonstrate, for those risks that are addressed by law or otherwise are required, that you're earnestly trying to control for them. As a federal examiner from the NCUA frankly put it: "The entire compliance process is there to determine if the institution is being negligent given their risks. Are we, as an insurance company, going to get screwed because you didn't know better?" So it is the chief requirement for regulated businesses that they *know* how risks apply to them. While this may seem way too simple, there are so many details in the realm of risk that organizations get lost in the weeds. A large banking client in New England had been taken to task by examiners, not for a lack of controls, but for their inability to speak to it. If things are so complex that they cannot speak to their organization's process for understanding risk (ERM), discussing risks, controls, and demonstrating an audit trail, then the examiners begin to worry.

The reason for this background is that there is a clear need to make this GRC simple and standard. If we think back to email, maturity came with a standard: Simple Mail Transport Protocol (SMTP). As information security matured, we had vulnerability IDs. So as we look to the future, history would indicate the need for a "Simple Risk/Compliance Protocol." Much as the world of electronic communications was changed by a standard mail protocol, the same could and perhaps should happen with a Simple Risk/Compliance Protocol (SRCP).

So what might this look like? At the core are risks and their counterpart controls. Much as there is a central shared source of information security vulnerabilities in OSVDB, there could be a shared source of risks. As legislators or other overseers craft regulations and guidance, they can simply associate a given legal citation with the risk which it was written to address. On the flip side of this we'd have vendors or internal staff that provide solutions to address the risk, and associate their solutions with

this RiskID. A simple description of *how* **it addresses the risk would go a long way.**

In this new world a regulated business would be able to easily see the superset of risks to be addressed by looking at all applicable regulations and showing their associated risks. Those that serve this industry would know clearly the range of risks to be addressed for them. This simplified world would be able to spend far more of its scarce resources on mitigating risk, than guessing about compliance and being fleeced by consultants. And I think it's a world we can get to by 2020.

Litigation

Currently, data security breaches are almost connected at the hip with class-action lawsuits. Law firms are taking full advantage of companies that experience data security breaches. The natural assumption is that there was some negligence involved. Based on the vague nature of regulations, known best security practices, lack of deep security knowledge in corporations, and how few organizations adhere to best practices and compliance, it isn't difficult to prove negligence.

However, these organizations are beginning to fight back. In some cases, this liability is being diverted effectively to the companies that have tested and certified the company as compliant. In one case in 2009, Merrick Bank filed suit against Savvis, a security consulting company, that certified CardSystems as compliant less than one year before their data breach. Merrick Bank claims to have lost 16 million dollars in that breach that was not their fault.

Financial breaches will continue to happen and, so far, the banks have taken the brunt of the losses. They do not want a bunch of case law that leaves them paying out millions of dollars for breaches they didn't have anything to do with.

At the same time, lawyers will continue to file suit against anyone who has a data breach. These cyber-ambulance-chasers are making it so that many organizations will not disclose data breaches and will leave their customers exposed, not knowing their identities are in danger or that fraud may be committed.

As a result of the negative impact of a data security breach, and specifically the fear of class-action lawsuits, only a small percentage of organizations disclose these breaches although nearly all states require it. In a 2008 survey at RSA, researchers found that only 11 percent of companies report data breaches. Furthermore, when they do disclose the breach, more and more are not reporting the number of records lost. The graph in Figure 2-4 shows the percentage of reported data breaches between 2000 and 2009 where the number of records compromised was disclosed.

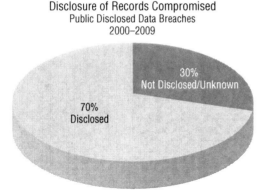

Figure 2-4

The number of organizations that did not disclose the number of records compromised in their data security breach incidents increased so dramatically during 2009 that the average across nearly a decade increased by 7 percent in one year. While that may not seem like a large increase, when looked at year over year, 2008 had just over one-quarter of data breaches that did not include the number of records compromised, whereas in 2009, nearly 4 out of 10 breaches did not include the number of records compromised (see Figure 2-4).

There appears to be a disturbing trend whereby we are getting close to where half of publicly disclosed data breaches do not include the total number of records compromised. The chart shown in Figure 2-5 illustrates this trend.

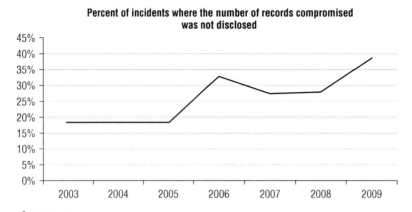

Figure 2-5

Breach Impact on Public Companies

Sometimes companies fear more than litigation. It can be the impact on a public company's stock price that should worry companies. In a data security breach study I wrote in early 2010, I looked at all public companies that had security breaches in 2009. Some of the findings were interesting.

There are simply too many factors that impact a public company's stock price from moment to moment to know definitively how a data breach impacts it (at least in most cases). Data breaches are not all equal. Some are very large like the Heartland Payment Systems breach, where 130 million records were compromised. Others are insignificant, such as California Pizza Kitchen, which had 50 records compromised. In still other cases, we don't know how many records were compromised. Then, there is the insider impact, which may negatively impact the stock price just prior to notification of a data breach, and, of course, there is the aftermath once public disclosure is made. How much media hype and exposure the breach gets will impact the price as well. Table 2-1 shows the list of public companies that reported data breaches in 2009.

Table 2-1: Public Companies Reporting Data Breaches in 2009

NAME	DATE	RECORDS COMPROMISED	STOCK SYMBOL
Continental Airlines	1/12/2009	230	CAL
Occidental Petroleum Corporation	1/6/2009	5,673	OXY
Heartland Payment Systems	1/20/2009	130,000,000	HPY
Circuit City	1/10/2009	0	CC
SRA International, Inc.	1/20/2009	6,617	SRX
Best Buy	2/2/2009	3,990	BBY
California Pizza Kitchen	2/19/2009	50	CPKI
Developers Diversified Realty Corporation (DDR)	2/27/2009	4,000	DDR
Sprint Nextel	3/30/2009	0	S
Aetna Inc.	5/27/2009	6,5000	AET
Hewitt Associates	3/11/2009	0	HEW

Continued

Table 2-1 (continued)

NAME	DATE	RECORDS COMPROMISED	STOCK SYMBOL
Pfizer	5/7/2009	0	PFE
AT&T	7/8/2009	2,100	T
WaMu Investments Inc.	4/30/2009	0	JPM
Wells Fargo	7/17/2009	500	WFC
IBM	6/19/2009	0	IBM
Blue Cross Blue Shield Association	10/3/2009	850,000	WLP
Boeing Co.	7/1/2009	0	BA
HSBC Holdings plc	11/20/2009	0	HCS
Textron	12/1/2009	0	TXT
UnitedHealthcare	8/28/2009	0	UNH
Dollar Tree	12/14/2009	0	DLTR
Kraft Foods	9/18/2009	0	KFT

While not quite an empirical study, it is perhaps meaningful to analyze these data breaches by dividing them into three categories:

- Large public breaches where more than 10,000 records were compromised.
- Small public breaches where less than 10,000 records were compromised.
- Public breaches where the total number of records was not known or not disclosed.

Often when a breach exposes less than one million records, the media doesn't give it much exposure. Heartland Payment Systems currently holds the title for the largest U.S. breach in recorded history. There isn't anyone who doubts the impact this breach had on the stock price of Heartland (see Figure 2-6). A very stable stock for the previous 2+ years dropped more than 90 percent shortly after the notification. Some experts see the stock fluctuation the few months prior (see circled data points in Figure 2-6) as a sign of insider trading on the knowledge of the breach. Within about a year the stock had almost fully recovered.

On average with small information security breaches of public companies, there was a 12 percent drop in the stock price two weeks after disclosure. On average, the stock had recovered to the level of the day of initial disclosure within 60 days.

There appears to be little impact in 2009 on the stock price when an information security breach is publicly announced for public companies that do not disclose the number of records lost. In cases where there appears to be a large impact, it seems to be the result of other factors impacting the stock price.

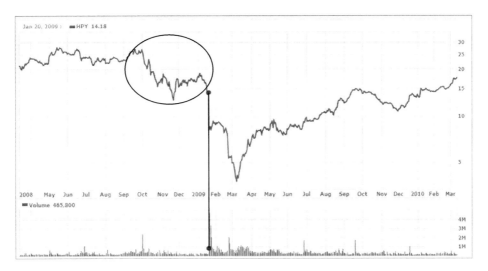

Figure 2-6

In summary, it would appear that the impact to the stock of a public company is largely based on the nature and information in the disclosure. When it is a high-profile, greatly publicized breach, it seems to impact the stock heavily. When a company does not disclose the total number of records lost, there appears to be no statistically meaningful impact on the stock. It is no wonder that more and more companies are choosing not to publicize this type of information.

I believe that over the next decade we as a society will continue to become more numb to data breach announcements unless they are record breaking. We will likely pay more attention to cases when fraud and identity theft occur as a result of these data breaches. While fraud and identity theft are at all time highs, there is little evidence that proves this is being caused by data breaches. Only in a very few instances do breaches result in any cases of identity theft. When they do result in fraud or identity theft, the number of individuals impacted is usually very small as well.

Regardless, lawyers can make a case and win when a breach occurs. Take the Veterans Administration data breach, for example. A laptop was stolen with 26.5 million veterans' information on it. The laptop was recovered. It was determined that no one accessed the data. No fraud cases were ever reported or linked to the breach, and still the VA had to settle a class-action lawsuit for $20 million dollars.

Cyber-criminals may not be targeting a particular company for customer or employee data at all. Perhaps they are targeting the company for trade secrets, intellectual property, and other valuable information. These types of breaches do not need to be publicly disclosed and can cost a company much more than some public discontent, fines, and a lawsuit.

FROM OUR CONTRIBUTORS

Eric Shepcaro, Chief Executive Officer, Telx

Today, it is not enough for a corporation to have established physical and virtual security and IT policies. It is also not enough for corporations to just achieve various certifications such as SAS 70 Type 2 or other ISO certifications. These policies have become the table stakes — the "must-haves" to do business with customers, vendors, and others in the supply chain. In fact, I have come across many firms that have deployed these policies, processes, and certifications to meet some legal requirement or even a Sarbanes-Oxley requirement. Corporations need a rigorous ongoing testing program, they need to conduct business impact analyses on processes, close gaps where appropriate and hold everyone accountable from the CEO down through the organization. This includes ongoing risk assessment and governance. Now, even while following this approach, a breach of systems may occur and it may result in fraud and even theft of your customers' identities. If you believe that trust equals customer loyalty as I do, my recommended approach if this occurs is to, of course, plug the hole — but to also notify everyone as soon as possible and to over-communicate. Yes, you may be worried about stock price impact and class action suits and users' recommending that others not use your product; however, I have found that corporations that are totally transparent in this situation do best. A good recent example is Network Solutions. After a hacker penetrated the ecommerce system on their site, they quickly put up an informational website on what occurred, actions they were taking, and even included a blog for those affected to ask questions and receive answers in real time. Communication is critical in these situations!

Dave Meizlik, Director of Product Marketing and Communications for Websense, Inc.

The rationale for preventing data breaches has moved from risk and compliance to simple common sense. The impact of data loss can never accurately be forecasted because it's based entirely on content, context, and conditions — all of which are speculative. What was lost, how much was lost, your position in and perception of the market at that point in time, external market conditions entirely independent to your business, and many more factors all play a role in assessing the impact of a breach. Sure, you can build models, risk mitigation plans, and instrument compliance controls, but at the end of the day whether

to invest (and how much) in preventing data breaches all comes down to an argument that's based on common sense. And here's a hint, the answer is *yes*.

Stocks go up and they go down; consumers are finicky and their attention spans are short; and the priorities of an organization, its customers, and its stockholders change. As a further example, even the sensitivity of data changes, as in the case of a company's earnings release that loses its confidentiality once it is publicized at the end of a fiscal quarter. Fundamentally, no organization wants to have a data breach, ever. The decision then isn't whether to make a best effort to prevent one, it's how best to get started.

Most organizations today have yet to invest in data loss prevention (DLP) technologies because of their well-founded reputation for high cost and complexity. Mitigating those two inhibitors is key for organizations that must build an irrational business case for what is a common sense problem.

The Security Culture

Will companies and individuals value protecting their information enough to invest in it, to defend it, to even understand what the risks and benefits are? Are businesses willing to spend the money necessary to protect all of their endpoints, employees, and data? Certainly they have invested in antivirus and anti-malware software, but what happens when the software costs more and has to be applied to 3 to 10 times the number of devices that it does today? What happens when companies must do real-time security monitoring of all systems, not just the ones where the data at rest (presumably important data) resides? Even now, software vendors are good at writing code that does not apply updates and patches unless it has been properly licensed. These solutions will rely on updates to keep the device safe. Are home users willing to spend tens, if not hundreds of dollars each year in security software for their devices? Unfortunately, the answer is probably "no" in most cases.

What happens when the cyber-criminals have the upper hand . . . or more specifically when organizations become aware they do? When the environment, culture, and technology all favor the hacker? There is a growing unhealthy division between corporations, the government, and consumers regarding information security. For the past several years, laws, regulations, and financial institution policies have completely eliminated any financial liability a consumer has regarding fraud. This has been so effective that consumers worry very little about potential risks because they know they will experience no financial loss whatsoever.

Unfortunately, this mindset has bled into corporate and executive cultures. Those same consumers who don't worry about their personal information and financial liability, go to work each day for corporations that have a high degree of responsibility and liability for information security. The complacency, lack of awareness, and apathy impact organizations that really do need additional security precautions but either do not implement the right solutions or do not implement them in a timely fashion.

Companies over the next 10 years will become more and more educated regarding the threats to their information security. There will be more and more regulations, each with ever-expanding auditing and enforcement. Some companies will come to the determination that doing everything they should to protect their sensitive data is not financially feasible. Others will feel this investment in a strong security program is critical to their viability as an organization.

FROM OUR CONTRIBUTORS

Mike Cote, Chairman and CEO of SecureWorks

Information technology has created the opportunity for wide-scale change in the way that corporations do business and, despite security challenges, the costs of not using technology far outweigh the risks of technology-enabled systems. Consumers will continue to become more savvy about secure technology use, but hackers are likely to stay ahead of this awareness curve with increasingly sophisticated and cloaked attacks. Consequently, the security community must work together to layer security technologies, processes, and expertise into an increasingly seamless web of visibility and protection to protect users regardless of their level of sophistication. We are playing a game of security chess with a very competent adversary and we will increase our chances of winning by more thoroughly understanding their game strategy and their likely next moves. If we can ultimately impact the economics of the underground by making it more expensive for the hacker to steal the data than it is worth, perhaps these highly skilled technology pros would have incentive to contribute in a more positive way to the world economy.

Dennis Devlin, CISO, Brandeis University

What will information security and privacy look like in 2020? Will the operant model be "innocent until proven guilty" as it is today, or the reverse? And what can information security professionals do to best prepare the organizations and individuals we serve for such an uncertain future?

The ARPANET began as an open electronic communications infrastructure that assumed everything was trustworthy until proven otherwise. Before the Morris worm in 1988, there were rarely even security demarcations separating its interconnected networks. When the ARPANET became the Internet in 1990, that open architecture and culture continued. Even today, messages, software, and information sources are generally considered to be legitimate unless there are malware signatures or spam filters indicating they are not. As new threats occur faster than signatures and patches can be developed, today's model is collapsing.

The openness and naively-assumed trustworthiness of the Internet gave rise to email, social networking, open sharing of information, and free exploration. In 2020, will our interactions be limited to pre-vetted individuals, information sources we already know about, and software only from a small number of very large software providers? Are we destined for a more Orwellian future where someone else determines what is safe for each of us to see and use?

Information security involves people and process, in addition to technology. Increasingly, people and process are proving to be the weak links in the chain. Who will be responsible for bad security decisions in 2020? Will the cost of failures shift from credit card companies to individual cardholders? Are we preparing our digital citizens for this brave new world?

As information security professionals, our primary role has shifted from implementing technology-based security solutions to educating our constituents to think the way that we think.

Creating a digitally-literate populous with the skills and knowledge to better discern good from bad seems to be the most cost-effective strategy to prepare for 2020. Technology and information security professionals cannot provide all of the *in loco parentis* security protection needed today. A decade from now we will likely be facing new information security threats we haven't even imagined yet, and we are going to need all the help we can get.

The Path to 2020

So, companies in 2020 and beyond will have some difficult choices to make. They will have to make a conscious decision to walk down one of two roads (unlike the fence sitters of today). The first path is an insurance-based approach to security. The other path is a genuine comprehensive best practices model that incorporates regulatory requirements as a minimum standard. Many, rather than attempting to achieve best practices, will choose to gamble by choosing the first path. They will do the minimum necessary to be technically compliant with whatever regulations govern their industry (if any). They will then hope for the best. If a data breach occurs, they will try to sweep it under the rug. If that doesn't work, they will bite the bullet when it comes to fines, lawsuits, and other negative repercussions.

Data breaches will seem more common in 2020 than they are today. This may be because more breaches actually occur. In part this will likely be because fewer and fewer will be able to be kept secret. Naturally, if breaches are commonplace, the novelty will have long ago worn off. Media outlets will no longer report on them. They won't have the same strong negative impact that they have today, so businesses will be more willing to tolerate the risk.

This may, however, be altered by legal cases that occur over the next several years. It is almost a given that if a data breach occurs today, a class-action lawsuit is not far behind. It doesn't matter if fraud occurs, if the data was actually exposed, or if negligence was present. Worse yet, many current suits are filed by individuals or groups that are not a party to any loss, potential loss, or personally involved in any way. These are typically the result of lawyers who are trying to make a quick and easy buck. So, if case law leans toward the success of those suits, there may be less tolerance for data breach risk. If case law moves toward finding proper fault and placing blame and liability at the feet of those who deserve it, then the negative repercussions of a breach are limited to fines and the loss of customer loyalty. History has shown us that customers have quite a short memory for these types of things. So, with breaches likely to be more common in the future, it may not be nearly as big a deal to weather the storm of a breach in 2020 and beyond.

The higher path of implementing a compliance-based security framework based on best practices will be selected by those who have greater regulatory requirements (financial institutions, for example) and feel a greater responsibility to their customers to protect their sensitive data. They will have to invest heavily in security technology and solutions to mitigate threats. Technologies will continue to advance and be combined. This approach is similar to the way that firewalls, intrusion detection and prevention systems, gateway antivirus, spam filtering, web content filtering, and virtual private networking technologies (which were all separate technologies requiring installation, management, maintenance, monitoring, etc.) all became available on a single appliance and with an easy-to-use interface. Then, that appliance got less and less expensive. Over time, this same collapse of technologies will include data leakage prevention, security information event management, event correlation, and other elements in easy-to-deploy, -use, and -manage systems.

So, those who choose the best practices and compliance path will not find it extremely expensive to achieve adequate security. The delta in 2020 between those who implement the minimum required solutions and those who strive for best practices may not be as far apart as some might think from a cost standpoint; however, it could be significant in terms of risk mitigation.

FROM OUR CONTRIBUTORS

Charles J (CJ) Spallitta, Global Services VP, Security Services Global Services VP, Security Services, Verizon

Information technology (IT) is all about enabling a business to accomplish its goals efficiently and effectively. IT security is all about allowing IT to accomplish its goals within an acceptable level of risk for the business in a financially prudent manner. Often organizations focus on doing so much security "activity" without taking a step back to really understand what they are trying to accomplish in support of the business. In my view, organizations could spend an infinite amount of money on security and never adequately address the risk requirements of the business. Said another way, many organizations could spend a lot less on security and get better results (reduce risk — or at least understand their risk, measure compliance in a satisfactory manner, implement good-enough identity services, etc.) by focusing on fewer things that really matter.

So for an organization with five global locations, is one firewall enough? Probably not. Are 100 firewalls enough? That is probably too many — yet organizations tend to lean this way. The point is that at some point you cross over into a situation of diminishing returns and begin wasting your limited security budget on things that don't actually advance the organization's security posture or reduce its risk. Back to the example on firewalls, the answer is that such an organization needs probably more than 1 and a lot less than 100 firewalls. Let's just say the answer is 10 firewalls.

The budget for the other 90 firewalls can be used to advance the organization's risk reduction in other areas — say actually monitoring the event logs of your security devices and application servers. Evidence pertaining to roughly 80% of all breaches, according to research and investigation by Verizon, is likely to be in those logs, but this information is neither noticed nor acted upon. Typically, organizations implement a bunch of tools to monitor attacks on their perimeter (FW/IDPS), malware attacks (anti-malware), attacks on data (in motion traffic analysis and logging and data at rest), and trickery attacks (anti-phishing). Each component obviously provides valuable information, but organizations rarely seem to look at all these discrete sources of security data holistically (i.e. correlate all the data into something meaningful that can be acted upon — ideally proactively, but at a minimum reactively should an attack occur).

Continued

FROM OUR CONTRIBUTORS   *(continued)*

While there are many things to consider going into the next decade of IT security, I feel these basic tenants hold true as we move into the future:

- **User privileges:** While the majority of data breaches occurred from the efforts of outside criminals, insider data breaches rose in 2009. So it is important for organizations to not give more privileges to users than they need and have a way to audit user activity.

- **Monitor event logs:** As I mentioned above, monitor the event logs of your security devices and application servers. Buy a SEM and implement it properly or go to an MSSP.

- **Do the easy things:** The attack methods bad guys are employing are not highly difficult. They are looking for easy ways in, because the unfortunate truth is that because so many organizations don't do the easy things, most breaches or hacks could have been avoided by implementing simple controls.

Douglas W. Barbin, CPA,CISSP, CFE, GCFA, PCI-QSA, Director, Assurance and Compliance Services, SAS 70 Solutions, Inc.

The unfortunate reality is that many companies will tacitly adopt the insurance method described in this section. They will aggressively market adherence to compliance and best practice standards, doing only what they need to get by and look attractive to an acquiring company. There are two things that will act as counter to this:

- **For the customers:** Ten years from now, the increase in access to information will rival the growth we have seen this past decade. In 2000, Google was just getting started and Twitter was non-existent. With even greater access, customers will demand transparency around what is being done to protect their business. The absence of such data, including independent audits and/or certifications will be a red flag as to the legitimacy of a company. More important, expect that in 2020, contracts with outsource providers will include detailed requirements for information security by default, and not by exception.

- **For the companies and providers themselves:** Security technology continues to converge, providing more control for less. In 10 years we hope to see the same for audits and certifications. Today, companies are bogged down with audits ranging from SAS 70 audits to PCI DSS validation, not to mention audits by regulators and their own customers. More often than not, a security audit is a rehash of many of the same topics ranging from administrative to network and application security controls.

Some argue that a universal standard for security would alleviate much of this stress. This is a particularly hot topic in cloud computing. The practical reality is that an audit or certification is designed to meet the needs of an end user. Until those end users can agree to accept the same output, we will not see a lot of audit or certification consolidation. That said, it is well-known that many security controls span across multiple regulations and industry requirements. As a result, the opportunity for leverage lies in the ability to reuse information and testing at the control level (and forcing your auditors not to reinvent the wheel on your dime).

An organization with a good grasp on its controls and a mapping to all of the regulatory and best practice requirements should be able to spend much more time on customers and less time with auditors. Most importantly, the companies on this path will have no problem sharing this level of information with their customers, and those following the "insurance" approach will be hiding in plain sight.

Note

1. Racz, N., Weippl, E. and Seufert, A. (2010). A frame of reference for research of integrated GRC. In: Bart De Decker, Ingrid Schaumüller-Bichl (Eds.), Communications and Multimedia Security, 11th IFIP TC 6/TC 11 International Conference, CMS 2010 Proceedings. Berlin: Springer, pp. 106–117.

CHAPTER 3

Technology Influences on Security

Any intelligent fool can make things bigger, more complex, and more violent. It takes a touch of genius — and a lot of courage — to move in the opposite direction.
—Albert Einstein

In the future, many technological changes will affect our lives—changes such as the transition to IPv6 and to such familiar technologies as remote access, search engines, web browsers, web services, and virtualization. There will also be movements affecting things such as identity management, mobility, how domain names are used and managed, and how software development is managed, that we must adapt to both from an operational and a risk perspective.

Current threats, including malware, botnets, and Advanced Persistent Threat (APT), will continue to evolve. Each will impact the way IT, IT security, and IT risk management are applied and managed.

The Movement Toward National Identity Management

Many scenarios create momentum toward a national identity management program. There are few people we talk with who do not believe that eventually the United States will have a national identity management program. Most, however, believe a national identity management program to be something that isn't likely to be implemented until well past 2020. That said, the next 10 years will move us significantly closer to this becoming a reality. In the Enhanced Border Security and Visa Entry Reform Act of 2002, the U.S. Congress mandated the use of biometrics in U.S. visas. This law requires that Embassies and Consulates abroad must now issue to international visitors, "only machine-readable, tamper-resistant visas and other travel and entry documents that use biometric identifiers." Additionally, the Homeland Security Council decided that the U.S. standard for biometric screening for all visa applicants seeking to come to the United States should transition from two fingerprints to ten fingerprints at all embassies worldwide, originally planned to be implemented by December 31, 2007.

In May 2009, President Obama's National Security Telecommunications Advisory Committee unanimously approved a report on Identity Management and recommended that the White House play a key leadership role in advancing this topic as a national priority. In the President's 60-Day Cybersecurity Policy Review, released at the end of May 2009, President Obama identified the development of a national strategy for identity management as one of the 10 short-term priority action items.

Since the end of March 2010, there has been a U.S. government national security agency called the Biometrics Identity Management Agency (BIMA). It supersedes a Biometrics Task Force that was established in 2000. Currently, its reach is limited to the Department of Defense, but it could possibly have greater reach in the future.

As we are all painfully aware, September 11, 2001 changed our nation and set the stage for increased security in airports. The government moved swiftly immediately after that attack to make changes in an effort to ensure that it won't happen again. But imagine the effect of another terrorist attack on U.S. soil—or even just a credible threat of another serious attack. Would the Department of Homeland Security decide to use the biometric program within the country rather than just at border crossings? It's not too far-fetched. In fact, today, many if not most, legislators are in favor of making this program mandatory, even for travel within the United States, in an effort to eliminate terrorism. Why? It's rather simple. The majority of the experts believe a terrorist attack will take place again in the next 10 years, and if you believe this as a lawmaker or politician, you had better be seen as working to move the program forward. Can you imagine the political leverage gained if a politician can openly criticize his opposition for not advocating border security measures using biometrics, the lack of which could be seen as the single reason that led to a terrorist entering the country?

Biometrics may not be the technology or platform that pushes this national identity management agenda along at all. Advancements in radio-frequency identification (RFID) technology have been remarkable and its uses for national identity management are compelling. RFID comprises two parts. One is known as the "tag," which is an integrated circuit that stores and processes information, including modulating and demodulating a radio-frequency signal. The second is an antenna used for receiving and transmitting the signal, known as an interrogator or reader. The tags are placed on products, on animals, and even on people. The tags can contain a tremendous amount of information that can be read via the readers from up to several meters away. In other words, it is an ideal way to track where something or someone is.

Those who wonder how RFID could be used for national identity management need look no further than the Baja Beach Club (`http://www.bajabeach .es/`) in Spain. (In addition, there's a BBC article about this available at `http:// news.bbc.co.uk/2/hi/technology/3697940.stm`.) They insert an RFID tag under your skin when you arrive. From that point forward, there is no need for access cards, room keys, credit cards, or anything else that would be used to conduct transactions or access rooms, resort areas, or systems. When you eat, the RFID tag automatically bills you without your ever having to give your credit card to a waiter, or telling them which room you are in. Plus, you can keep tabs (literally) on exactly where your children are and what they are doing.

Right now, however, especially in the United States, people express outrage and disdain anytime someone promotes the idea of RFID tracking in human beings. Of course, advocates cite the benefits for emergency paramedic drivers, locating kidnap victims, and a host of other scenarios. One of the uses that is discussed most often is in the prison system. RFID tags would help tremendously to reduce violence and track illegal and other antisocial behavior. It could even help identify prison guards and other workers who help inmates procure contraband items, including drugs.

When some people consider the use of RFID in humans, however, they believe that is exactly what we would become: prisoners. Government and law enforcement agencies, and even private security companies, could track where you have been, with whom you associate, and the things you own, all with RFID technology.

Another area of concern related to national identity management is the American Recovery and Reinvestment Act that President Obama signed on February 17, 2009. This act included provisions relating to Health Information Technology; Title XIII of Division A and Title IV of Division B together are known as the Health Information Technology for Economic and Clinical Health Act, or the HITECH Act. Billions of dollars are allocated for building a nationwide healthcare database. This could be the way and means to fund a national identity program, because the uses for healthcare and medical information are enormous.

If the nationwide healthcare database does in fact become the foundation of a national identity program, many organizations would want to piggyback on this system for other purposes. Some could use it to authorize access to government buildings. Others could use it to validate identity for the purchase of firearms. Still others could use it for the purposes of ensuring the identity of those taking out loans or to establish credit accounts in an effort to reduce fraud and identity theft. There are an endless number of applications, processes, systems, procedures, and organizations that could benefit from a nationwide identity management program.

NOTE Of course, participation in a national identity program wouldn't start off being mandatory for anyone (except for some government employees and specific programs run by the government) but the same can be said for requiring a driver's license or passport as a form of ID. Of course, states will be under pressure to ensure that people who get a driver's license are properly identified. It's not a stretch to see the federal and state governments wanting to link national ID with the process for obtaining a driver's license.

Why does anyone care? Because fraud and identity theft are rampant right now and are growing every year, and identity management can help to slow that. The technology to support biometrics or RFID at an individual endpoint level is reasonably affordable. If programs using those technologies were put in place, they likely would use independently deployed systems that are not networked together. However, multiple individual systems might cascade into a management problem that forces the organizations managing them to integrate the systems together to be more usable. It might just be easier to work from a common, master database of legitimate citizens. Merchant systems and the systems used by other companies that facilitate day-to-day commerce and trade could all tie into this master system in a global effort to eliminate fraud and identity theft.

Perhaps it's not necessary that a single method or system be the standard; perhaps several technologies could be supported. Maybe a scan of your right hand and some kind of facial or retinal scan could be the default requirement. This potential new system of commerce, based on biometrics, RFID, or both, could be so effective in reducing fraud and identity theft that the government might decide to make it mandatory for all commerce and transactions.

Wait! We are Americans and get to vote on this before it happens, right? Well, that's why you should think about it now. For example, imagine cyberterrorism where there isn't a physical attack, rather an attack in which a large percentage of the credit cards in the world is compromised. This is not really outside the realm of possibility given the concentration of a few card processors (companies that process credit card transactions) and a few brand cards (like Visa, MasterCard, and American Express). Now imagine the world without credit cards for a day, a week, a month, or more because the legitimacy of every transaction is uncertain. Citizens would look to the government to restore that basic requirement for security, which might be incentive enough to implement a national identity program.

Regardless, at the current pace, it is not likely a national identity program would all happen prior to 2020. However, national and world events that create high degrees of emotional impact can cause major changes to happen in weeks and months rather than years and decades. In our opinion, it really isn't a question of whether a national identity management program plays out, but rather how quickly it comes to fruition.

Frankly, a national identity program scares me to death. While it sounds like a perfect solution to many problems, once this is in place, the government has a tremendous amount of control over its citizens. This opens the door for segregation, especially for groups that choose to not participate. Basic human services may be refused unless a person is part of the program. What if their religious beliefs or other reasons prohibit their use of the system? Persecution of these minorities will undoubtedly begin. Giving one group, even if it is the U.S. government (or some might say "especially if given to the U.S. government"), this level of access and control in general is a very bad idea and sounds a little too Revelation 13:16-17 for me. That being said, there are many countries that already do this. Primarily these systems are in regions of the world where I don't think too many Americans would feel comfortable with the rights and freedoms those countries offer their citizens. I also think that each of us is part "lemming," so likely this will eventually happen with little push back.

— Kevin Prince

I'm not sure if it's my background from being in the military or my general lack of concern for hiding anything personal that leads to me not really caring if the U.S. government had a National Identity Program. If properly deployed, the benefits in my opinion outweigh the personal liberties that I might give up. If the government really wanted to collect data on me there are many sources and resources they could apply. If they had easier access to my data and could set up some automation that maybe in some scenario caused me some discomfort, so be it if it saved lives.

While I do understand there are still many racial and religious biases in the world, I believe those, from a government's point of view, are controlled significantly by public opinion and find it hard to believe there would be widespread abuse of using this information wrongly. On the flip side, I'd hate for anyone to have unnecessary access to anything and everything I do each day for no good cause. I also understand and respect other people have unique experiences, backgrounds, and concerns.

I'd also really hate to be a politician or a movie star when this is implemented, it'll be code-named "the Blackmail database!!"

— Doug Howard

FROM OUR CONTRIBUTORS

Dipto Chakravarty, VP Engineering, Identity & Security Products, General Manager, Cloud Security Services, Novell

Identity management in traditional computing is a complex issue to begin with, and this complexity will only increase with the advent of virtualization and cloud computing. To deal with it, those responsible for managing identities and those creating technologies for identity management have had to continuously innovate. The latest innovations we have seen in 2010 are in the area of intelligent workload management, specifically toward intelligently managing identity-aware workloads. Considering how we got to where we are today and where we will be in 2020, consider the four pillars of Identity Management:

■ **Authentication:** In order for a user to access your systems, one needs to authenticate that he is who he says he is. Authentication methods can be very basic, such as simply requiring that the user enter a password, or they can be stronger and involve fingerprint readers or other types of biometrics. Of course, the number of systems that an individual may have to access during the course of a workday has proliferated, and many of these systems have migrated off-premise. In order to deal with multiple password issues and the varying authentication requirements of different systems, some organizations have moved to single-sign-on methodologies. At the same time, we've become better at correlating different types of identity data to allow for the behavioral analysis of users. We can know, for example, when "John Doe" swiped his ID badge in order to enter the campus as well as when he tried, and perhaps failed, to enter his password correctly. If someone is trying to use John Doe's password when he's not on premise, we know there's a problem!

■ **Authorization:** Once we know who a user is, we need to be able to authorize his use of this or that application or system. The traditional authorization method is roles-based. "John" may be a marketer who should be authorized to access marketing assets at various levels; he may also manage a P&L, so he needs authorization to access financial systems; and he may be a "super-user" for some infrastructural elements like a website. Role-based authorization is often supplemented with policy-driven authorization. For instance, John can only be a root-user while he's on campus, so the question becomes, "How do I delegate this privilege to him for the time he's on campus and then rescind it once he's left?"

■ **Provisioning:** With authentication done and authorizations in place, the system is then responsible for rolling out the appropriate attributes based on relevant credentials.

■ **Auditing and Monitoring:** Finally, the system needs to log activity, perform audits, generate reports, and track events as they happen.

These functions in themselves are by no means new: provisioning users is two decades old and likely to persist for another decade (2020) as well; authorization has been around as long as client-server or time-share systems have been around, etc. What is new is the way that these get connected and work together. People have gone from multiple tools addressing individual functions to bundles or platforms where you have authentication and authorization and auditing all sorted in a systemic way so that you can cut across and report across them. This bundling or platforming has become necessary as SLAs have become stricter and regulations have gotten tighter. With tighter regulations has come ever-increasing complexity. You not only need to have these tools in place, but you've also got to map the various technologies to specific controls — compliance controls, security controls, governance, and on and on. These controls have six to seven different components which in turn get mapped to the actual regulations which could be PCI for financial records, Sarbanes Oxley for the password retries, HIPAA for any health records, and so on.

And now, to add to the complexity, you have to deal with the fact that some of these components are actually "out there" in the cloud, thereby making this new layer of "intelligence" for managing workloads a necessity in 2020's ubiquitous computing paradigm.

Internet Protocol in 2020

A major upgrade to the Internet is under way and will continue to progress over the next 10 years. This is the movement toward IPv6. IP, or Internet Protocol, is the language spoken between computers on the Internet. Currently, most systems still utilize version 4 of this protocol. The need for IPv6 came about largely because of the limited number of IP addresses (unique numbers assigned to each computer accessible from the Internet) available in version 4. On April 15, 2009, the American Registry for Internet Numbers (ARIN) (the organization that distributes IP addresses for the U.S., Canada, and most Caribbean nations) sent a letter out that stated that within two years, the IPv4 address space will be depleted. They encouraged everyone to get their infrastructures prepared for IPv6, which has immensely more address space. Substantially increasing the number of addresses isn't the only change in this version, however. There are many security enhancements in it as well.

Most good information security professionals are bracing for IPv6 because they understand that any technology that has not had wide adoption and use inevitably has an enormous number of security flaws that are exploited in the early days of deployment and use. Worse yet, history shows that because there is little business benefit in moving to IPv6, organizations will not migrate until they are forced to do it because they cannot get any IPv4 space. Organizations will therefore move to IPv6 without developing an understanding of the security and other implications it has. Because of that, it will be deployed haphazardly, and we will again begin a cycle of security threats and breaches like those we have seen with every other new technology, including email, instant messaging, wireless, VoIP, mobile devices, social networking, e-commerce, cloud computing, and, of course, the grand master, web browsers and web applications.

To get an idea of the enormity of the task facing us, consider the following mandatory elements of IPv6:

- Mandatory IPSEC (with all the associated crypto code)
- Mandatory multicast
- Mandatory QoS
- Automatic configuration of interfaces (DHCP replacement)
- All devices Internet addressable (no more NAT)
- Massive packet sizes (up to 4GB)
- Many new rules for routing, private addresses, DNS, packet analysis, fragmentation, and so on.

All of this trickles down to new code at the driver, network, and application layers. New code means bugs, flaws, and vulnerabilities for many years to come. This means a large learning curve for developers, information security professionals, network architects, and technical staff. There is a good chance that most of these individuals will treat IPv6 like IPv4 (but with more address space), leading to many configuration problems and vulnerabilities that will be exploited by knowledgeable hackers.

With IPv6, foundational concepts like firewall, NAT, and IDS must be rethought and perhaps redeployed. While there are some guides, such as RFC 4942,[1] available to help, a full makeover of personnel training, policies, standards, and procedures will have to be done. Without it, we enter the next generation of methods to compromise networks and systems, such as finding source routing flaws, IP spoofing, tunneling, cache poisoning, exploiting buffer overflows, denial of service attacks, and more. Round 2 (ding ding).

Testing tools will have to be developed and enhanced. The tools most security professionals have used for years, such as NMAP and Nessus, have limited IPv6 support. Other popular tools at this time have no IPv6 support at all. Unfortunately, the way we as an industry have handled this in the past is to allow the attackers to lead the way. We reactively build in security features once a series of exploits has occurred.

FROM OUR CONTRIBUTORS

Frank J. Ricotta Jr., Chief Technology Officer, Enterprise Information Management, Inc.

The fear that we will run out of Internet IP addresses has been around for years and concern about that has increased with the explosive growth of wireless data. In practice, the address space utilization has not occurred at the pace many suggested due to the introduction of technologies such as NATing, virtualization, and even SaaS. Regardless, the problem will exist in the minds of many until we fully implement an extension of the Internet that includes use of the IPv6 address range. Often, fear serves as a motivator for the progression of technology; however, more often than not it isn't motivation enough. Rather, expanding business horizons usually drives innovation.

As noted in this section of the book, IPv6 provides many new features that can enable further use of the Internet as a business enabler. Security is certainly one feature. IPv6 allows for secure transactions at the network level versus it being layered on as an afterthought. These capabilities will enable new and creative wireless and home devices as well as provide ambiguous client access from any location that has network connectivity.

The real question still centers on the IPv6 adoption rate. Today, government and educational sectors are the market's early adopters. Beyond these sectors, wide scale adoption will be driven by the ease and cost to do so. With that said, new products are being designed to support IPv6, so we should see a natural acceleration over the next 5 to 10 years just through normal refresh cycles. Near term, the next major adopter will be (or let's rephrase and say should be) major wireless network providers. In some cases they have already done so at the core of their network, but have yet to extend it to edge due to limited support for IPv6 in consumer devices.

2020: Remote Access Continues to Be a Problem

In 2008, gas prices rose past $4.00 per gallon in the United States. Almost overnight there was a 15 percent surge in employees working from home. Telecommuters traditionally have been a soft spot in the information security program of organizations. Many telecommuters still use unsecured remote access programs, which require open ports on the firewall and simple authentication to gain full remote control of internal systems. Others do utilize secure virtual private network (VPN) technology but lack endpoint security such as proper patch management, desktop security for host-based firewalls, IDS, antivirus software, and spam protection. That can be a problem because VPNs are great for keeping data private between the remote users and the corporate network, so if the remote workstation is compromised, viruses, hackers, and worms are encrypted by the VPN and can securely travel directly into the corporate network. The result is that the organization might get more than they thought from the telecommuter or traveler.

Worse yet, enterprise IT administrators usually have no visibility into these remote systems to know if the systems are protected or up to date. All too often, these remote computer assets are not owned by the corporation, and IT administrators have little power or influence over the software and levels of protection on these remote systems.

The reality is that, through a combination of policies, enforcement, and technology, the solutions could easily be put in place today to resolve many of these issues; however, most business owners aren't willing to make the investment or sacrifices in convenience to allow these solutions to be enabled.

The workplace and workforce will change significantly over the next decade as the demand for more flexible work hours, telecommuting (full- or part-time), and the use of mobility solutions continues to increase. In addition, over the next 10 years, with the increased demand for energy, the emotional impact related to the perceptions and realities of an energy crisis, and green initiatives, a greater and greater percentage of employees will work remotely. The security issues that surround remote workers will continue into 2020 and beyond. The demands for and of secure remote access and user activity will continue to increase, while our personal and business lives will continue to merge. Building an IT infrastructure, combined with a layered approach to security with a heavy emphasis on remote and mobile work forces, will pay dividends to business.

FROM OUR CONTRIBUTORS

Niall Browne, CISA, CCSP, CISSP, CCSI, CISO & VP Information Security, LiveOps

One of the fundamentals, and a primary benefit of the cloud is its on-demand nature, whereby you use only the resources you need, and only pay for what you use, as opposed to the traditional model of paying for resources independently of use. Up to this point, the cloud has been mainly associated with technology offerings, such as SaaS (Software as a Service), PaaS (Platform as a Service), and IaaS (Infrastructure as a Service). Recently, however, there has been a work-model shift toward allowing for more flexibility in the workforce, and a key component of this has been the rapidly growing model of *on-demand work-forces*, also known as WaaS (Workforce as a Service). WaaS will often operate in a far more flexible manner in relation to time (flexible work hours) and location (distributed locations). As a result of this, security will need to grow to become a critical component of this model by ensuring that security controls evolve from their current role of protecting the perimeter "walls of the building" to protecting this distributed data, and the workforce that accesses this data.

The Search Engine Impact

For years, Google has dominated the world of search engines and it doesn't appear likely that anyone will overtake them in the near term—although as we speak Microsoft is making a big push with Bing. Also for years, hackers have discovered ways of manipulating search engines, such as:

- Presenting false results that link to malicious sites
- Ranking their malicious sites at the top of the results
- Manipulating advertising elements to direct users to malicious sites

While Google and other search engines continue to get better and better about detecting and stopping these exploits, cyber-criminals find even more creative methods to exploit them. Because search engines are the major gateway to content on the Internet, search engine manipulation by hackers will continue to be a method of exploitation through 2020 and beyond.

What will likely increase is the use of botnets and website compromises to help with search engine manipulation. While Google and other search engines use very sophisticated and complex algorithms (which they keep very secret) to determine which search results are presented in what order, some things are clearly more important than others. For example, how many times a certain word or search string is entered and how often the resulting links are clicked will help raise the ranking of a website. How many times other websites link to certain content is another strong criteria used to determine search rank.

Recently, there has been a flurry of mass website compromises by botnets running automated exploit scripts. In a few of the most recent cases, the botnets compromised tens of thousands of sites, with a recent exploit compromising over 40,000 sites.

Now imagine adding hidden pages to these compromised sites that include a reference link to some specific malicious website on the Internet with embedded keywords that match the most popular search criteria of the day. If hackers want to compromise millions of systems in a very short period of time, here is how they could do it using this method. First, the cyber-criminals would identify a vulnerability in a website or popular web-based application. While they could just wait for the patrons of these websites to show up and be exploited, many of these sites are small and not frequently visited, so the hackers use a botnet to systematically exploit all these websites and add a hidden link to the home page of the site. The link directs users to a basic web page on the site. No active exploit is being run; no malicious code is being hosted; therefore, it isn't likely that the administrator would notice that anything is wrong with the site.

The new web page would be tailored around a specific keyword or key phrases that match some current event. This could be anything from celebrity news and gossip to political events to natural disasters, anything that draws people's attention. The page would include links associated with those keywords that would all point to a website or websites hosted (or controlled) by the criminal.

Within a matter of days, Google would have all those hidden pages indexed and this would likely put the malicious website (controlled by the criminal) at the very top of the search results for the specific terms and keywords they used. If it is a popular topic, millions of people each day would search on it. This could be simultaneously done for any number of popular search words. The criminal could "own" the whole first page of Google or any other search engine around whatever keywords they wanted.

When users go out to their favorite search engine and type in these keywords, they will be presented with "poisoned" search results that when clicked will lead to these criminal controlled sites where their systems can be compromised.

The Web Services Impact

Web 2.0 is a widespread standard for web-based development. Cyber-criminals have developed a variety of attacks that take advantage of this standard. Some of the most popular attacks include:

- Cross-site scripting (XSS)
- Cross-site request forgery
- Browser flaws

Many technologies that are part of this standard are at risk, including a very important one: web services. Web services act as middleware, allowing dissimilar systems to communicate and share data.

Web 3.0 is just around the corner and the next decade will likely include several new generations of web standards. Throughout the next 10 years and beyond, we will see a host of attacks against these technologies. Attack types will include the following and more:

- Extensible Markup Language (XML) parser DOS (DTD [document type definition] named entities, DTD parameter entities, attribute blowup)
- Simple Object Access Protocol (SOAP) array overflow
- XML external entity file disclosure
- SOAP web services injection
- Cache poisoning
- Transport hijacking
- DNS attacks

Systems running these technologies will be highly prized targets because they will be the nexus point where sensitive, valuable data is available for capture.

Darknet is a common term used to describe a closed peer-to-peer network designed to share information. In the past, darknets have been created through the use of applications running on computers. In the future this type of technology, as well as most other interesting software, will run right inside the browser itself, perhaps using some of the enhanced functionality of JavaScript. This opens the door for attacks in which, by accessing a website (perhaps through a pharming attack, web link, phishing email, search engine poisoning, or any of dozens of other methods), a darknet session is opened on your computer without your knowing it (right inside your browser). Your system can then be searched automatically for sensitive files, which can then be published for easy download by cyber-criminals.

Perhaps darknets, as a technology, could evolve into micro-virtual machines run directly inside the browser. Imagine the power of an operating system running inside the browser itself. While there could be many applications for such technology, cyber-criminals could use these to exploit systems and data in ways never before imagined. These and many other scenarios could be played out with the use of browser-based darknet technology.

The Impact of Virtualization

Hardware capabilities, including processing power, storage capacities, and so on have significantly outpaced the capabilities of software designed to run and utilize the full features of the hardware. Physical space requirements, environmental impacts, and energy consumption have everyone attempting to do more in a smaller technology footprint. As a result, an amazing technology has emerged, called virtualization or virtual machines.

Virtual machines are software technology that allows you to run multiple instances of a software environment on a single piece of hardware. For example, you can run an instance of Windows XP, Windows 2003, Windows 7, and Linux simultaneously on one server—even multiple instances of each one. Originally, this was used for test environments, but it quickly spread to hosting platforms, where a much greater density of hosted systems could be achieved. This is especially true for website hosting where a hosting provider can now have a single piece of hardware with hundreds or thousands of websites hosted rather than just one. This allows for the maximum density, while maintaining completely customizable environments for each customer.

But what happens if there are vulnerabilities in the virtualization software itself? That very thing happened in June 2009, when a UK web hosting provider was attacked by hackers.[2] The over 100,000 websites hosted in virtual environments were exploited, and the hackers destroyed all the data. The attackers seem to have exploited a zero-day vulnerability (a bug or weakness in the software that has no available patch or fix) in the virtualization application that allowed them to gain root access to the system. This, in turn, allowed them to execute administrative Unix commands. In this particular case, less than half of the customers affected had a data backup of their website.

Because virtualization is so useful and bridges the gap between hardware processing power and current software limitations, its use will expand from now until 2020 and beyond and ultimately become a major catalyst for the cloud computing revolutions we will see over the next decade. Unfortunately, this will also draw hackers in droves to look for ways to exploit these environments.

FROM OUR CONTRIBUTORS

Mark Iwanowski, Managing Director, Trident Capital

Few recognize, or they simply ignore, the serious impact weak security can have on an organization until serious damage occurs. The sophistication of the bad guys only continues to get greater, making consumers and less sophisticated small and medium enterprises (SMEs) especially vulnerable. No more apparent is the risk to organizations of any size than the risk created by virtualization, SaaS, and ITC services. Any time shared resources are introduced, risk increases. This complexity and risk/reward relationship is not missed by the bad guys either.

IT security "silver bullets" don't exist, although most companies offering security try to convince the buyer they do. Layered defense is the best ROI even when leveraging virtualization, whether within your own virtualized environment or if you are leveraging a SaaS model. Virtualization does often allow for more system cycles to be applied toward security problems, which in some cases is a deciding factor for providers and enterprises to implement security.

The success of virtualization will be based on the realization of its efficiency promises and resulting positive green impacts and financial economies of scale. However, security concerns must be addressed and, at minimum, virtualization must provide the same if not higher levels of security than standalone machines.

This must be an approach applied by hardware, software, and service providers alike. Howard Schmidt, who was previously a Trident security advisor until he took over cyber-security for the White House, is working hard to get government and industry to work much more closely together to combat both criminal and foreign government supported threats. Key to the success of this effort is to move from reactive to proactive by prioritizing risks (normalized by dividing risks by cost to mitigate) and then focusing on obtaining the highest bang for the buck.

Irida Xheneti, Product Marketing Manager, Security Management, Novell

With a new era of rapid technology innovation comes a new wave of security threats along with the broad proliferation of security vulnerabilities. Although an open IT infrastructure and innovative technologies such as virtualization, mobility, and cloud computing enable companies to increase productivity and reduce cost, they also open up the door to a plethora of security threats and vulnerabilities, business disruption, and security infrastructure challenges such as data breaches, data loss, non-compliance, decreased customer confidence and many more business challenges. Internal and external pressures continue to rise as a result of the high stakes between new technology investments and the risk that security threats pose to an organization.

Virtualized environments, web applications, mobility, and cloud computing initiatives have demonstrated significant cost savings and increased efficiency, but they also called for an integrated and proactive approach to security and risk management. This IT transformation has brought significant benefits to the enterprise, and it has also increased the opportunities for information security vulnerabilities and threats, data leakage, and compliance violations.

The disparate, ad hoc nature of these enterprise environments makes them vulnerable to security risks and, therefore, unable to fulfill the promise of security as a strategic business process. Network complexity makes it difficult for internal IT staff to detect and respond rapidly to attacks, partly because it provides hackers with a plethora of targets from which to choose. The problem will continue to intensify as hackers will continue to grow increasingly savvy and aggressive in their attack methods.

Today, many organizations have adopted disparate security strategies of confinement by building firewalls and deploying standalone security products to protect against potential threats, contributing to a limited and closed off enterprise infrastructure. Looking ahead to 2020, this approach would be highly detrimental to an organization as it would counteract the primary business objectives of becoming more competitive and profitable. Simply too much is at stake, in terms of financial impact, brand equity, and liability, to continue chasing problems rather than proactively eliminating them.

The Malware Problem

Malware in the computer world is analogous to disease in the body. Just as there are many types of disease that go by many different names and have many different requirements for treatment, so too are there many different types of malware with names like virus, worm, Trojan, spyware, grayware, root kits, crimeware, and many others. This software can sometimes be benign, but often it is not.

Malware has been in use since the creation of the computer. Any time someone builds a piece of software, someone else figures out a way to destroy it, or at least manipulate it for their own benefit. The malware of 2020 and beyond will be more difficult to detect and remove than the malware of today. Even now, we are beginning to see malware that is not written to a hard disk partition, doesn't appear in memory, and isn't listed as a running process. The risk of catching the flu can be reduced through vaccinations, cleanliness, reduced exposure, and similar measures. The same sort of precautions apply to reducing your chance of "catching" malware: use anti-malware/antivirus software, follow best practices for security, avoid high-risk websites, and so on. Malware is now, and will continue to be, the single greatest threat in 2020 and beyond.

FROM OUR CONTRIBUTORS

Tim Belcher, Chief Technology Officer, NetWitness

If you are not detecting a deluge of malicious code on your enterprise network, it only means that you are not detecting it — it does *not* mean that your network is clean. By far the most pervasive and difficult problem to solve is custom malicious code. A decade ago, it was obvious that with rudimentary obfuscation, malicious code would bypass all the protections provided by most antivirus and host IPS products. Security companies would use targeted spear phishing with custom malicious code to penetrate victim networks in the '90s, long before the terms "malware" or "spear-phishing" were coined. It is equally obvious today that if an adversary were willing to write custom attack code for a single victim, rather than spend time obfuscating code for widespread use on multiple victims and botnets, the success of these attacks and the length of time before detection would be enormous. Combine this approach with a highly targeted attack directed toward a small group or an individual, and it represents the single most difficult problem to mitigate.

Malware has also proven that compromise is and will continue to be inevitable. The concept of being able to prevent compromise is an illusion. We will always have users who can be fooled into downloading malicious content, and that content will only prove harder and harder to detect in the future.

The Web Browser

With most good software, updates, patches, and new versions are released from time to time to increase functionality, expand features, and eliminate discovered security problems. The problem is that most systems are not upgraded to the newest software and rarely are incremental updates applied in a timely fashion. For example, in May 2009 a study of Internet web browsers was conducted that revealed that nearly one half of all browsers used were Microsoft's Internet Explorer 6.0. IE6 was released in 2001 and is still by far the most used web browser even though there have been two subsequent free major upgrades (IE7 in 2006 and IE8 in 2009). In addition, there are several competing free browsers available. Eight years after the release of IE6, it is still the most used browser, and currently its use is not showing signs of diminishing.

Web browser flaws are one of the most common vulnerabilities used by hackers to exploit systems, so you would think organizations and individuals would be motivated to keep their software up to date, but that, unfortunately, is not the case. There are a number of reasons for this. Sometimes the hardware can't support the new version; some organizations have policies or procedures that prohibit the installation of new software without going through proper testing; other organizations don't understand the risks and might think that if it isn't broke, why fix it? Then, there are cases in which someone is using a pirated version of an operating system or program, and when the user attempts to download a more recent version, a check is made and they are disallowed from upgrading. Hence, they stay on the old version.

This culture of using outdated software versions is, of course, systemic and extends far beyond web browsers. From a global information security perspective, we will always be behind the 8-ball as long as the majority of systems use very old, outdated, and vulnerable software. In other words, the problems posed by global vulnerability exploits, especially browser exploits, cannot be fixed by the software vendors. They have already done all they can when they have fixed the bugs and made new software versions available. It is up to us to use the more secure versions of the software they release. This will require a culture shift that likely will not occur in a major way through 2020 and beyond.

The Portable Media Debacle, A.K.A. Mobility

The explosion in the use of portable media is changing the way we look at information security. While many smart phones use proprietary, closed software platforms, often there are cracks, hacks, and "jail break" methods to open them for customization. Other smart phones are susceptible to exploitation now. For example, when Apple released version 3.0 of its iPhone, it had patches for 46 security vulnerabilities. Possible exploits included the ability to make calls without the knowledge of the user, execute malicious code, or make the device crash. The future will introduce a whole new playing field for vulnerability exploitation on mobile devices.

In 2020 and beyond, we will be dealing with the malware threats of today, but on all types of mobile media devices. We will be dealing with Trojans and exploits that can track our every move, record our conversations (whether on the phone or not), and manipulate other connection technologies such as Bluetooth devices. Imagine the value of monitoring the telephone conversations, text messages, and emails of a corporate executive of a Fortune 500 company. The insider information that could be retrieved and used to make a small fortune would be very enticing to criminals. Imagine how scary it could be when cyber-stalkers use methods such as these to follow and monitor the lives of their victims.

Portable media devices include mini-handheld drives that can hold a tremendous amount of information. Even now many stores sell devices that are smaller than your thumb that can hold many hundreds of gigabytes.

Moore's Law is a concept regarding the long term trends of computing. Gordon E. Moore was the first to observe the trend that integrated circuit technology capacity was growing exponentially, doubling every two years. However, more than just the technology growth of integrated circuits are linked to Moore's law. Everything, including processor speed, memory capacity, the size of pixels in digital cameras, and even hard drive capacity roughly follow a similar exponential growth curve.

The growth of electronically stored information (ESI) is a phenomenon that well outpaces Moore's law and has a huge impact on information security. ESI has changed every aspect of the way in which companies do business. Between 2002 and 2006, there was an 800 percent annual growth in the amount of ESI produced in the world. In 2006 alone, the world created 161 exabytes of information, which is equivalent to 12 stacks of paper stretching from the earth to the sun. It is a good thing that it is electronic rather than on paper, too. If each tree can make 20 reams of paper and a ream is about 2 inches think, that is about 1.8 trillion trees worth of information, or roughly 20 percent of the Amazon rain forest.

Many industries are just now moving from paper to electronic records, including digitizing all old paper records. Imagine the impact on online storage for data at rest, bandwidth impacts, data backup requirements, authentication and access, as well as procedural changes.

How far beyond 2020 will it be before fingernail-sized petabyte storage chips are available? What will be the impact on information security when this volume of information can be stored on something that can be hidden under the ring on your finger? How do you control access to information when one wrong move and every piece of data your organization has ever created can escape in a matter of seconds?

Like the correlation of time and the exponential growth of technology, there is a similar correlation between the advancement of technology and the number of vulnerabilities and exploits that exist. Up until now and through 2020 and beyond, we will continue to see an exponential growth in the variety, complexity, and creativity of exploits used by criminals to compromise information security.

With technology physically shrinking but becoming more powerful, we will see uses beyond what we could imagine only a few years ago. High-tech companies have already developed medical devices such as heart defibrillators and pacemakers that can be connected to wirelessly and adjusted so surgery is not required. In 2009, a team of researchers was able to connect to one of these pacemakers remotely and reprogram the device to deliver jolts of electricity, and they were even able to make it shut down. Many medical devices today emit signals that have personal patient data. These signals could be captured to gain sensitive information about an individual. What type of data could you get by just having one such "sniffer" as you walk through a hospital, medical facility, or the subway? Will these devices be susceptible to infections from worms, viruses, or other malware?

FROM OUR CONTRIBUTORS

Suprotik Ghose, Head of Networks & Information Security, a leading financial service firm

Portable media has been the bad boy of information security news over the last few years. The reported issues have ranged from infected thumb drives being the conduit for a worm spreading through military computers[1, 2] ; free thumb drives containing worms distributed by a leading software vendor at a security conference[3]; "lost" thumb drives lying in public places being used for social engineering[4]; smart phones of celebrities and notable personalities being hacked and their contents disclosed to the media[5,6,7] to a slew of high profile information security breaches as a result of users losing unencrypted USB drives.[8,9,10] The ever-decreasing form factor, the ease of use of the USB drives, the increasing speed of transfer (USB 3.0 at 5Gbps as compared to USB 2.0 at 480Mbps) and the fact that the capacity of the drives (Lexar just released a 128GB USB drive) keep increasing every quarter poses a challenge for CISOs trying to block the "leakage" of data from the enterprise, as it allows unsupervised visitors, contractors, and employees to walk out with confidential data on a small drive with almost no chance of detection.

In spite of the security guidance provided by enterprise IT security shops and the release of multiple portable media security products, portable media and mobile security will continue to be a challenge for the CISO in the next decade. The threat of mobile malware, phishing, viruses, and spam is real as more and more applications are migrated to operate on smart phones and other mobile devices. These mobile devices try to look more like PCs, and in the future phones are slated to support RIA (Richer Internet Applications) using equivalents of Adobe Flash, Java, and Microsoft Silverlight, and browser plug-ins such as Ajax or Google WebToolkit. These new applications would require upgraded antivirus and malware detection engines, current scanning

Continued

FROM OUR CONTRIBUTORS *(continued)*

signatures and malware removal capabilities, as well as enforcement of "real time" identity management controls to deny network access to unauthorized portable media. The micro-USB interface being used as a standard to access and charge the phones may become a method of physical attack into the phones and will require updated security standards to be developed. The industry will need to continue to improve on the resiliency of the encryption being used on the USB drives as versions are cracked.[11] In addition, USB drives may incorporate public/private key and the PKI technology for positive identification prior to being allowed access into the network.

Another industry that will jumpstart the need for superior security is the rapidly expanding mobile NFC (Near Field Communication) market. Near Field Communication is a new, short-range wireless connectivity technology that evolved from a combination of existing contactless identification and interconnection technologies (such as the proximity-card standard and RFID) which enables the exchange of data between devices over about 4" distance. Mobile products such as smart phones embedded with NFC will simplify the method by which consumer devices interface, will accelerate the speed of interactions, and will make fast and secure payments. Several mobile applet developers will team up with financial institutions such as banks, credit card companies,[13] and transportation/logistic companies to enable these transactions.

[1]http://www.us-cert.gov/cas/tips/ST08-001.html
[2]http://www.kb.cert.org/vuls/id/940193
[3]http://www.darknet.org.uk/2010/05/ibm-distributes-malware-laden-usb-drives-at-auscert-security-conference/
[4]http://www.cmu.edu/iso/aware/be-aware/usb.html
[5]http://www.washingtonpost.com/wp-dyn/content/article/2005/09/13/AR2005091301423.html
[6]http://news.cnet.com/Paris-Hiltons-cell-phone-hacked/2100-7349_3-5584691.html
[7]http://www.ucan.org/blog/telecommunications/wireless/who_needs_a_private_eye_when_youve_got_a_cell_phone
[8]http://searchsecurity.techtarget.com/news/article/0,289142,sid14_gci1374839,00.html
[9]http://www.usatoday.com/news/washington/2007-05-04-harddrive-tsa_N.htm
[10]http://blogs.courant.com/connecticut_insurance/2010/07/attorney-general-reachs-settle.html
[11]http://www.h-online.com/security/news/item/NIST-certified-USB-Flash-drives-with-hardware-encryption-cracked-895308.html
[12]http://www.nfc-forum.org/aboutnfc/
[13]http://www.intomobile.com/2010/08/02/att-verizon-and-t-mobile-team-up-with-discover-for-nfc-payments/

Advanced Persistent Threat in 2020

The Advanced Persistent Threat (APT) is another name for an ongoing, sophisticated, and organized cyber-attack designed to access and steal information from compromised computers. Sound like hacking? Yes—however, the difference is that the intruders responsible for the attacks are targeting the Defense Industrial Base (DIB), including the federal government, financial industry, manufacturing industry, and research industry. The key difference between normal hacking and APT is the focus, perseverance, and resources applied to achieve success. This results in more than the typical hacker is after, who finds the weakest links in the industry and exploits those companies and organizations. Rather, the focus and organization of an APT result in achieving precise objectives that resources are applied to. This includes creation of custom malware, viruses, Trojans, and customer attack codes. It also includes social engineering and other means outside a normal vulnerability exploitation. Think of a team of really smart people, with no moral restraints, and high emotional, monetary, and/or political drivers, thinking of nothing but how to compromise a specific target!

That's the threat today. Now combine that with reduced IT and security spending in 2009 and beyond, and reduced research and development in the IT security industry in general. It's a perfect combination for success—for the bad guys. In almost any realistic scenario, we can't imagine where at least one of the major U.S. industries (meaning more than just a couple players within a single industry) or the U.S. Department of Defense does not suffer a major breach.

FROM OUR CONTRIBUTORS

Mike Hrabik, President and Chief Technology Officer, Solutionary, Inc.

The first thing that comes to mind when I think of Advanced Persistent Threats (APTs) in the future is HAL, from the film *2001: A Space Odyssey* (1968): "I am a HAL 9000 computer. I became operational at the H.A.L. plant in Urbana . . ." Undoubtedly the most complex character in the film, HAL interacted much like a human — even to the point of letting inner conflicts drive him to murder. While artificial intelligence has long been captivating material for computer scientists, philosophers, science fiction writers, and movie directors alike, HAL stands out both as a fascinating film character and a carefully thought out vision of where artificial intelligence might have been at the dawn of the new millennium. Clearly, nothing remotely resembling HAL can be found today and most likely won't be found in the year 2020, but the concept of a well-intentioned HAL, who is able to monitor all aspects of an organization's security posture, observe behavioral anomalies, and take proactive protective action, is what organizations will require to combat computer threats, including APT, in 2020.

Continued

FROM OUR CONTRIBUTORS   *(continued)*

In January 2010, Google announced that it and numerous other large orga-nizations — in the Internet, finance, technology, media, and chemical sectors, were the target of a highly-sophisticated and targeted attack. The resulting publicity from this incident has raised awareness of a class of attacks and attackers, which are termed the APT.

The concepts behind the APT are not new, only the term. The concepts themselves have existed since the dawn of intelligence gathering, and long before the existence of computers or the Internet. The U.S. Air Force coined the term APT in 2006, but the earliest known instances of network-based threats date back to the early 1990s. At that time, the Department of Defense colloquially referred to them as "Events of Interest."

There are significant differences between an APT attack and a typical hacker attack. Hacking attacks are commonly perpetrated by individuals or small groups of attackers to demonstrate the existence of security vulnerabili-ties, to prove their own technical abilities, or to steal information.

The intent of an APT attack, however, is to develop a long-term clandestine infiltration of a targeted organization. APT sponsors are willing to provide a significant amount of time and resources to establish a presence in an envi-ronment they have targeted. Their goal is to obtain access to an environment, and then make that access permanent. Unlike typical hacking attacks, current APT attacks are organized, well-funded, and focused on achieving precise objectives. Attack techniques of APTs can include creation of custom malware, viruses, Trojans, and attack code designed for their target's unique environ-ment. It can also include social engineering and other means outside normal vulnerability exploitation. The teams responsible for APT attacks are typically highly intelligent computer professionals with no moral restraints and high emotional, monetary, and/or political drivers, who are working together to compromise specific targets. APTs are intended to operate quietly, seeking high-value data such as research data, military intelligence, software source code, or other intellectual property over a long period of time. Instead of find-ing the weak links and exploiting them, the APT uses multiple attack vectors and a higher level of sophistication to accomplish the attackers' (or team of attackers') objectives.

Therefore, the APT attacks present different challenges than common com-puter security breaches. The Senate Select Committee on Intelligence recently said, "we assess that a number of nations ... have the technical capability to target and disrupt elements of the U.S. Information Infrastructure ... we expect disruptive cyber-activities to be the norm in any future political or military conflicts."

The rise of APTs by state-sponsored espionage has changed the game of security. The new adversaries and the methods they employ require new tools and practices to counter targeted attacks. Despite years of investment and efforts to comply with frameworks such as ITIL and COBIT, most organizations are not prepared to counter sophisticated, targeted attacks. APTs are becoming increasingly advanced, and their targets are shifting from government agencies to trusted technology providers and enterprises. As societies become increasingly dependent on the Internet, from individual enterprises to defense operations, the risks of successful attacks by hostile regimes and terrorist networks becomes more apparent.

Most individuals are dependent on cyberspace in one form or another as we rely on it in our personal lives as a form of communication and entertainment. Countries are also dependent on the Internet for commerce. National critical infrastructure (such as the electrical grid) depends on cyberspace. Military organizations utilize interconnected computers to conduct operations. The advanced weapons and communications systems, which underpin the U.S. military, rely on the uninterrupted functioning of the IT backbone and protection of the information it contains. Hostile nations and terrorist groups recognize this. "Defense Department systems are probed by unauthorized users roughly 250,000 times an hour, or more than six million times a day," according to U.S. DoD officials.

Commercial IT systems, which form the backbone of the nation's industrial base, play a similarly critical role.

As cyberspace grew and the dependence on cyberspace increased, malicious attackers developed new tools and technologies to exploit it. The information security industry has developed new tools and technologies to combat malicious attackers, but the nature of the attacks has changed. Hacking has moved from being a mere inconvenience to being financially or politically motivated. Many cyber-criminal organizations are well-funded and employ trained computer scientists to develop new malware and the means to distribute and install it.

To look into the future evolution and impact of APTs, we first need to understand how technology will be used in 10 years or longer. The Internet is becoming increasingly geographically dispersed, and is interconnecting all types of devices, applications, databases, and so on, and now encompasses a wide variety of non-traditional resources such as medical devices, ATMs, physical security systems (e.g., cameras, electronic card access, safe locks, etc.), utility, and environmental control devices (e.g., UPS, generator, HVAC, etc.). This has also enabled real-time connectivity and information sharing across all platforms and systems. It has become a network of things, not computers. Today, the Internet has over 575 million host computers. At the same time, billions of Internet-connected sensors are being installed on buildings, bridges, and other key infrastructures around the world.

Analysts estimate Internet traffic will grow to 44 exabytes per month by 2012, doubling today's volume. The number of mobile broadband subscribers is increasing by 85% year-over-year, utilizing intelligent devices (e.g., smart phones, tablets, laptops, etc) via 3G/4G, WIMAX, and other high-speed technologies. At the end of 2009, 257 million people were accessing the Internet via a wireless device. By 2015, the number of wireless subscribers is expected to grow to 2.5 billion.

Continued

Technology convergence by the year 2020 will provide a single personal email/phone number for life and "always on" connectivity coverage, which (technically at least) will have 100% global coverage. Software as a service will be the norm. Everything from video conferencing to supply chain management will be outsourced and streamlined. Mobile Web and Internet interfaces will not only be present on luxury gadgets, but will become standard on all devices. We will still think of them as tools, but by 2020 they will have become "transparent." By 2020, we will be largely living in "immersive virtual reality worlds," where wireless connectivity and computer-generated environments will have radically altered our daily lives.

To see the future of APT, it is instructive to consider how much more dependant our lives will be on technology in 10 years, but also to look at the details of Google's January 2010 press release related to the APT incident — *"a primary goal of the attackers was accessing the Gmail accounts of Chinese human rights activists."* An attack is launched against one of the world's most profitable, and technologically advanced, companies. But the attackers weren't necessarily interested in money or intellectual property – they were interested in accessing the hosted email accounts of a few key individuals.

The future of APT will likely encompass two extremes: threats against nations, by attacks against the critical technology infrastructure they are growingly dependant upon, and threats against individuals, by accessing and utilizing the growing amounts of personal information accessible via the Internet. By 2020, APT will have taken the form of "virtual spying," not only against defense, government, and industrial assets, but also against the personal information of individuals that APTs deem important. Attempts to access the personal information of high-profile individuals in government, technology, and industry will continue to grow. But the attacks will not even be against the individuals themselves — they will be against organizations that maintain critical data of the individuals — their email provider, bank, insurance provider, phone company, and so on.

There are already a staggering number of new APT variations surfacing daily, and current conventional defenses cannot adequately protect individuals, enterprises, or critical infrastructure against the sophistication of these attacks. At best, many current defense systems are reactive, but cannot prevent an attack. They cannot detect new unknown threats. Some APT variants have become extremely difficult to eradicate, even when their presence is detected.

APTs in the future could be the equivalent of today's Navy Seals and Mossad: elite tactical teams whose goal is to penetrate defenses and extract targets without being detected. They will plan, rehearse, and launch attacks from anywhere in the world against their target and will be successful.

Organizations must recognize they are a potential target of an APT attack and clearly identify critical assets, which may contain or process information of interest to an outside entity. Even if an organization believes it would not be the direct target of an APT attack, it should recognize the potential to be used as a base of attack against business partners, or that attacks may be conducted against them, not to obtain financial or intellectual property information, but personal information about customers.

Protecting against future threats will require a cultural change in how we address cyber-threats. To continue the advancement of state-of-the-art security technology and to protect and safeguard critical resources, we must change how we value and treat our information in cyberspace.

Real-time operation will be required for appropriate network defense. Threats must be anticipated before they materialize. Attacks must be pre-empted before they impact the network or the endpoint. When attacks are successful, we must be able to terminate the attack and thoroughly expunge the attackers from the environment. Resources must be dedicated to and focused on cyber-security to protect critical operations. To protect against the APTs of the future, these threats must be treated as clear and present dangers.

There will always be certain fundamental precepts to threats and conflict — that's why we continue to read Clausewitz and Sun Tzu even after all these years. These principles translate to technology environments. There also exist dynamic variables that will demand a different approach to how we recruit, train, and organize our information security resources.

One key takeaway is to think globally and act locally, understanding the drivers of APTs, and employ a holistic security strategy, while focusing on the local resources available to address them. The future technology environment will present a unique set of challenges, which will require both doing the same thing differently, as well as doing different things altogether.

We may not have a HAL by the year 2020, but we will see significant developments in technologies, which can build behavior baselines from user activity and its context in the environment. These technologies must be situationally-aware, self-maintaining, and have the ability to adapt and learn. This approach will be the only way to detect and combat persistent and skilled attackers in the future.

The Network Edge

Following trends, cycles, and patterns can help bring clarity and focus to a picture of information security in 2020. One such trend is the movement of what IT administrators like to call the *network edge*. When companies first began connecting their networks to the Internet, they implemented security devices, such as firewalls, to keep the bad guys out. This distinction between inside and outside was valid at the time. Unfortunately, the idea of a demarcation point where bad ends and good begins is no longer valid but still exists today in the ways many organizations attempt to secure their systems and networks.

The value of a corporate-level edge- or perimeter-based security model is slowly eroding. Hackers have developed several methods of subverting or bypassing edge-based security solutions. One method used was to scramble the packet sequence as data was sent through the network. Computers are smart. They realize that a total communication stream is made up of many different packets or pieces of a total message. When sending a message, a computer will break it apart into manageable pieces and send those pieces sequentially to the receiving computer. Each packet is tagged with a sequence number so that the message can be reassembled properly. Many security systems traditionally would use pattern matching as a way to detect malicious behavior. In many cases, this was predicated on the belief that these packets would be sent sequentially (as they normally are). Hackers have written applications that scramble the packets and do not send them sequentially. This effectively renders the security device useless, while the receiving system reassembles the message without any problem. This is just one of several methods employed to get around edge-based security systems.

Security vendors consider each of these methods and develop a method to address it, but there is a larger fundamental issue with edge-based security: encryption. With the broad use of encryption protocols and applications for communication, an edge-based solution becomes nearly ineffective, because systems cannot analyze encrypted traffic. As a result, network-based solutions (which are effectively in the middle or between the two communicating devices) begin to have little value. This is something that security vendors cannot do much about. Some have attempted to implement "man-in-the-middle" systems that terminate one end of the encrypted tunnel and reestablish the encrypted session, creating a place where they can analyze traffic. Unfortunately this only works on certain protocols and applications and usually requires modification and configuration on the end user system. These are also fairly easy to subvert by even nontechnical employees. Some vendors have accomplished monitoring SSL traffic on IDS and IPS technology by loading the SSL key on the appliances.

What has happened more frequently is a change in marketing message: The companies that realize it is futile to try and monitor encrypted traffic spin the problem differently. They say that encrypted traffic is likely "secure and authorized" and, therefore, doesn't need to be monitored. That is their way of saying that because we can't do anything about it, let's just call it "good." Unfortunately, this traffic is all too often *not* good. Worse yet, the proliferation of encryption technologies is such that soon everything will be encrypted—obliterating the idea of edge-based security altogether. This means that, soon, most security protection will only be effective when deployed at the endpoint.

Of course, there is some information security protection that can be done outside of the endpoints. The infrastructure side of data security will largely have to be dealt with by network service providers, Internet service providers, and telecommunication companies. Attacks such as distributed denial of service (DDOS) and network infrastructure attacks will have to be warded off and addressed by these organizations, as opposed to the endpoint systems.

All other technical attacks (not social engineering attacks) will have to be defended against at the endpoint itself. This creates an enormous problem and opportunity for the information security industry. It is a huge problem because endpoints traditionally have been left largely insecure (being behind the strong outer defensive layers of the firewall and network intrusion detection systems). We treat our networks like candy: they have a hard outer shell and a soft gooey center. We spend a great deal of time and effort protecting systems that are accessible from the Internet and other external networks, but far less on the internal systems we believe are behind our strong defensive walls.

As a society and industry, we aren't really good at creating a hard center. The opportunity for software vendors, of course, is in the development of robust endpoint security solutions. This is software that will need to be loaded on all "Internet-aware" devices. With the endless number of devices that fall into this category, security software vendors have a vast untapped market heading toward 2020.

It doesn't mean sunny skies for all security software vendors. It will be a huge challenge to write and maintain software for so many devices, each of which has any number of versions that need to be supported. Then, there is the challenge of deployment, management, maintenance, monitoring, and reporting across this sea of electronics.

Many high-end, critical systems of the Internet will be housed in collocation facilities around the world. These are network access points where companies host racks and racks of servers and systems in a physically secure, temperature-controlled, fully redundant environment. Recently, I had the opportunity to tour one of the most advanced collocation facility in the world. It was in the Nevada desert, just outside of Las Vegas. Switch NAP founder Rob Roy took me on a tour of this revolutionary Super NAP. His customers include Sony, Disney, Google, MySpace, Facebook, and almost everyone else in the "Who's Who?" of the Internet. This facility allows for high-density computing (at least four times that of other colo's) managing heat, power, physical security, and redundancy. A blastproof perimeter, biometric security, man traps, and highly trained armed guards wearing bulletproof vests are just the beginning of the security protocols in place. His facility has been selected by several government agencies because it has the lowest threat from the 19 natural disasters the government tracks by region. As a result, he can offer his customers 100 percent uptime. While this is the future of protecting critical systems, physically, it is still up to the individual customer of Switch NAP and other collocation facilities to protect their systems from hackers and cyber-terrorists.

FROM OUR CONTRIBUTORS

C.J. Spallitta, Executive Director, Global Product Marketing Security Solutions, Verizon

The network edge or network perimeter is becoming less relevant because organizations around the world are transforming their business to operate within a new business model often referred to as the "extended enterprise." In this model, customers, partners, suppliers, and employees are widely distributed in remote offices, in airports, in hotels, at home, in a partner's office, at a customer's location, and so on, with laptops, PDAs, and smartphones connected to the corporate network accessing critical data required to conduct business. So the days of putting security around the four walls of headquarters to protect an organization's most critical data has passed because now the data is everywhere. This extended enterprise model certainly creates additional complexity in IT, network, and security — and much of the legacy infrastructure no longer meets the needs of this new business operating model. Starting now and looking out over the next decade, organizations need to ensure that security controls span the extended enterprise and they should be executed where they are most effective and cost-efficient. So for example, DOS attacks (which are network-based) should be mitigated in the network before they even get to an organization's network. Identity management, AV, compliance monitoring, and so on, are best handled at the endpoint. The firewalls, IDSs, and other security infrastructure in the DMZ on an organization's edge still play a role in thwarting attacks and doing security monitoring, but their relevance has diminished given that the risk and threat landscape are changing so dramatically. "Edge" protection, for the most part, really only looks at the network layer. Security needs to span the entire IT stack, including the network, data, applications, and users. The growth in data breaches and hacking is coming at higher levels in the stack than the network layer — it is occurring at the application and user levels where the data can be accessed. Lastly, as we move towards 2020, security decisions should be based on risk, not on threats and vulnerabilities. By taking a risk view of security, organizations better understand the impact of lost or stolen data, system unavailability, and so on, and the effect on their business operations. Consequently, better decisions can be made about what data and systems to protect, how and where those should be protected, and how limited IT and security budgets should be used to meet the risk requirements of the organization.

The Security Software Vendor

Another challenge is writing software that can truly protect devices from the infinite array of attacks being targeted at them. New attacks come swiftly, limited only by the creativity of very smart, malicious people. Against this are the complications faced by the writers of security software. Any device has root firmware or an operating system that runs the basic code and functionality of the system. There are usually additional applications that can be loaded for enhanced features. The security software needs to effectively detect and block attacks, detect and stop malware, detect misbehavior, stop unauthorized access, maintain the integrity of system data, ensure the privacy of communications, and enforce proper authentication by authorized individuals. In today's terms, such software will have to combine the technologies found in firewalls, host-based intrusion detection and prevention systems, antivirus programs, malware detection and removal software, virtual private network technology, encryption, strong authentication, data leakage prevention, security information and event management, and more! It also needs to work on everything from a core router to a smart phone.

FROM OUR CONTRIBUTORS

Eddie Chau, Chairman, Firmus Security

With the onslaught of new attacks detected daily, the role of a security software vendor can quickly become a nightmare, or it can represent a plethora of opportunities.

Traditionally, security software vendors were often specialists in a particular area of security (e.g., firewall vendors, antivirus vendors, web content filtering vendors, and so on). With the exponential growth of attack types and methods, security vendors have now realized that by playing in just one particular area of security, they would never be as effective as they might be. Many vendors now go on sprees acquiring technologies that can work together to form an ecosystem of security protection, where the various security technologies can work hand-in-hand. Truly, in security the whole is more than the sum of its parts. The vendor that plays in the most layers of security technologies will likely be the winner in crafting a solution that fits today's threat-scape.

An interesting development has been the increasing use of white-listing in security software. In white-listing, the user defines the activities that are allowed. This makes sense compared to the traditional blacklisting approach which requires the user to continuously play catch-up in defining what activities are not allowed (as antivirus does).

While new security threats and related protective security technologies are constantly developed, the only certainty seems to be that this jousting will continue on for the foreseeable future. While the winner is yet to be determined, constant vigilance and a deep entrenchment in relevant security R&D will likely differentiate between the security vendor that thrives and one that slips into oblivion.

Personal Information and Data Correlation

Through 2020 and beyond we will see social engineering attacks go to a whole new level. The power of search engines with social networking sites and other publicly available systems will combine to give criminals all the information they need to commit fraud.

Consider this scenario: After not much effort, on LinkedIn you notice that Atlanta-based "Big Corp" CEO Bob Bighead has recently become connected to Denver-based "Mega Corp" CEO Pete Hugego. You then see that Bob has a flight scheduled to Denver in two weeks. (LinkedIn has a service where you can be notified where people are going so if you happen to be in the same city at the same time, you can connect with them.) Perhaps the stock from one or both companies begins to have some unusual behavior. Could there be a merger between these two companies in the works?

Often one bit of information by itself is pretty innocuous. With so many systems tied together and so much information available in near real time, however, lots of harmless bits of data can be combined and correlated into a picture that can do companies or individuals great harm.

In 2006, AOL released an "anonymized" database of real search queries from 658,000 customers. Several web databases popped up almost immediately, as a result giving people the ability to deeply analyze this information in detail. Some people have claimed that through analysis they can determine who the individual user was that searched.

Search engines aren't the only place where information useful to criminals can be obtained. On December 21, 2009 Netflix was sued[3] for violating customer privacy. This wasn't your ordinary data breach or employee mistake. Netflix ran a public contest looking for a new system or method to recommend movies to customers. In so doing, Netflix provided the contestants with information about the viewing habits of nearly a half a million customers, without those customers' consent. Netflix felt the data was sufficiently anonymized. The plaintiff, who is identified as Jane Doe in the suit, is a closeted lesbian. She believes that in-depth analysis of the data could reveal who she is and her sexual orientation.

In April 2010, several privacy groups filed complaints against Google and other online providers stating that the providers were capturing and correlating cookies from each other's sites in order to present more relevant ads to users. Google has been doing this individually for some time. Just type an email using Gmail, and you will notice that the ads you are presented with match the content in your email.

Having organizations work together in such a way that they can reference and use the information that each of them collects can get even more scary for those concerned about their online privacy. Imagine all the bits of data that are collected about you and your family by vendors, retailers, government, healthcare providers, employers, search engines, schools, Internet service providers, phone companies, and so on. Many of these bits of information you might consider small or insignificant. When these little bits of data are correlated and analyzed, however, the result could paint a very clear picture, and one you may not want others to know about.

As we have said many times in this book, the Internet never forgets. Here's a question for the IT administrators and executives of the future: What advantage will all this historical information give to criminals? The years 2020 and beyond will see corporate leaders who have grown up on technology. They will have been "plugged in" to technology, the Internet, and social networking their entire lives. They will have used blogs, social media, online games, and every other imaginable online medium for years. The information posted by these individuals throughout their youth and early adult lives could be traced, correlated, and used against them. How difficult would it be to commit fraud, identity theft, or system compromise through social engineering techniques if you know everything about your targets?

FROM OUR CONTRIBUTORS

Dale Cline, Chief Executive Officer, netForensics

The right to privacy is a fundamental part of the American character long codified in our laws and culture, famously in the once again popular motto "Don't tread on me." Often interpreted as a warning or challenge to the British military, the motto also encapsulates the very American attitude of the need to respect an individual's boundaries and privacy (notice the use of the word "me" as opposed to "us," in the motto). Our right to privacy in theory extends large around us as citizens: privacy in your home, your associations, your worship, and so on. In practice, however, those rights have all but disappeared, not through titanic legal battles waged in our courts of law, but rather through an accelerating change in how we generate, manage, distribute, and track the data that makes up our lives. The rise of the World Wide Web has resulted in a massive shift in how consumer goods are purchased, information is consumed, and societal interactions are performed. Recent and impressive technological advances in massive data aggregation, correlation, and mining have converged to allow commercial, private, and governmental organizations to identify the most private details of your life and use those details in ways both beneficial and nefarious.

While technology has allowed massive data correlation to occur, it is the cultural shift in attitudes where consumer convenience trumps transactional security, and social connectivity trumps privacy that has propagated the massive data deluge itself. And that data is rich, providing insight and causal correlations into every aspect of our lives to those persons and entities with

Continued

FROM OUR CONTRIBUTORS   *(continued)*

the desire and resources to look. With an ever-increasing amount of accuracy, correlation of an individual's available data can predict everything from consumer preferences to preferred entertainment to your actual physical movements and location. The positive use of this is clear: more open and engaged communication with our friends and family, more choices presented in all areas from companies competing for our business. The negatives, however, are emerging as rapidly: corporations abusing predictive correlation to lower their own corporate risk, closed governments surfing their databases looking to suppress, early on, perceived threats to their power from individuals and groups.

What to do? Privacy rights today are not being challenged by correlation technology so much as ignored. Security of a transaction is not the same as privacy and there are few enforceable laws that prevent your data from being gathered and correlated without your prior consent. Moving forward, individuals, organizations, and governments will need to raise the preservation of real privacy to as high a priority as the security of the data if we are to begin the road back to reclaiming the fundamental right of privacy that is a cornerstone of our democracy.

The Domain Name

In late 2009, Internet Corporation for Assigned Names and Numbers (ICANN) decided to allow domain names using non-Latin characters. So sometime in 2010 you will be able to register domains in Japanese, Arabic, Hindi, Greek, Chinese, and other languages. This makes sense for ICANN because the Internet is not limited to populations that use Latin characters as part of their alphabet. In fact, even now, about one-half of all Internet users do not have Latin-character-based languages as their primary or native language. The change will certainly allow other areas of the world to navigate the Web more easily and develop websites that include the domain in their native tongue. As with any new technology or major change deployed, criminal minds find some way of exploiting this.

One of the most obvious security concerns relating to allowing non-Latin characters is the way in which we as individuals attempt to evaluate a website as legitimate. When we see a website at http://z8d7daf.com, a red flag goes up and we are cautious to stay away or not click on that link. What happens when there are literally billions of legitimate websites that we cannot evaluate by looking at the domain name to know if it is legitimate or not? At first blush some might say that those who use the Latin characters would naturally stay away from non-Latin domains because it wouldn't be in their native tongue anyway. Others might say that if your keyboard is not converted to use a non-Latin alphabet, then you couldn't type in the domain anyway. While there is some truth to this argument, most sites are accessed via links, not by typing in the domain.

Because domain names are completely unique (there can be only one `kevin.com`... which I do not own) people will continue to be driven to select names that are available. In the last year or so, all five-character domain names (Latin based), regardless of alphabetic sequence are registered. Six-character domains are getting pretty scarce. Having a short domain name is very desirable. In the case of websites that utilize services such as Twitter where there is a 140-character limit on messages—including any links—short domains are paramount.

Perhaps this is a good thing. People who rely on their analysis of a domain to determine if it is malicious are often wrong. While there are certainly some domains you would obviously want to stay away from, names that look legitimate are easy to register. There are also all those domains that look similar to, but not identical to, a legitimate domain (like `wellsfargo.com` where the L's have been changed to the number one). Then, of course, there are times when a legitimate site is compromised and can infect the systems of users who access the site. In reality, on our way to the year 2020, we will need to rely less on our "domain spidey sense" and more on better technology to distinguish between legitimate and malicious sites.

Notes

1. The text of RFC 4942 is available at `http://www.ietf.org/rfc/rfc4942.txt`.

2. For an article about this attack, see The Register at `http://www.theregister.co.uk/2009/06/08/webhost_attack/`.

3. An article about this suit is available from The Register at `http://www.theregister.co.uk/2009/12/21/netflix_privacy_flap/`.

Where Security Threats Will Come from in the Future

People don't want their lives fixed. Nobody wants their problems solved. Their dramas. Their distractions. Their stories resolved. Their messes cleaned up. Because what would they have left? Just the big scary unknown.

–Chuck Palahniuk

Since the inception of computers, and more specifically our global reliance upon them, the number, severity, complexity, and source of threats have all increased exponentially many times over. At the same time, threat mitigation solutions and tactics are developed and used to address and mitigate our risk from these threats. These solutions evolve over time in an attempt to keep up with each new threat.

Threats evolve for several reasons. Sometimes it is the result of the developer wanting notoriety. That was the primary motivation in the late 1990s and the first few years of the new millennium. The desire for notoriety quickly evolved to the desire for monetary gain, which is the current force behind the evolution of threats. There are other motivations as well. Political and religious motivations, for example, are driving threat evolution more than ever before.

Solutions evolve in direct response to emerging threats. The motivation for a company to continue to deploy new risk mitigation strategies is to counteract these new attack methods and the risks they pose. This balance between risk mitigation strategies and attack methods is maintained while threats emerge and solutions are developed and implemented. The problem comes when these get out of balance.

The relationship between what are known as "white hats" (the good guys who help develop and implement solutions) and "black hats" (cyber-criminals) is similar to the relationship expressed by the concept of yin-yang in Chinese philosophy. The concept of yin-yang is used to describe how seemingly opposing forces are interconnected, giving rise to each other in turn. There is a symbiotic relationship between the two. According to Wikipedia, yin and yang are thought to

> arise together from an initial quiescence or emptiness and continue to move in tandem until quiescence is reached again. For example, dropping a stone in a calm pool of water will simultaneously raise waves and create lower troughs between those waves. This will radiate outward until the movement dissipates and the pool is calm once more.

According to Chinese philosophy, yin and yang (and for the purpose of this chapter, the forces of good and evil in the world of information security) will always have the following characteristics:

- **They are in opposition.** The good guys are always trying to stop the bad guys. The bad guys are always looking for the next way to outsmart the good guys.
- **They are rooted together.** For example, the discovery of a critical vulnerability will simultaneously start a flurry of development of patches and fixes by the good guys, and malware and scripts to exploit it by the bad guys.
- **They transform each other.** New technologies and tactics are developed to counteract the effects of previous technologies and tactics.
- **One cannot exist without the other.** If all the cyber-criminals disappeared tomorrow, you would have no need for security professionals. The multibillion dollar industry could go away overnight. I and many others would be out of a job. The very fact that these criminals exist and attempt to do harm necessitates the ever-growing need for the industry.

There is one characteristic of information security that is not always in line with the philosophy of yin-yang, however. Yin and yang are always balanced, while information security is sometimes out of balance (although, over time, the good and evil forces of information confidentiality, integrity, and availability will return to a balanced state).

There are several elements that cause these forces to become out of balance.

- **Speed of new attack development:** New threats can emerge and evolve so quickly that mitigation solutions are not available quickly enough to prevent attacks.
- **Cost of deploying solutions:** Usually, new risk mitigation solutions are available, but they can sometimes cost so much that organizations do not deploy them, or only the largest and wealthiest of organizations can afford them.
- **Lack of security expertise:** Some solutions are complex and therefore difficult to understand, deploy, manage, or monitor, which creates barriers to successful use.

- **Lack of awareness:** All too often most individuals and organizations do not understand the current threats and how to mitigate those threats. This is often true of IT administrators. Even when a security expert is on staff, there is sometimes a managerial or political disconnect between that individual and those who control the purse strings of the organization.

- **Rapid threat landscape changes:** When the preferred or common method to compromise systems quickly changes from one method to a completely different method, organizations have a difficult time transitioning their thought, policies, procedures, and technologies.

- **Threat scope:** A new threat may be so large and complex that no single solution can counteract it.

Any of these elements individually can cause problems in the information security space. When all of these elements are true at the same time, you have a perfect storm for massive, global impact that can cause catastrophic damages and enormous economic loss. Only through this process do the masses learn of the threats, refocus on solutions, and appreciate and value security once more. The environment then is brought back into balance.

Spam

Spam is a good example of how a slow and steadily evolving threat is countered over time through deployed mitigation solutions. Spam is the slang term for unsolicited email. Spam is arguably the greatest scourge of the Internet age.

The term *spam* is believed to have come from a Monty Python skit that first aired in 1970 about a group of Viking singers who chant a chorus of "SPAM, SPAM, SPAM . . ." at increasing volumes in an attempt to drown out other conversations. Unsolicited email is seen as drowning out regular communication on the Internet. Others have associated the term with the luncheon meat clogging arteries the way that spam clogs bandwidth on the Internet.

Analysts estimate between $49 (Radicati) and $1,400 (Osterman) is lost per person each year dealing with spam. The wide range in estimated cost exists because the methods by which they calculate this statistic are very different. Needless to say, the number is staggering when you apply it to all employees across all businesses worldwide.

Bill Gates, in 2004, said that "spam will soon be a thing of the past" and predicted the end of spam within a couple of years from that time. He made this statement because he believed that technology would be developed to validate email messages, effectively killing spam. Mr. Gates believed more in technology than in the evolution of threats.

We began to see spam in large quantities at the end of the 1990s. Laws began to emerge about spam. Technology was developed to help identify, quarantine, and/or delete spam. For example, there was a time when IT administrators would import blacklists into their systems that were based on world geography. An IP address block that was assigned to the Soviet Union could be blocked by many organizations in the United States, but this didn't last long. With the use of botnets, spam began to be sent from everywhere and the world got smaller, making it difficult, if not impossible, to use geographic blacklists.

The spammers used text, so the good guys developed keyword matching for detection. Cyber-criminals then used replacement characters, such as a lower-case "L" for a capital "I", two slashes (\/) to create a capital "V", and so forth. The good guys created a rating system for spam to classify, quarantine, deliver, or delete messages. Criminals used graphical images to subvert text analyzers. Security vendors allowed image blocking. Solution providers figured out a way to detect the operating system of the sending system from the spam message and block non-server-based operating systems. If an email relay is sourced from a Windows 95 computer, it is likely spam. This cat-and-mouse game has and will continue. Spam messages are not just targeted toward email systems but SMS text, social networking sites, instant messaging, and every other communication method. Solutions are continuously developed to filter and block these annoying and malicious messages on each platform and application used. As of 2010, spam is at its highest recorded levels, accounting for between 85 and 95 percent of all email messages sent.

The number of spam messages will continue to increase. Technology will continue to evolve to detect, block, or quarantine spam. The percentage of bandwidth utilized for spam will remain about the same over time, but it will account for an ever-growing percentage of the total number of email messages, as the number of legitimate messages will not grow at the same pace. While the total number of spam messages will increase over time, so will our bandwidth and detection methods. So spam, from a threat perspective, has reached an equilibrium relative to the mitigation solutions in place and will remain that way through 2020 for the Internet.

Private, secure, encrypted email communication systems will spring up as "spam-free" systems (as well as offering other benefits—in fact, this will be one of the lesser benefits) and will have some success. Because these systems limit their membership to specific users and groups and are controlled by other parties, they will not reach global use by 2020.

FROM OUR CONTRIBUTORS

Gus Harsfai, President & CEO, Ceryx

Email presents a unique security concern in today's business world. Businesses want, and need, to be able to receive email from many users, even those whom they don't yet know and trust, while avoiding email from hackers, spammers, and those that include malicious viruses. Given the inability

for technology to provide absolute protection without occasionally blocking legitimate email, you typically see solutions that either let too many bad emails through or block too many good emails. As a result, email creates a potential vector, or pathway, which allows intruders or threats into production systems. These production systems are the same systems we use to communicate with those whom we trust, and who trust us. There is a fine line between being the effective protector and being seen as a business hindrance; overprotection results in containment of valid messages while less aggressive or under-protection results in increased risk. In either case, the business suffers. Protecting users from spam is therefore a complex multipronged problem involving many elements, but in my mind there are two broad categories: technology and education.

On the front lines in the fight against spam, blocking and containment are the two primary features that provide visible functionality to users. Blocking typically occurs at multiple layers; most, if not all, of which end users never see. Containment, often referred to as quarantining, captures the email en route between users and places it where it will not harm an end user's system or where the end user can view it in advance, before making a decision about whether it is a legitimate email or something they wish not to receive. In some cases, a group or an individual company employee may decide on behalf of the end user whether or not to "release" the message, or in other words let it pass to the end user. When thinking of either option, user enablement is a paramount variable. We again must strike a balance between transparency, where users have minimal awareness of the security being applied, and protection. An interesting phenomenon is that when users trust the containment engine, they forget that the problem exists. When they do, they often stop proactively managing their quarantines and greatly increase the risk of lost email. The most effective way to keep users engaged is through ease of use. User enablement has to consider easy access to the quarantine, so that it becomes part of a user's daily routine, and initiates on an impromptu basis from any device the user might be using.

End user education, and, speaking candidly, sometimes the education of the email administrators, is paramount to protecting your business from being negatively impacted from threats originated via email. Our training plans need to educate users to ensure they know how to use the tools as well as encourage the habit of reviewing their quarantines; users must value the rewards and understand the consequences associated with email security. User education also needs to teach them that there are always evolving threats, and how to identify risks in daily use. They must understand that regardless of how effective containment is, and how effective the security may appear for days, weeks, or months, there will always be times when dangerous messages get through. Users need to be aware not only of what information or attachments are within the message, but also of phishing techniques, as well as other forms of social engineering. An educated user is your last line of defense, but sometimes the best line of defense against sophisticated attacks.

Botnets

So, if we don't have to fear the scourge of spam, what do we have to fear? The mechanism that is used to send spam is the answer. Botnets (as discussed in a previous chapter) are hundreds of thousands, and sometimes millions, of compromised computers under the command and control of one individual or group.

Nearing 2010, the speed at which botnets evolved was staggering. What was once some basic malware was transformed into sophisticated systems that can receive commands and completely control an infected system. Once compromised, the zombie can perform almost unlimited types of attacks, remain concealed, spread to other systems effectively and quickly though several methods, utilize encryption technologies for stealth communications, and disable, subvert, or sabotage software that attempts to detect or remove it.

Early on, botnets were generally thought to be a Fortune 100 and Internet service provider problem. This was primarily because there is little that can be done to stop them, from the enterprise level down to small and medium-sized businesses, and even less at the end user level. The cost of building a botnet-proof infrastructure can be staggering, specifically as pertains to protection against distributed denial of service (DDOS) attacks.

Even security professionals often look at the botnet problem as a spam problem. That is analogous to a doctor thinking that coughing is the problem rather than pneumonia. This lack of expertise often leads to the wrong technologies being deployed, or the right ones at the wrong times or in the wrong places.

Additionally, security professionals hear about botnets but think they are someone else's problem to deal with. They don't feel it will impact them directly. Some IT folks don't take infections seriously. They think, "The worst that can happen is that they will send some spam email from one of my systems. So what?" On the other hand, some IT folks understand the serious nature of the botnet threat but can't get executives to release the budget dollars to properly protect the network environment from them. Still other organizations are heavily infected with botnet software and simply don't know it.

Many IT folks are still focused on protecting the outer edge of the network and are neglecting the core. Botnets spread in a variety of ways, most of which completely bypass edge-based security defenses.

Lastly, those who do understand the size, scale, and capabilities of botnets can be quickly overwhelmed by the scope of the problem, and they give up trying to do anything about it. It is true that no one person, organization, or even government can stop the botnet threat that exists today.

Not only do all these elements create the perfect storm for cyber-criminals, but botnets are the perfect global Trojan horse—not just technically but psychologically as well. Sure they are stealthy and spread virulently, but what is the harm? With few exceptions, they are used to send spam and that is it.

So what is next for botnets? Several things remain that will reach center stage between now and 2020. Some have begun but are in their infancy, while others we have not yet seen.

First is to use the power of a botnet for large-scale DDOS attacks. These will also encompass a growing use for non-monetary motivated attacks, such as political attacks (like the one in Estonia mentioned in Chapter 1); infrastructure attacks as part of cyber-warfare; religious attacks, such as the individual who used a botnet to perform a DDOS attack against the Scientology network; and strategic attacks against critical computer systems upon which modern societies rely, such as the New York Stock Exchange, ATM networks, and credit-card-processing systems. This is likely where we will see the first human death caused by hackers in the next few years. There have already been close calls with hospitals taken offline or losing power from DDOS attacks, as well as speculation that some power outages have been caused by coordinated cyber-attacks. Whether it is a power outage in the middle of summer that causes fatalities or critical care systems losing power or being modified, it will be a sad yet very newsworthy day when this occurs.

Second, botnets include infected PCs all over the globe. They exist everywhere. Not even the botnet owners have a good understanding of where all their systems are, what information is loaded on those systems, what those systems are primarily used for, and what access those systems have to other valuable assets. Perhaps having a botnet rootkit on a home PC in Alberta, Canada is no big deal. However, a loan processor at a bank, an administrative workstation at the power company, and a laptop at the FBI all could have the same software and be of high value to cyber-criminals. In fact, all of these scenarios have happened several times over. Even if malware associated with botnets is only on 1 percent of computers worldwide (which is the lowest of estimates, and the actual number is unlikely to be anywhere near that small), that is a very big number and likely to only get larger. Infected systems are everywhere. When a system is infected, the botnet owners see another blip on a computer screen, but they know very little about the value each zombie computer represents. There will be a massive inventory performed of infected systems by botnet owners in real-time as they are compromised. The infected systems will be programmed to automatically evaluate their own environment and even automatically rank their value through a series of checks and tests. Some inquiries will likely include:

- **What type of system is it?** Faster processors, more memory, and large disk stores may all indicate a high-value system.

- **What type of data resides on the system?** Does it have a customer information database, intellectual property, financial information, or employee information?

- **What type of software is loaded?** The applications that the system runs could establish its value. A computer that has children's games may be of low value but a system running the latest Oracle database may be of high value.

■ **What network resources does it have access to?** What other systems are connected to it? When the user is logged in, does the computer have rights to other systems? What is on those other systems? Can I spread to any of these other systems?

■ **What does the user on the computer do when they are logged in?** Do they surf porn, manipulate a database of patient records, perform stock trades, or maintain an electrical grid?

■ **What type of user is he or she?** Is he or she an IT administrator where I can use the credentials that are typed in to access other network resources?

■ **What company is the system installed at?** Is it a Fortune 100 company or some home user's PC?

The list can truly go on and on. Establishing an inventory of what the hackers currently have access to and control of has only happened on a very small scale. One reason is that there are so many infected systems, and right now, the majority of the money hackers make is in spam relay. An analogy can be made between zombie computers and real estate. Right now, the only thing the "land" is being used for is a weekly swap meet (sending spam). As time goes on, the owners will find the "virtual properties" they control can be mined, thereby providing much more value than can be realized from the swap meet. At present, these criminals don't really evaluate the value of the these virtual properties. Metaphorically speaking, they will find lots of gold mines, a ton of silver mines, a few platinum mines, and a never-ending supply of copper mines. Each one has some value; some systems more than others. When this analysis and classification is performed by the cyber-criminals, I think even they will be totally shocked at the value of some of the systems they have complete control over.

Extortion will happen more frequently. As these botnet controllers discover the valuable information on the systems they control, they will request payment for a variety of actions or inaction. An organization may have to pay to keep their system from going offline (there are several instances of this happening already). They may have to pay to keep their customer and employee records undisclosed (this too has already happened). They may have to pay to decrypt their data. They may have to pay to maintain the confidentiality of their proprietary information. They may have to pay to keep information undisclosed that would be embarrassing if publicized.

Additionally, those who control these botnets will start using them for espionage. Recently, several government agencies discovered that malware had enabled the audio and video on computers and recorded what was going on in private meetings. Essentially, their own computers were spying on them and sending the information securely and secretly out of the network. No longer do you need to install bugs, just use the fully multimedia-enabled system right in front of the person you want to spy on.

Lastly, I believe we will see a coordinated use of botnets to solve single problems; specifically those that need a tremendous amount of computing power. If you need to break an eight-character password of random alphabetic, numeric, and special characters (which would be considered a strong password), that would take a single computer 177,408 hours (over 20 years). However, 10 million computers working on the problem simultaneously in a coordinated effort would allow you to break the password in about 72 seconds. Even a 10-character password with random alphabetic, numeric, and special characters (which would be considered very strong) would only take about 156 hours to crack (using a botnet with 10 million zombies). When one system systematically tries each combination of a password to see if it will work, it is called a brute force attack. When many distributed systems are doing it together, it is called compounded execution of processing procedures, or a CEPP technique.

The password scenario would have to be done offline with most live systems having limited retries before the account is locked, or delays enabled between tries. The more interesting scenario is to break encryption algorithms. The inherent strength of an encryption algorithm is based on how long it would take to break. With millions of systems at the disposal of a single person or group, the time needed to break any given algorithm is exponentially smaller.

Botnets are not the only thing that we need to worry about over the next decade. There are several existing threats that will morph and evolve over time. Those are discussed in the following sections.

FROM OUR CONTRIBUTORS

Tim Belcher, Chief Technology Officer, NetWitness

Botnets have, to date, largely impacted individuals, meaning they have been very successful at identity theft for financial gain, and for co-opting millions of systems for DDOS or spam. I believe that the problem will rapidly get to a point where "personal identity" will need to change dramatically. To some degree, we may be there already.

Certainly botnets have become the scourge of small and large financial institutions, responsible for stealing hundreds millions of dollars. What we have *not* seen so far is wide scale destruction of assets. The compromised "eco-system" has intrinsic value if your target is money. Financial exploitation of botnets will continue to accelerate, and cause radical change in the ways we perform all manner of personal identification.

While financial gain has been the primary goal of those employing botnets to date, how long will it be before we see states make use of them for espionage or warfare? How long before radical groups make use of this repeatable process to bring about real damage? Both scenarios point to a much more destructive end result, and I believe this will be a trend over the next decade.

The Ph-enomenon: Why so many attack methods start with "Ph"

Many people ask why so many threats begin with the letters "ph". To answer that question, you need to know a little about the history of "phreaking." Phreaking is the first term to use "ph" in this way. Phreaking is the earliest form of hacking and happened on telephone networks in the 1950s. Phreak is a portmanteau word (a blend of two words) meaning "phone freak." In other words, a phreak is someone who manipulates the telephone network in order to place free long-distance or international calls. Some also say that phreak stands for "phone frequencies," which was the earliest method used to compromise these systems.

Phreaking was done underground by only a small handful of individuals and small groups until the mid-1980s, when bulletin board systems (BBSs) became popular. BBSs were computers connected to modems that other computers could connect to for information exchange and gaming. Phreaking became a frequently used tactic because individuals wanted to connect to BBSs outside of their local calling area (without paying long-distance fees). So, phreaking techniques were used to call long distance and internationally.

With the advent of dial-up and later high-speed, always-on, Internet connections, these BBSs morphed into what is now the Internet and the World Wide Web. The "ph" prefix endured to become associated with more modern threats even though they didn't rely on phones.

Phishing, Pharming, SMSishing, Vishing

Phishing attacks occur when a cyber-criminal sends an email message to someone, usually disguised as coming from a legitimate person or organization. Within this email there are usually instructions for the victim to follow, such as clicking on a link, opening an attachment, and the like. When the recipient follows those instructions, usually one of two things will happen. The user will be led to a place where they are either tricked into giving their personal information or tricked into allowing malicious software to be installed on their computer. Both can lead to fraud, identity theft, data breaches, and more.

We have spoken at length about those threats that evolve over time. Other threats move in more of a cyclical pattern. Those threats that move in cycles often go through the following phases:

- **Unveiling:** When the attack is either completely theoretical or, if executed, fairly benign. There's a lot of speculation about what the attack type could do on a large scale.

- **Hype:** When some of the first attacks are launched using the method, they attract widespread media attention, but in reality the attacks do not affect the vast majority of people or organizations.

- **Global impact:** When widespread exploitation occurs.
- **Mitigation:** The monetary loss and emotional impact have reached levels where organizations or individuals are willing to invest money and resources to mitigate the risk.

Then, the cycle starts again with a new variant or new ways to exploit vulnerabilities and systems.

Pharming attacks provide a good example of this cycle. In the early 1990s, there was talk about an attack type that could poison a DNS (Domain Name System) to route traffic to a false site. In such an attack, a DNS server is used to translate the friendly name (such as www.security2020book.com) to the numbered address assigned to each publicly facing Internet system. At the time, we called it DNS poisoning, and it was largely theoretical. Shortly thereafter there was a series of vulnerabilities discovered in DNS systems that would allow a remote attacker to compromise the DNS and change the records to point to different IP addresses, effectively rerouting all traffic that relied upon that DNS for name resolution. Hackers exploited these systems and rerouted sites through this DNS poisoning technique. These attacks were widely publicized and shortly thereafter, patches were made available and applied to the DNS servers, effectively fixing the problem. After that, we did not hear about DNS poisoning for almost a decade. In fact, so much time had gone by that when, in late 2008, a new series of DNS exploits would allow for the same thing, we had a new name for it: "pharming," which is a spin-off of the term "phishing." Again, the same attack (with an up-to-date name) allowed the rerouting of traffic. Again patches were created and released. And so the cycle started again.

The cycle, however, is not the same each time. The complexity increases each time, making it more difficult to detect and thwart. Often the scope increases, making the vulnerability and exploitation impact a greater number of systems. The impact increases as more and more businesses and individuals rely on these systems for day-to-day critical operations. The time between learning about newly discovered vulnerabilities and when malicious applications are released that utilize these exploits decreases. This relationship is illustrated in Figure 4-1.

SMSishing is phishing, but the lure is an SMS text message to a mobile phone rather than an email. With the explosion of Internet-connected mobile devices, this became an effective way to direct unsuspecting users to malicious websites. Usually, there is a message meant to panic the end user into action. Messages include things like "Your debit card has been frozen due to fraudulent account activity. Please visit our website at {link} to reactivate it." The site looks legitimate and asks the user for login credentials to "validate" them as well as asking for other personal information. Once they do this, the criminals can use this information to perform fraud or identity theft.

Vishing means voice over IP (VoIP) phishing. In other words, phishing attacks using the telephone rather than email. This method uses digital telephone systems to perpetrate fraud. While there are many ways a VoIP phone system can be used for nefarious purposes, one common method is for the system to make an automated call and use a recorded system to ask the person on the other end of the line to use the keypad on their phone to "verify" information. For example, someone might get a call that sounds like it is from their bank. The recording might say, "We are experiencing some difficulties with your account . . . for security verification, please enter in your account number . . . thank you. Now enter your PIN. Thank you. Now enter your Social Security number . . ."

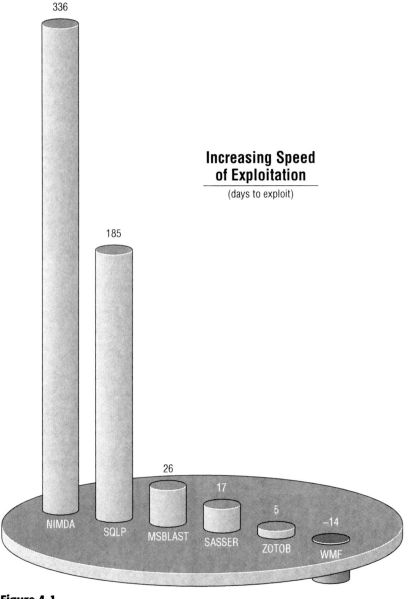

Figure 4-1

The reality is that any method of communication can be used to lure individuals into compromising their personal information or the computer system they are using. While there are many terms for the various specific methods (with more likely to come), they all essentially rely on social engineering techniques to trick users into doing something they wouldn't normally do.

Vulnerability Exploits

What is commonly known as hacking occurs when hackers break into a computer by exploiting known vulnerabilities. A vulnerability exists when the software running on a system can be manipulated into doing something it wasn't designed to do. This manipulation can often lead to root or command-level access on the system. Once an attacker gets root or command-level access, they can usually modify permissions and install back door software for later entry and control.

On average there are about 20 new vulnerabilities found on a daily basis. Not all of these will apply to each system in your environment. However, over time no system will escape from having some, and likely many, vulnerabilities. Figure 4-2 shows the per-annum number of discovered vulnerabilities from 2001 through the first half of 2010.

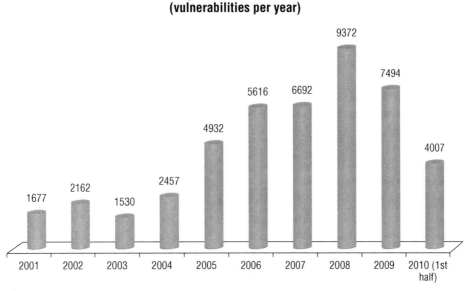

Figure 4-2

In the early days of computers, vulnerabilities were commonly discovered at the operating system level and service level. This is the most fundamental access point to a computer. Operating system vendors have gotten better about developing their code with security in mind. That has not eliminated OS vulnerability exploits, but it has reduced it to the point that hackers have begun moving up the stack to find vulnerabilities.

NOTE The *stack* refers to the layers described in the Open Systems Interconnection (OSI) model:

- **Layer 7: Application**
- **Layer 6: Presentation**
- **Layer 5: Session**
- **Layer 4: Transport**
- **Layer 3: Network**
- **Layer 2: Data Link**
- **Layer 1: Physical**

Where traditional attacks focused on the Network layer (layer 3) and Transport layer (layer 4), attackers are now commonly finding vulnerabilities to exploit in the Session layer (layer 5) and Application layer (layer 7).

Operating systems and services were targeted because they were accessible from a remote system. If you have an email server, you need to keep port 25 open to allow inbound email to be received. Hackers could run exploit scripts against port 25 to gain entry and access to that system. With applications, it is different. Most applications do not "listen" on any port waiting for a connection. They are designed to be used by the person sitting at the computer. This is why new attack methods that target internal systems and the applications running on those systems are the weapon of choice by current cyber-criminals.

In order to exploit an application, you need to get the user to essentially compromise themselves. The user must be led out to a website that can exploit the application, install malicious code on the internal system with a back door, and then create an outbound connection back to the hacker (usually using encryption to bypass traditional edge-based security solutions). Applications can also be exploited through a file attachment that the user opens, and in a variety of other ways.

Application exploitation was believed to be more difficult and less fruitful than traditional vulnerability exploitation, but on the contrary, it is actually easier.

The number of application vulnerabilities have significantly outpaced operating system vulnerabilities (see Figure 4-3). This trend will likely continue for many years to come. There are tens of thousands of applications, many of which are developed with little or no security framework or process followed. The focus currently is, of course, on applications that are loaded on most computers. Adobe Acrobat is the application that is usually on the top of that list. Adobe is loaded on more systems than any other vendors' software. Naturally, the hackers would explore ways of exploiting this before some more obscure application that is loaded on only a small percentage of systems worldwide.

Source: National Vulnerability Database

Figure 4-3

Cyber-criminals still must get unsuspecting users to compromise their own systems. Malware sites are one of the most effective ways of doing this. This technique literally exploded in 2008 (see Figure 4-4), although it was commonly seen for several years prior to that time. Then just when some thought we had seen the worst of it, 2009 made all previous years look like the hackers had taken a vacation (see Figure 4-5).

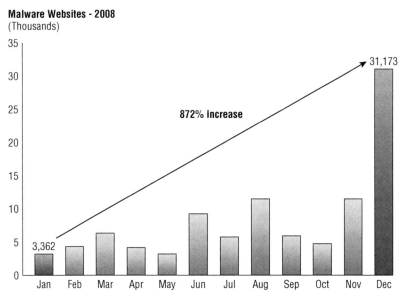

Figure 4-4

Hackers would either compromise a legitimate website and load malware on it, or would build and host their own malicious website. The effectiveness of compromising a website that is visited by millions of users every day is of high value to criminals. That is why (according to Websense) the majority of the top 100 most accessed websites were compromised between 2007 and 2008. Although a lot of users' systems are compromised in a very short period of time, the exploitation is soon discovered and eradicated.

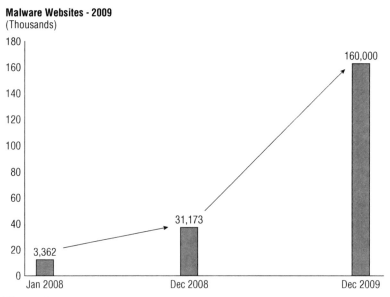

Figure 4-5

Hosting a malicious website oneself provides the advantage that the site will stay up longer. The downside is that the hacker doesn't naturally have millions of people accessing their site daily. Therefore, they must utilize other methods to drive users to their site. One method is search engine manipulation. This is where the hacker develops their website in such a way that it naturally makes it near to top of an organic search. Hackers will usually use the top search words and build their site around those. When someone types a word or phrase into a search engine, the results they are presented with may actually take them to a website that will compromise their system. This method will undoubtedly continue to be used in the future.

Search engines also have their advertisers. Their ads are often on the top or side of the screen when searching for something. These ads are paid for with credit cards by legitimate vendors . . . usually. Cyber-criminals have been known to use stolen credit cards to place ads to direct traffic to their malicious websites.

Because search engines are the window to the Internet world and all the amazing information that exists there, they will continue to be a target for hacker manipulation.

A growing problem is the lack of a secure method for what is known as "single sign-on." In other words, we usually have a different set of login credentials for each system we access. Our corporate email requires one set of credentials. Our personal email requires another. Our online banking system uses still another. We have reached a tipping point where we have so many different online systems that use different passwords, we can't possibly manage them any longer. You might ask, what does this have to do with vulnerability exploits? Well, because there is still no universal solution in sight for single sign-on, system providers have developed ways of helping users remember their usernames and passwords. For many sites and services, when users forget their usernames or passwords, it is relatively easy to have them reset. Often, when setting up a new account, you are asked a series of personal questions, the answers to which are needed if you forget your login credentials. When you do forget your username or password or both, the system will ask you these questions to validate your identity and allow you to reset your username or password. The problem is that the Internet has an amazing memory. Cyber-criminals can search online records for the answers to these questions. If a system asks what street you grew up on, or what the name of your elementary school was, these are not difficult questions to obtain the answer to on the Internet. This is how David Kernell, a 20-year-old college student, broke into vice presidential candidate Sarah Palin's email on September 16, 2008, in an effort to derail her campaign. David is the son of Tennessee Democratic state representative Mike Kernell. David reset the password for Sarah Palin's email account by answering one of the standard questions at the time: "What is your date of birth?" David used a Wikipedia article to determine her birth date in "15 seconds." David went by the online name "Rubico" and was prosecuted for four felonies, punishable by up to 20 years in federal prison. In April 2008, Sarah Palin testified against Kernell in regard to the incident. On April 30, 2010 Kernell was found not guilty on the wire fraud charge, but guilty of both the unauthorized access and obstructing justice charges. The jury remained deadlocked on the final charge of identity theft. We will see an enormous jump in incidents like the Sarah Palin email incident: data compromises and system exploitations through the creative use of the limitless information on the Internet.

FROM OUR CONTRIBUTORS

Eric Yeow, Co-Founder & VP, Firmus Security

In this age of the Internet, information is being shared round-the-clock at an explosive pace and updated almost on a real-time basis. In similar fashion, security vulnerabilities are also being discovered, shared, and exploited at such a fast pace that it leaves many organizations struggling to protect their IT infrastructure. Examples of newly compromised web destinations are available with such a high frequency that it is mind boggling that corporations are still not fully awake to the risk posed to their users when they decide to take their business online.

Continued

FROM OUR CONTRIBUTORS   *(continued)*

The typical IT environment has become more complex and consists of many components that work intricately together (infrastructure, operating systems, applications, databases, etc.). Within each of these components lies the potential for a hacker to discover security vulnerabilities. Akin to throwing a wrench into the intricate workings of an engine, exploiting vulnerability in a single component within the whole eco-system may result in catastrophic consequences. In order to ensure the safety of the users, vendor corporations constantly battle to keep their products free of vulnerabilities.

While many corporations are now aware of the risks posed by vulnerabilities, they are nevertheless unable to respond fast enough to protect their users. Addressing new vulnerabilities will require many things to fall into place: the vendor corporation must develop the required fixes to address the vulnerability, then the internal testing of the compatibility of the new fix with other system components (necessary because a patch might break an application), and finally the harnessing of resources to implement the fix. All this means that there is a substantial window of time between the discovery of a vulnerability to the time when the system is secured again. This cycle then repeats itself each time a new vulnerability is discovered.

Combine this with all the malicious threats being targeted at the user and you really have a complex and scary environment. As IT security professionals, we try to create solutions and provide advice about protecting the infrastructure of our clients, our networks, and their end users, without negatively impacting the user's experience. This is a delicate balance. Over the next ten years we will see this balance change as technology advances, the economy rebounds, and user demands shift. The magic, as it always has been, will be to make security transparent to the users. Day to day this is, and will continue to be, a challenge to the best security professionals.

Insider Threats

Most of the threats listed previously are initiated by individuals we don't know. These threats are very real and could literally be coming from anyone, anywhere in the world. Insiders pose a tremendous threat to organizations. On the one hand, insider threats are actually one of the threats you can do the most to reduce your risk from. On the other hand, you can never entirely eliminate the threat.

An insider threat is defined as the misuse or destruction by employees, contractors, and other trusted individuals of sensitive or confidential information, as well as the IT equipment that houses this data. Insider threats are caused by actions such as mistakes, negligence, reckless behavior, theft, fraud, and even sabotage.

Insiders are a broader category of people than most companies realize. An insider is any individual who has been entrusted with physical or electronic access to nonpublic systems or information. Insiders can be employees, contractors, and even some third-party partners and service providers. Even former employees can count as "insiders" when they leave some residual processes, code, or access features that can assist them or others in a nefarious act.

It is also important to recognize where these "insiders" are. These individuals do not have to be sitting in an office at your company headquarters. They can be at a branch or remote office. They can even be a traveler or telecommuter. In other words, long gone are the days when an insider could be defined by a brick and mortar location.

There are typically four classifications of insider incidents. In other words, there are four different root causes when it comes to insider incidents:

- accidents
- malicious behavior
- pretexting (falling prey to social engineering scams)
- negligence

According to a mid-2009 study, 80 percent of chief information security officers (CISOs) believe that employees and contractors present a greater threat to their data than hackers.[1] Only 18 percent of the respondents considered hackers a greater threat.

We often hear things like, "The insider threat actually outweighs the threats from cyber-criminals, hackers, and the random malware that most organizations concentrate on." These statements are often unsubstantiated, have no concrete statistics behind them, are referenced in a narrow context, or are based on surveys of people's opinions rather than facts. So, what are the facts?

For all reported data security breaches in the United States between 2000 and 2009, insiders were the source of 22 percent of all records compromised and 31 percent of all incidents (see Figure 4-6). "Inside" and "outside" are classifications of many individual incident types. Outside incidents include hackers, lost or stolen backup tapes, stolen computers and laptops, viruses, and so forth. "Inside" can also include stolen laptops, lost or stolen backup tapes, as well as accidental exposure and malicious activity. It all depends on if the culprit involved in the incident is classified as an "insider" or not.

Insider incidents can further be broken down into categories, including accidents, malicious behavior, and other events. Between 2000 and 2009 in the U.S., malicious insider incidents account for 25 percent of all reported data security breaches (see Figure 4-7). In other words, less than 8 percent of all reported data security breach incidents and records losses involve malicious insiders.

Contrast this to accidental data breach incidents caused by insiders, which constitute more than 20 percent of all data breaches (67 percent of insider incidents) in the United States over the past nine years. Malicious insiders account for over one-third of all records compromised by insiders with the balance (64 percent) being caused by accidental loss and exposure. 14 percent of all records compromised result from insider mistakes. The number of records compromised can be misleading because in many data breach incidents it is not known, or is not reported, how many records were actually involved in the incident. The statistics and graphs below represent the number of records reported.

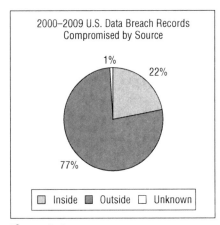

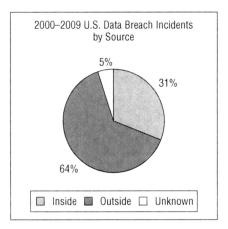

Figure 4-6

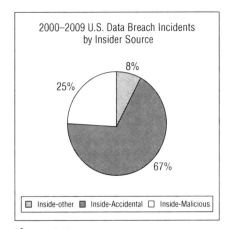

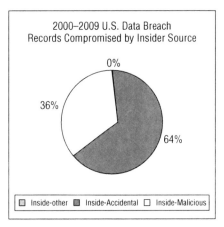

Figure 4-7

The sharp rise in reported insider data breaches (see Figure 4-8) came in conjunction with the many states that passed data breach disclosure laws during these years. Today, nearly all states have such disclosure laws with proposed national legislation being discussed.

With all of these statistics, one might conclude that the insider isn't the greatest risk to a company; however, we have only been reviewing reported data security breaches. According to an RSA survey, only 11 percent of companies that experienced breaches in 2008 reported them. It is widely believed that it is both easier and more desirable for a company to hide a data security breach caused by an insider. Additionally, there are many insider incidents that, while severe, costly, and embarrassing for companies, do not involve sensitive data that would require a company to disclose it publicly. So in reality, these statistics only show one classification of insider risk, and while the statistics are great data points, they are far from a representation of the whole story. But wait, things get more complicated.

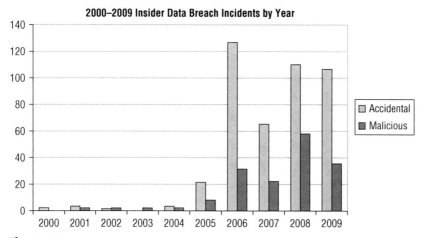

Figure 4-8

Statistics by their very nature are quite binary. This static black-and-white approach doesn't always do justice to the reality of the story behind the numbers. When a company formally announces an information security breach, usually it includes details surrounding the incident. These details often include the source of the breach, the number of records compromised, the industry, data type, and so forth. If a hacker exploits a vulnerability that grants him or her access to a system with sensitive data that is extracted, then it would be classified as an external hacker breach. What if in that same example, the hacker used network credentials of former employees that had not been removed? This would likely still be classified as a hacker breach; however, the cause was clearly internal employees not removing accounts when employees leave the company.

It seems to be less and less often that we see clear causes of a data security breach. When a hacker compromises a system through a well-known vulnerability, is the cause of the incident the hacker, or the IT administrator that didn't patch the system? If an organization performs a vulnerability scan of their external systems (such as their web or email servers) once a quarter, and a hacker does it every day, who is at fault when the system is compromised?

A survey[2] conducted on behalf of *eWEEK* magazine found that 57 percent of the respondents that recorded a security breach cited "users accessing resources they shouldn't be entitled to" as one cause of the breaches, while 43 percent cited breaches as a result of accounts left open after an employee had left the company.

When you perform deep, contextual analysis of data breach incidents, you quickly see just how at fault internal employees are, often being negligent. One of the main differences with insider negligence compared to other categories of security breaches is that these insiders are hired, trained, and responsible for the security and integrity of the organization's sensitive information. These individuals are often derelict in their duties, committing technical and procedural "sins of omission" that lead to a data security breach.

In the same survey cited above, one-third of respondents believe firewalls alone provide adequate protection against data leaks. One-quarter of CISOs reported either not having the correct data leakage protection technology, or not knowing what they should have. In other words, more than half of companies either believe they are protected and aren't, know they don't have the solutions required to protect sensitive information, or don't have a clue what they need or how to protect themselves.

Experts agree that an insider's fear of getting caught is one of the main deterrents to malicious behavior. Video cameras at a financial institution are more about employee honesty than robberies. Using technologies that can restrict and monitor access and behavior are important.

Mobility Threats

Portable systems have become a popular item for nearly every American. If it isn't their smart phone, it could be their iPad, laptop, or any number of other devices. These devices can become infected and then be plugged into or connect to internal networks where those infections can spread. They can be used to extract sensitive data and leave the network. They can be a powerful tool for malicious insiders. They can be the perfect access point for hackers.

Software is now available that can track stolen mobile devices by using IP tracking and wireless triangulation techniques. The same software is usually designed to wipe out the hard disk or any sensitive information if it is stolen. Solutions such as these will become commonplace over the next decade; however, criminals will get a lot of mileage out of exploiting these systems prior to widespread use of these solutions.

FROM OUR CONTRIBUTORS

Christopher Hart, CISSP, Chief Information Security Officer (CISO) for Life Technologies

When Apple launched the iPod in late 2001, it revolutionized the handheld music player space. Cassette Walkmans reigned supreme from about 1979 through 1984, when portable CD players took over as the dominant portable music player technology — both of those are now relics. The Apple iPod was not the first portable digital music player, nor was it the cheapest. However, it was the sleekest, sexiest, most polished, non-geek device around. It was not targeted at the technology junkie, but rather at the everyday consumer.

Apple's movement into the cell phone space with the launch of the iPhone in 2007 brought that same consumer community bursting into the high-end, ultra-capable smart phone community. Up to that point, smart phones and data-centric phones were either business tools (RIM's BlackBerry, Palm Inc.'s handhelds, etc.) or the novelty tools of the tech community. Apple brought it mainstream.

Now in 2010, the iPad goes one step further. It is not a phone. It is not a laptop. It is a new type of device. New devices with little history and with paradigm shifting potential make for big threats.

Bringing new consumer devices into the corporate world has always been frowned upon by corporate information and support groups. But with the exceptional marketing of some of today's technology companies, the speed to market of these technologies and, let's face it, some really great technology, the line between consumer electronics and business technology has become gray at best, non-existent at worst.

The impact of the bridging of these two markets has some very interesting threat consequences:

■ The technology refresh cycle for consumer technology has traditionally been much faster than that for business technology. There have been four generations of the Apple iPhone in four years. Part of this can be attributed to its lack of maturity, but it is primarily simply the way the consumer electronics world works. More change means more costs and more potential for vulnerability.

■ Consumers have different needs than does the business community. This drives the increase in capabilities ahead of improved reliability and security. The business market is being seen in many crossover technology spaces as a bonus market which is marketed to but not necessarily focused on.

■ Many of these devices are personal devices which can often cause issues around data ownership, liability, and control of the device. We see a blending of data and data ownership.

The corporate world has already begun to wrestle with these new and ultra-capable devices. There is certainly a great deal of business value to be had by adopting a more mobile device-focused business posture. This business value will not come without a cost. Business leadership must find the right balance of technology, process, capability, and control to manage the threat to acceptable level. This will become easier with time, but we are at the bleeding edge of this technological shift.

Infected Software

Open source and free software is commonly used by most organizations. Hackers have been known to manipulate these programs and post them back to the Internet for download by unsuspecting users. An insider that downloads and installs one of these software packages can compromise that system, or perhaps the entire network. This will continue to be a problem for many years to come.

At some point, I believe there will be a software registration and validation process that legitimate software vendors will go through. It will be similar to the way in which we validate websites through a PKI (public key infrastructure) digital certificate that can be traced back to a source of authority. There is so much rogue software out there, which often leads to infection, that a software registration process would seem to be inevitable. This is especially necessary with such a strong open source software movement.

Peer-to-Peer (P2P) Software

Peer-to-peer software programs by their very nature are a very large threat to information security. This software is commonly used by end users to download illegal music, videos, movies, and applications. P2P software, when it gets installed, usually will scan the system and any connected systems for files to share with others on the Internet. These programs have been used by criminals to scan for sensitive information such as databases and present them for download from anywhere in the world by someone with the same P2P program. These applications are very stealthy and easily subvert traditional edge-based security. There are liability, security, bandwidth, and productivity issues associated with P2P sharing. This will continue to grow as a serious problem over the next several years.

Third-Party Threats

More and more companies rely on third-party organizations for part of their critical business functions. These relationships often require trusted network connections between the companies and systems. Currently, there is little in the way of security filters between these connection points. There is also often a lack of enforced policies, procedures, and access controls within systems and software. There are many cases of a third-party provider being compromised, which allowed the perpetrator access to the company's system through the trusted connection. This has even happened to the U.S. government at the Pentagon. This threat will decrease over time as partners do more to protect their clients and network connections, but solutions will be slow in coming. We will see data security breaches utilizing this method for some time to come.

Social Networking Threats

Social networking as a phenomenon has grown out of control. I mean that literally. It has grown to the point where neither the users nor the social networking companies themselves can control these monsters that have been created. It reminds me of the movie *Jurassic Park*, where John Hammond, the rich old guy, wanted to build something no one else ever had: a fun theme park combined with a zoo of cloned dinosaurs. He built what he thought would be adequate security, but he didn't understand nearly enough about the environment he was trying to control. People naturally trusted that proper security was in place and that they would of course be safe. Quickly things spiraled out of control and nearly everyone gets eaten by the end of the movie.

The creators of social networking sites . . . yes all of them . . . are just like John Hammond in *Jurassic Park*. Their unique ideas caught on in such a viral way, just keeping up with the bandwidth, processing power, storage, development, and everything else to keep the system online is an amazingly complex, never-ending project. For most of these sites, adequate security is, and always has been, an afterthought. Not that some of them don't try. It is just a bit like closing the barn door after the horse has bolted . . . and boy did it ever bolt!

A better example might be why it always seems like road construction is happening wherever you drive. The truth is population growth leads to heavier use of popular traffic arteries. Naturally, this means that more road repairs need to occur as well as seemingly never-ending expansion and enhancement. But do you ever get home faster? These social networking sites are working tirelessly just to keep up with the growth and adoption of their service. Simultaneously enhancing security in a meaningful, robust way can often take a back seat. This is the first half of the problem.

The second half of the problem relates to the back seat as well. I remember a short skit by Jerry Seinfeld where he talks about taxis. He found it interesting (and disturbing) that when we get in our own car, we fasten the seat belt to stay safe, but when we get in the back seat of a taxi, we don't even think about fastening the seat belt. It is almost like we are going on an amusement park ride with surely a professional with years of experience at the wheel who is swerving in and out of traffic. This is how users of social networking sites act. They are absolutely reckless when it comes to their behavior on these sites, specifically when it comes to security.

As a social networking experiment on Facebook, I created a new user profile based on a free email account I set up on Gmail. The name of this Facebook user was Rebecca Johnson, age 26, with a profile picture of a 3-year-old girl in a dress that I snagged from a department store website. No other information was in the profile. I wanted to see what would happen when I invited random strangers to be friends with this fictitious person. Lucky for me, Facebook presents you with people it thinks you might know. Because I didn't have any relevant information in the profile, Facebook presented me with people that live in my same county (obviously they were looking at my IP address and correlating that with my local city). I of course knew none of these people but went ahead and invited all of them to be my friends.

I invited 250 totally random people to be my friends. People of every imaginable age, sex, city, number of friends, and even country were invited. The only criteria I used was that I would only select "friends" that had profile pictures. My logic behind this was that if you don't have a profile picture, you are probably not a serious or frequent user of Facebook. Here is a timetable of what happened next.

8:00a.m. – Invite friends

8:02a.m. – My first friend accepts my invitation

9:00a.m. – 6 friends

10:00a.m. – 12 friends

3:00p.m. – 28 friends

After 1 Week

140 friends

47 people ignored my request

3 people questioned me with an email saying, "I am kind of embarrassed, how do I know you again?"

60 "pending" requests resulted

1 friend invitation resulted in an email saying "Hey, I must know you because we know 3 of the same people"

If you remove the "pending" requests, nearly 75 percent of requests ended in the person accepting me as a friend (see Figure 4-9). After 1 month I had 187 friends out of those initial 250 friend requests. In other words, a staggering percentage of people will accept a friend request from someone they don't know. But does that really matter? What harm can come from it? Well, let me tell you.

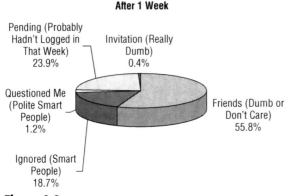

Figure 4-9

Rebecca Johnson now has an intimate knowledge of the lives of those 187 friends she gained. Most have posted recent photos of themselves and their loved ones. One took pictures of every room in their house after a recent remodel and then began "a much needed vacation" to California and announced she wouldn't be back for two weeks. Several were young kids still in high school. Facebook is a cyber-stalker's dream come true. For many people on Facebook, you can know their every move. For others, you know the major events in their lives. Even a mildly creative person can come up with hundreds of ways this information could be exploited. Think of the information that most of us have entered into Facebook: name, sex, birthday, relationship status and interests, political views, religious views, email address, schools, employment, location, other friends, photos, videos, not to mention whatever comes into our heads and gets posted on our walls. I know when people are coming, when they are going, who they will be with, and much, much more.

Users who don't think about security are often those who become victims of identity theft and fraud. One of the biggest problems that cause identity theft and fraud is that people are not careful about their passwords. All-too-often people will use simple passwords that are either easy to guess, short, or the same one they use on many different systems. So naïve, trusting, apathetic, and unsuspecting users are one-half of the problem, which bleeds over into the other half of the problem: the software as a service, software on-demand, or "cloud computing" providers. For example, in 2009 a hacker broke into a Twitter executive's personal email account. While this has happened several times, in this case this account was linked to shared Google Apps (a cloud computing system) documents. Exposed were hundreds of company-related, and some sensitive, Twitter corporate documents. Is the user to blame or the cloud-based services? Several comments were made by Twitter's founders blaming cloud computing, while others blame poor password policies. Still others blame a lack of policies and procedures that should prohibit the connection of personal email accounts to corporate resources.

How many times has Monster.com, the job-hunting site, been compromised? What about Lexus-Nexus? How about Facebook, MySpace, Twitter, and others? And there are many other examples. Cloud-based application providers think application first, and somewhere down on the list is security.

Social networking sites are simply one type of cloud computing service. They have (in my opinion) one of the biggest targets on their back, which will remain through this next decade for fraudsters and criminals. This isn't a surprise given the popularity of these sites, most of which have already had many security breaches . . . far too many to discuss individually here. Social networking sites contribute to the problem by making it easy to register, log in, remember your login credentials, and even reset your password. They also make it very easy to spoof other users, install malware, send spam, or perform any number of other nefarious acts. Then, there is a host of third-party applications and service providers that interact with these services with little in the way of what most security professionals would consider adequate security. The combination of weak security procedures built into cloud computing services, third-party interactions, a user culture of "ease of use" trumping security, and the blending of corporate and personal lives is a formula for disaster.

Each of us being responsible for our own identities and demanding security protection from the services we use (especially social network sites) is our obligation; however, we will likely trust that these providers are taking care of it in the coming years.

FROM OUR CONTRIBUTORS

Steve Addison, Vice President Business Development, Cosaint

You can't eliminate with technology all of the security risks posed by social networks.

Banning the use of social networks in the workplace could certainly reduce some risks (e.g. malware infection resulting from rogue Facebook applications), and possibly improve workplace productivity (although the jury's still out on that one). But most of your staff are probably using social networks from home, or from the local coffee shop, or even from their phones. And, while they're doing that, they could be leaking your secrets to your competitors, or to hackers.

Before we go any further, don't think it's just disaffected and/or careless employees who are the problem. You also need to worry about IT staff posting technical questions to support groups that might give a hacker a hint about the systems that you're running, or a security hole you're trying to fix; former employees posting information to their LinkedIn profiles or Monster resumes that detail the systems that they worked on when employed by you; executives posting sensitive information in your organization's blogs; the list goes on.

So you're going to have to start working to change attitudes throughout the organization about what should and shouldn't be posted online to help your staff understand that posting sensitive information could have very serious consequences. And that means awareness training.

What should you cover in your training? If social networks are being accessed from your company systems — either with or without your permission — you probably need to remind people about the precautions they should be taking with any Internet access: use strong passwords, don't download files that might be infected, watch out for links and pop-ups that might install spyware, and so on, but with the added complication that your staff might be lulled into a false sense of security because they're "among friends." And don't forget basic email security, since most social networks include their own messaging capabilities that could bypass antivirus tools installed on your email gateways.

Don't forget the issue that you're going to have whether you ban social networking at work or not: staff posting inappropriate and/or sensitive information online. They should be taught that privacy controls are critical, and that information posted online should never include anything that might compromise the security of your organization. In particular, you should point out how online support forums can be a treasure trove of information for hackers. They should also try to avoid posting information that might be used as a security question, such as their mother's maiden name, their pet's name, or the name of their high school. Posting this online could be making it easier for an identity thief. And they should be selective when adding friends and connections, and (as far as is possible) try to ensure that they really are who they claim to be! Make it clear that this applies just as much to IT staff and executives as to other staff.

This may seem like a Herculean task, but you can start with one really big advantage. If you engage your staff's self-interest by offering them advice that will make them personally safer — not just hammering the company line and quoting your acceptable use policy — they *will* listen, and everyone will be better off.

Digitization

For a few years prior to 2010, there was an overall movement from paper records to electronically stored information. This was particularly true within the healthcare industry, but many other industries had similar initiatives as well. This opened many new doors for cyber-criminals to target. For the next several years, we will see a huge upswing in the number of data breaches related to this type of information. As a result, we will have a sharp increase in healthcare and retail fraud and identity theft.

Star Wars

Prior to 2020, it is possible that we could see attacks against satellite systems, including denial of service attacks (uplink/downlink jamming, overpower uplink), orbital positioning attacks (raging transponder spoofing, direct commanding, command replay, and insertion after confirmation but prior to execution). We will have to see if this type of attack disrupts military systems or GPS systems, or if you don't get to watch the season finale of *American Idol*. Sometimes I wonder which would cause greater social chaos.

FROM OUR CONTRIBUTORS

Rob Kraus, Senior Security Consultant, Solutionary

The future of satellite attacks and vulnerabilities will likely follow a similar suit to those previously experienced. However, as new technologies are deployed, additional attack vectors will likely make themselves apparent. Satellites play a critical role in commercial and military communications infrastructure, an infrastructure in which flaws can be identified not only in the

Continued

satellites themselves, but also in other mission-critical components. A great example of a flaw was identified in the Mars Polar Lander crash in December 1999. During the decent of Mars Polar Lander, critical coding errors led to the lander crashing into the surface of Mars at an estimated 50 miles per hour. The official cause of failure and subsequent crash was identified in the Mars Program Independent Assessment Team Summary Report (ftp://ftp.hq.nasa.gov/pub/pao/reports/2000/2000_mpiat_summary.pdf), which states: "Spacecraft operating data needed for navigation were provided to the JPL navigation team by prime contractor Lockheed Martin in English units rather than the specified metric units. This was the direct cause of the failure."

Furthermore, the report also indicated that "specifically, software testing was inadequate." These findings can help us directly conclude that as long as there is a human element involved in the deployment of systems, whether it is software for satellites or your home security system, there will be vulnerabilities, which may be leveraged by attackers.

One example of exploitation of satellite systems involves hijacking transponders of U.S. military satellites. An article posted by Wired in April 2009, reports that 39 individuals were arrested for abusing U.S. Navy communications satellites and illegally accessing and using the satellites for communications in March of 2009. The article also states: "The practice is so entrenched, and the knowledge and tools so widely available, few believe the campaign to stamp it out will be quick or easy." (http://www.wired.com/politics/security/news/2009/04/fleetcom?currentPage=all)

As the U.S. government increases its reliance on technology to further the success of battlefield communication and operations, more opportunities to identify and leverage vulnerabilities will surely arise. Some examples involving modernization for weapons and communications platforms are explained in the article titled "Soldiers test the latest battlefield equipment" in the U.S. Army NCO Journal. The article, dated May 2010, outlines some of the future technologies, which may be used to support military units and includes proposed timelines leading up to the year 2025. (https://usasma.bliss.army.mil/NCOJournal/Soldierstestthelatestbattlefieldequipment.pdf)

From the perspective of an attacker, we can only imagine the types of communications protocols used to control some of these technological advances in warfare. Command, control, and real-time updates from systems can be implemented via satellite communications or long and short range wireless technologies. It is feasible that given time and appropriate resources, attackers (funded terrorist organizations, individuals, or foreign governments) will be able to identify vulnerabilities and manipulate the command and control protocols for some of these advances in military technology.

One scenario we may entertain involves the use of weak encryption algorithms to secure the communications link between a command and control station and military field units. What if an enemy is able to defeat the encryption and position themselves in the communication stream of our friendly units? (This would be similar to how a malicious network attacker would use readily available software to perform a man in the middle (MITM) attack on a network to capture user credentials.) Hijacked communications can allow our enemy to modify communications and instructions from the command and control station to the field units causing confusion and likely resulting in casualties.

Another article, posted on Wired in December 2009, provides insight into how insurgents are already using techniques similar to those discussed previously to capture real-time video from Unmanned Arial Vehicles (UAV). The article describes how insurgents were able to use software costing only $26 USD to capture sensitive video streams from unencrypted communications being transmitted between the UAV and ground units. The article also indicated the vulnerability described has been known to U.S. officials for over ten years. (http://www.wired.com/dangerroom/2009/12/insurgents-intercept-drone-video-in-king-sized-security-breach/)

If significant vulnerabilities such as these have been known for longer than the last 10 years and have not yet been fixed, what is in store for us 10 years from today in 2020? My answer: History repeats itself.

Infrastructure Attacks

The next 10 years will include major reconnaissance and attacks against networks that control infrastructure and utilities around the world. A few of our incident scenarios later in the book fall into this category. Some may target mobile phone towers and communications. Others may aim for emergency service communication. Still others might mark hospitals and other critical care facilities. But whether it is air traffic control, water systems, or nearly anything else, they are all controlled by computers that would be highly prized conquests of a cyber-crime organization. We are just now starting to discuss openly that unfriendly nation states are behind many attacks and which countries are leading the way in cyber-espionage. More and more frequently we will see that many of these attacks are state sponsored. We will find that the former Soviet Republic and China are some of the top leaders in this area of cyber-warfare.

Social and Financial Threats

Attacks that could disrupt the social and economic flow of a country would be a prized trophy for most cyber-criminals. A large-scale disruption of several systems could accomplish this. If ATM and credit-card-processing systems are taken offline, this could create widespread public panic. Disruption of various stock exchanges would cause large-scale panic. However, a bigger disruption would be if the attackers were able to bring into question the integrity of the system. Even disruption to the flow of goods and services is possible if coordinated and executed correctly. Imagine the chaos that would ensue if the shelves at the grocery store were empty. People would be shocked to learn how dependent these logistical systems are on information systems. Disruption of oil, natural gas, and gasoline would be a major source of social unrest. People see a fuel truck driving down the road and assume the process to get that fuel from point A to point B is a very manual one where a driver is simply taking fuel from a central station to a series of local fuel stops. In reality, these processes rely heavily on technology that is vulnerable to exploitation and compromise that can disrupt the flow of these basic goods and services.

Website Middleware Threats

As more and more organizations use middleware to host their websites, these will become targets for hackers. Website-hosting software that makes it easy to host, update, and maintain a website has become very popular. Some software applications such as WordPress are becoming so popular that tens of thousands of sites use this software. When vulnerabilities are discovered within this management software, it will be open season for hackers. Often website administrators do not upgrade the software for fear it will break some page or process. So revision after revision becomes available, many with security patches and updates, but go unused until a breach or other incident occurs. Through "Google hacking" techniques (using advanced searches on search engines sites) where indexed pages within search engines are used to identify all similar sites, it will be easy for hackers to identify and exploit these systems. When criminals do exploit these sites, they can literally compromise hundreds if not tens of thousands of sites within a matter of minutes.

FROM OUR CONTRIBUTORS

Scott Simpson, Director, Security Consulting Services, Solutionary

Part of the maturation process of the Internet has been the evolution of middleware to facilitate like processes. In the beginning, everyone built Web applications from scratch. While this was not the most efficient method, it did result in a very diverse population of applications. Each developer solved development challenges in their own unique way. As things have progressed, we have come to find that it is much more efficient to rely on others' abilities to solve for "X". The result of this realization has been the birth of middleware.

IT companies have been built for the sole purpose of solving for "X". They do it efficiently, and provide interfaces for others to leverage their work.

In some cases, the code developed to solve for "X" is freely available, which makes using it that much more attractive. In the case of commercial middleware, the benefit remains because of the cost of development and the efficiencies gained in the overall development life cycle. If I rely on a commercial middleware application, I know up-front the cost of development and maintenance. I also know that the specific portion of the project that will leverage the middleware will come in on time because of the limited code development required to integrate with most middleware.

The evolution in the application development and deployment process should have been obvious. It is the same evolution we have seen in so many other areas of society. The development of specific skills to gain efficiency has facilitated economic booms and an ever-increasing rise in the standard of living. However, it has also increased the dramatic nature of any disturbance in processes that have been specialized. The U.S. auto industry leveraged the financial knowledge and skills of the banking industry to facilitate automotive manufacturing and sales. When the financial sector failed, the automotive industry also experienced significant issues. The same scenario is developing in the application development world.

Today's applications often utilize multiple middleware components, each of which facilitates a specific function. In some cases, the entire purpose of the application is to integrate otherwise disparate applications. This re-use of the best solution for "X" does create efficiencies; however, it also increases the overall risk presented by each widely-adopted piece of middleware. Beginning today, and into the future, attackers will spend more and more time developing targeted attacks on middleware and highly integrated applications to increase the devastating affect of their attacks.

One common use of this homogenization of code is in the website-hosting software niche. Utilizing web hosting solutions makes it easy to host, update, and maintain a website, and has become very popular (see the WordPress example in this section).

These types of attacks will be difficult to defend against because the attacker will not have to make multiple requests before identifying a vulnerability and exploiting it. These attacks will be developed in a lab. Targets will be identified through passive means (e.g., Google hacking). The applications will be exploited without incident, and the compromises will leave the intruder with a comfortable spot to observe the traffic between the applications and their middleware components. This is often the most advantageous position to be in to inspect and harvest sensitive data, understand the application's syntax, and develop more advanced attacks. Managing your middleware components to ensure they are up-to-date and monitoring your application's interactions with middleware providers will be critical techniques for ensuring a secure computing environment.

Doppelganger Attacks

Individual user profiling will begin to be popular. This is where enough is known about an individual (where they shop online, where they bank online, what email provider they use, what social networking sites they belong to, etc., etc., etc.) that the knowledge can be combined with information from a data security breach. So once your credentials are stolen from one site, the thief can use the same or similar usernames and passwords to access the other sites that you may use. Far too many people use the same login credentials for multiple Internet sites, which makes this type of attack possible. We call this a doppelganger attack because the criminals mirror the credentials from one site to others.

These and many other types of attacks will be discussed throughout the book. We will likely see these and many others throughout the next decade. Criminals are limited only by their imaginations, and history has shown us that isn't much of a limitation at all.

FROM OUR CONTRIBUTORS

Zachary Scott, Chief Executive Officer (CEO), Ironlike Security Consulting

I agree with the authors' belief that we will see the meaningful emergence of the newly coined "doppelganger attack." While this concept is new, the criminal idea behind it is as old as that of the "patsy." Criminals, cyber or otherwise, know that, in theory, unanswered questions will lead to further investigation. Doppelganger attacks will be of particular concern in insider threat scenarios, where the motivation for spoofing the identity of another user may range from the desire to sabotage a specific individual's career or personal reputation, to simply wanting to remain undetected in order to launch further attacks. In any case, the long-range repercussions of being the "doppelganged" individual are striking. Perhaps someday soon we will see a data-breach case in which the suspected parties declare that they are innocent and assert that it was in fact the man with the laptop on the grassy knoll.

More extreme methodologies of targeting are on the horizon. With the promise of profit driving the major increase in data breaches, I think we will see new, evolved methodologies that from a high level could be viewed as more specific and more random.

Psychological profiling is emerging as a strategy in attacks. With huge dollar amounts and political motives tied to future breaches, attackers will take reconnaissance to a new level. Gone will be the days of ping-sweeping the firewall looking for open ports; we will see groups using commonly available information to target key individuals in the organization using socially engineered, psychologically-based attacks. Much to the chagrin of CIOs everywhere, the "security through obscurity" concept will need to extend to them as well: Facebook pages and LinkedIn resumes will need to come down.

Any information that could be used by groups to develop a profile of an individual that could later be used as leverage, insight, or simply to narrow the scope of an attack, will be a risk. In the attempt to gain access, nothing will be considered off-limits. Hackers may decide that the best way to get a keylogger onto the CEO's home computer will be to give his daughter a rootkit-infected USB drive at school or send it to them via one of the many social networking sites. In the new era of attacks, knowledge equals power, and all knowledge can and will be used against you.

In the future we will see an increase in randomization in an attempt to create less-traceable attacks. To quote from *The Secret History* by Donna Tarrt: "If we attempt to order events too meticulously to arrive at point X via a logical trail, it follows that the logical trail can be picked up at point X and followed back to us. Reason is always apparent to the discerning eye. But luck? It is invisible, erratic, angelic."

As information and security methods continue to improve, it is natural to assume that the criminal justice investigation arm of our industry will also continue to improve. Better investigation techniques and better detection should lead to an increase in criminal prosecutions and ultimately convictions. The cyber-criminals' adaptation will be to increase the randomization of attacks to avoid detection and conceal motive. Currently, most hackers are primarily concerned with whether they can do the hack — not with getting caught. In fact, many hackers actively seek credit and notoriety for the most networks hacked or the most websites defaced.

In the future, to conceal its origin, a virus may only propagate to randomized network nodes or random users. No longer will we see the typical pandemic spread which can ultimately be traced back to patient zero and ultimately back to the perpetrators. For decades the holy trinity of "means, motive, and opportunity" have been needed to guide investigators to suspects and convince juries of a perpetrator's guilt.

When looking at the following two groups, the motive and means of attack for Group B would be much more clear and would help investigators narrow down the list of possible suspects:

Group A:

■ The American Cheese Society (ACS)

■ The Department of Defense (DoD)

■ The Society for the Advancement of Little People (SALP)

Group B:

■ The Department of Defense (DoD)

■ North American Aerospace Defense Command (NORAD)

■ National Security Agency (NSA)

Because randomization of attack targets (as in Group A) will help an attacker conceal motive, means, and opportunity, it will be employed in future cyber-criminal endeavors.

Notes

1. You can read this report at `http://www.darkreading.com/insiderthreat/security/app-security/showArticle.jhtml?articleID=218100924`.

2. Information about this survey can be found here: `http://findarticles.com/p/articles/mi_m0BJK/is_9_12/ai_78355284/`.

Secure Communications and Collaboration

We can't solve problems by using the same kind of thinking
we used when we created them.
—Albert Einstein

As we put finger to keyboard in preparation to publish *Security 2020*, the most rapidly evolving technology is Unified Communications (UC). This category includes significant advancements in many communications subcategories such as email, instant messaging (IM), video conferencing, streaming video, voice over IP (VoIP), and collaboration tools. It's common to lump in collaboration and call the category Unified Communications and Collaboration (UCC). Collaboration tools come in many packages, such as shareware and open source peer-to-peer sharing tools, as well as commercial products like SharePoint. Often, and in this chapter, we will include supporting technologies such as archiving and storage. While not always successful, each of these technologies strives to improve our ability to effectively communicate and collaborate in our personal, social, and professional lives. As security professionals, it is not our role to restrict the efficiencies that these tools bring to businesses, but rather to leverage our skills to effectively apply security and controls as an overlay in a way that is transparent to the end user. Information technology (IT) security should not restrict a user's ability to perform his or her job, rather it should liberate both the employees and overall business to perform at a more efficient level than they could without the security controls. In order to accomplish this, we need to do more than secure today's technologies and apply current best practices, which will provide nothing more than a short-term patch. Rather, we need to understand and map out a long-term strategy that tactically secures our content today, but also allows our controls and monitoring to adapt as business needs, regulatory requirements, and technologies change. This is difficult when a thousand tactical projects are coming at you from the business, and new risks are evolving every day.

Businesses today are under extreme pressure to perform more efficiently and to integrate technology and automation into their arsenal of improvements. UCC is driven by businesses demanding business applications that can help them achieve higher efficiency from their workers in their daily work. Historically, IT security has been driven by multiple market influences, compliance and regulatory requirements being the most prominent in recent years. Unfortunately, IT security is often seen as a barrier to progress in business. The perception is that incremental security requirements will increase cost, slow a project, and create usability issues for the users. As a result, when compliance and regulatory requirements drive any expenditure, the bare minimum to achieve those requirements will be spent, and often in areas that have no measurable impact on lowering the actual risk to an organization. Some business leaders respond to media headlines, where obvious risks for security breaches (and actual breach events) are reported regularly. For example, when TJX suffered their credit card compromise, security vendors around the globe leveraged this as a threat to every prospect customer they called. Obviously, many security firms called TJX as well. Given the clear and present problem TJX had, they probably made purchases, some of which were certainly needed and others which were probably simply to say to the public that they were making investments. CISOs can rarely attribute the purchases they make to increased threats, but rather to an increased willingness of their bosses to spend more money. While the headlines were accurate, no new threat or increased risk was generated at that point in history; rather, the existing risks were simply emphasized. Unfortunately, this often results only in tactical fixes and a limited focus on broader issues that allow for higher impact, higher risk problems. Don't misinterpret this statement: any improvement in security is good; however the opportunity cost of not looking at the longer-term objective and addressing higher-risk elements are the key points of concern. All information security decisions should be based on reducing risk to an acceptable level, not simply being able to fill in the checkmark for compliance requirements or addressing a single known threat. That certainly is simple to say, but far more difficult to achieve in the real world. Hope is there, however, as most businesses now recognize that the relationship between achieving compliance and reducing risk is not always direct. In fact, there have been numerous cases where companies have been technically compliant, yet have suffered a breach. In the end, they were still found not to have performed their duties to provide adequate protection relative to industry peers. Today, more often than not, most business executives and legal advisors benchmark not only to compliance and regulatory requirements but also to the level of effort and expense that like companies, in like industries, are performing. Peer company and organizational relativity will become more and more important within governance, risk, and compliance (GRC) as the IT and IT security industries continue to mature.

Another flaw in the industry is with determining the return on investment (ROI) and total cost of ownership (TCO) for security. Demonstrating to a business that security investments provide value is difficult. Much of this problem is driven by the fact that, historically, IT security investments have been built around protecting existing applications, often applications that have been present within the enterprise for years or tens of years. This leads the business owner to believe that, since there hasn't been a security event in the past, there won't be one in the future. These applications have evolved and changed, but in reality the primary driver for increased security protection is increased accessibility, as these applications and the networks that they reside on are connected to the Internet, as well as the ever increasing threats that are evolving as attack technologies and techniques evolve. In other words, business owners must recognize that, while their IT environment might have served them well in the past, and had no known security breaches, this is no indication of future viability. The risk to this environment has evolved and increased; thus, the only way to protect it is to evolve the countermeasures.

The industry usually approaches IT security from a perspective that investments are made to counter risk. However, rarely do security professionals use the phrase "counter risk." "Reward" (or sometimes "opportunity") is the usual term used. Reward is what IT security provides to the business when it transforms high risk into acceptable risk. Risk occurs when a business application introduces technical challenges and increased threats into a business environment. Reward is when IT security makes this same business application an enabling tool to improve efficiency or generate more revenue. Success is when IT security enables business innovation to thrive. When IT security enables the business to generate profit through efficient use of resources with acceptable risk, business leaders take note. UCC is evolving rapidly, and this rapid evolution presents a significant opportunity to show that IT security can provide high value to the business. By getting ahead of the projected changes in UC/UCC and investing in security as a core function of the project, security can be seen as an enabler, rather than an afterthought that both slows the project and adds expense.

In addition, it's often hard to judge if technology is driving social change or social change is driving technology innovation. Today, far more communications are transacted via email than any other medium, including the phone. This applies to both our social and business lives. New applications are quickly being introduced, tested, and adopted to keep up with our evolving needs. (To be fair, it's worth noting that for all these obvious successes and advancements, more technology introductions fail than succeed.) Innovations by large companies such as Google and Microsoft with its collaboration suites (combined with easy-to-use options such as hosted services or, in some cases, complete end-to-end SaaS solutions), are allowing for quicker adoption of technology changes as well. Likewise, small, innovative startups are also introducing solutions. A byproduct of these rapid changes is the way users operate and exchange information, which has created many security and compliance issues across the globe for organizations, businesses, governments, and individuals alike. A point of significant issue, and often confusion, is the convergence of technology that has both personal use and business use. The historic separation of our work from our social lives is gone, and those two areas have now become a single intertwined fabric. Dual use of smart phones, laptops, and mobile media devices is a norm today, not an exception. Further complicating things is the ease of use for many consumer and prosumer applications that allow for efficiencies and improved quality of life experiences in our personal lives, but which many corporations attempt to block, as they are seen as interfering with employees' productivity. Examples include LinkedIn, Facebook, YouTube, online television and radio, numerous peer-to-peer applications, and other social media sites. There is no denying that, for some employees, and some companies, these applications are useful tools. In some companies, these applications have been embraced as a medium to improve marketing, communications, and information sharing. In other cases, however, they are undoubtedly not being used for business purposes. In this rapidly changing technology environment, and with the merger of personal and business data, corporations must be diligent to keep up with their legal and industry requirements. In addition to maintaining the integrity, confidentiality, and availability of data, issues now include capturing and retaining user-generated traffic for compliance and legal purposes.

The two primary issues in the industry that we must focus on to make it over the next hurdle in the evolution of IT security for communications are:

- **User identity:** First, we must be able to manage and track user identity and activity across the enterprise, then we must find a workable way to implement *federated user identity*. Federated user identity refers to user identification credentials that are portable across IT systems and even across enterprises. That way, if users leave one system or enterprise, they don't have to create another, unique set of credentials to use IT systems in another enterprise.

- **Content control:** Equally important is being able to effectively control who has the ability to access, modify, and distribute content. As our business and personal worlds merge, businesses run a great deal of risk that unauthorized content will be stored on company-owned assets. In addition, most enterprises have valuable content that they must control.

User identity is a security problem that has existed from the first day IT systems were enabled to take inputs from users and not just programmers. We wouldn't go so far as to say effective and user-friendly user identity is the holy grail of IT security, but it's certainly an elusive prize that most have not been able to accomplish. Now, with UCC, the identity of users has become more critical than ever, both for auditing and for making sure that the user can move between communication applications transparently.

Content control is top of mind for most online consumers and businesses alike. Most businesses want to distribute content in some way. The content may be marketing materials to prospects and customers, or it may be internal documents for development, or a myriad of other types. Enterprises, like many commercial content owners, seek to protect their data in order to capitalize on its value for as long as possible; thus, the advent of Digital Rights Management (DRM) and other ways to protect and control data. DRM and other content control methods seek to allow some content to be distributed freely, while other content is controlled tightly . . . and many variations in between.

The environment we must perform business in today is like none in history. Individually and in some combination, we've had times of war, times of financial stress and recession, rapid technology development, and even social change before. However, in no other time have we had the quad-facto all at once. That being said, we continue to perform business successfully in most cases. So, good times or bad, the resilience of business will continue to surprise people. The same applies to the technologies and networks that support our businesses.

Business requirements are supported by the trusted and reliable delivery of communications. Most users may not understand all the technical nuances or risk associated with performing their day-to-day business. Nonetheless those of us tasked with enabling business to be performed seamlessly must anticipate risk at multiple levels. To break this down, specific to UCC, we must account for:

- **Confidentiality:** Users must be able to communicate to another user, or group of users, in a way that does not expose the data to users for whom it was not intended.

- **Availability:** Users must be able to communicate whenever and from wherever, without interruption; they must perform business. Endpoint and network resources must be available under both normal and adverse conditions, including denial of service (DoS) attacks.

- **Access Control:** Access control has two components: authentication and identity.

- **Authentication:** A system must have the ability to connect to a resource (network, system, endpoint). Often this access to a resource is not restricted to a specific person or system; thus, authentication can be approved without identity being provided.

- **Identity:** Identity, which often may provide authentication, is in many cases the second level of access required to provide the critical component of who the user is, so that activity can be tied back to an individual.

- **Authorization:** Authorization is the process of mapping an authenticated user to a predefined selection of rights or resources they may access.

- **Integrity:** Integrity provides the endpoints or users with confidence that the data has not been tampered with.

Technology coupled with motivation, whether for financial gain, political motives, bragging rights, or simply for fun, is a very dangerous reality for today's IT managers. Fortunately, many new UCC applications have been built with some practical way of securing them. Unfortunately, many deployments don't take advantage of the technologies and techniques that are available to secure them.

Sometimes an example is the best way to communicate the important features of a useful technology. Data leakage is an obvious risk in UCC. A friend, Amit Yoran, the CEO of NetWitness, has developed a powerful tool for monitoring IP traffic of any type or protocol. With a single tool, you can monitor IM, VoIP, email (both SMTP and webmail), IP addresses user-specific details, and so forth. It also creates pivot tables that allow you to build relationships between variables, and allows a security administrator to follow user communications regardless of what machine he or she is on in an enterprise. More importantly, it allows you to search and monitor content as well (e.g., Social Security number, name, user name, address, file name, special symbols, etc.). It is powerful to the point of being scary. It truly shows the level of access to network information that can be achieved with today's technologies.

FROM OUR CONTRIBUTORS

Amit Yoran, CEO, NetWitness

As the pace of innovation quickens and the adoption of new communications reaches a critical mass, opportunities for new attack vectors and methodologies will thrive. Apple products, such as the iPhone, have forever changed the way we interact with people and technology, and further blurred the line between personal and professional communications. Consequently, the new mobile experience enabled by an arsenal of third-party applications has forced IT security groups to address the risks of a non-corporate-owned asset, with all its applications and exploits against the software stack; meanwhile, users demand access to corporate systems and data. Social and business communications tools will only increase in their complexity and become increasingly unmanaged by the organization.

The challenge is achieving a calculated balance of end user awareness, preventative controls, and accurate detection capabilities to satisfy the risk appetite of an organization. As the promise of UCC becomes a reality, the only certainty IT security teams can anticipate is that new methods of compromise through the use of embedded exploits in the business logic of communications such as hyperlinks, images, PDFs video, and voice over IP will be employed to trick users and evade security controls. A new approach to information security needs to evolve and gain acceptance in order to expand our visibility into IT risks and detect attempts of compromise against the communications ecosystem that is destined to deliver long-term business value.

Rick Howard, Director of Intelligence, iDefense, a Verisign company

In the business world, there is such a thing as *business disruptors* new technologies or ideas that emerge that fundamentally change how a business is run. Apple Inc.'s iTunes/iPod combination is the perfect example. Other companies were selling digital music at the time, but when Apple released these products at the right price point, the event fundamentally changed how we all buy music. Some music experts predict that the music CD will no longer exist by 2020. That is a business disruptor. There are cyber-security disruptors too; technologies or ideas that emerge that will fundamentally change how we all protect the enterprise. The smart phone is one such disruptor.

"Smart phone" is a bit of a misnomer. Walt Mossberg, noted technology pundit, said in 2008 that the difference between a BlackBerry cell phone and an iPhone is this: a BlackBerry is a mobile phone that through some trickery with short message service (SMS) allows the user to view Web pages in a "vulgar and ugly way." The iPhone is a handheld, wireless UNIX box that just happens to allow the user to make phone calls.

Cell phones are getting smaller and more powerful. In the span of a few short years, engineers and designers have reduced the mobile phone from the size of a thick suitcase in the early 1970s to smaller than the famous Star Trek communicator today. At the same time, engineers and designers have exponentially increased the functionality and bandwidth capability of these devices.

The basic cell phone has become ubiquitous to the general populace, not just in the West, but across the entire world. As the form factor continues to shrink and wireless networks get faster and faster, there will be a gradual transition in stages from the basic cell phone to the smart phone to whatever comes after that. Indeed, early adopters of products like Apple's iPhone are already experiencing this shift. During this transition, the cell phone will morph from the calling device that we know today into something else: a personal communication device that is much more than simply a telephone. It

Continued

will become a device that allows us to communicate with our friends and our colleagues via multiple channels and media, a device that allows us to store and experience entertainment in various forms and a device that facilitates our engagement of the global market and social spaces via the Internet. In the future, we can expect these devices to get smaller, integrate more functionality, and run longer on their own power.

Mobile communications have deployed across the world at dizzying speeds, and even more so in developing countries with no broadband access to users' homes. During the last few years, many people living in the developing world have begun to use their mobile phones as sole access points to the Internet; many do not even have a computer at home.

Of course, the news is not all positive. With new functionality comes exposure to new security risks. The kinds of cyber-security attacks that we see today on our home computers and laptops are the same as those we expect to see on these new mobile devices in the future. At the 2010 Black Hat USA security conference in Las Vegas (the annual and infamous hacker conference where white hat security researchers demonstrate their latest discoveries), there was not one talk that addressed security issues on mobile phones. If the white hats are trying to discover the security flaws in these devices, it is not much of a stretch to imagine that the black hats are pursuing them too.

Regardless of the security issues though, the smart phone is here to stay and will most likely completely disrupt how we all currently communicate with each other.

Email, Instant Messaging, and SMS

No longer is voice communication the primary way of communicating. Email, instant messaging (IM), and Short Message Service (SMS) represent the majority of communications tools that we use today. Each communications technique now easily straddles the gray zone between mobility and fixed location, as well as personal and business use. Not many people would have imagined 10 years ago how the business world and our social lives would be impacted by the changes in communications capabilities. Even with the rapid change over the past 10 years, few can imagine the changes that will occur over the next 10 years. Integrated presence and location data for each individual user is technically available today but has yet to be fully optimized. Embedding interactive multimedia into most business applications, even when mobile, is just now starting to be done. Virtual reality for gaming is widespread but has not been fully integrated into business applications. That integration could be highly productive as the workforce becomes more and more reliant on telecommuting.

New-generation applications which attempt to take collaboration to the next level, are starting to gain notice with younger generations. Video messaging and prosumer quality, and affordable video conferencing are now just starting to take hold, with examples like Skype having millions of users.

It's clear that these new-generation tools will replace many of the applications of today, but they will also introduce increased risk. The complications to IT security will be:

- Continued blurring of personal/social use applications and business applications

- A multitude of new access points and device types

- Requirements for federated user identity and presence regardless of location, connectivity method, or application in use

The question isn't how much the technology will change and evolve, but how we will use technology to support our business requirements. Success can be achieved in this area, assuming that some level of control and auditing must be applied to communications in one or both of the following two ways:

- All communications must be captured and analyzed at the endpoint (e.g., mobile device, PC, attached device [USB, local drive, etc.]).

- All communications must be forced through a common point so that they can be analyzed and retained (copied and stored).

Furthermore, you must evaluate the user base and corporate policies to understand what acceptable use and risk are for your enterprise or organization. Remote users who are allowed to access business applications from personal or public computers add incremental risk, but remote use may be necessary to give users optimal flexibility. This is where business needs and IT security must collaborate. It is true that both of the above could be very difficult to retrofit if the business is already operating in some other way; however, if each of them is built in from the beginning, the impact on the end user is transparent.

FROM OUR CONTRIBUTORS

Tom Dring, Director of Enterprise Infrastructure, Noble Energy

In today's environment, companies across the globe struggle with various aspects of email, mobile, and instant messaging. In B2B organizations, it is often the customers with specific business requirements that dictate the communications and security model for business transactions and communications, rather than the IT groups. It is common for each business and industry to have different

Continued

de facto "standards" for IM and collaboration tools. In this environment, it becomes very challenging for a business to establish and adhere to a unified security model and system. More and more business will be done this way but, hopefully, as messaging/collaboration tools mature there will be convergence in that market and a couple of leading solutions will evolve that better address security and identity management.

Demographics are also an important factor. Many younger employees prefer SMS texting to email and may tend to use that medium for communications both internally and with customers. This has obvious security implications and can be an impediment in organizations that are more email-centric.

These technologies are further complicated by mobile device management, since one of a few scenarios will occur:

1. In order to maintain his personal phone number, and privacy, for calls and texting, the employee will carry his personal mobile phone in addition to his company-issued phone or smart phone. This can be burdensome and the person may tend to not carry and monitor his company phone as much as he otherwise would.

2. The employee will use his company phone for personal calls and texting, often requesting that the company "port" his personal number to the company phone, with the provision that he can port it back again if he leaves the company. This situation raises obvious concerns about privacy and personal use and/or abuse of company equipment.

3. Rather than issuing and managing company-owned mobile phones, some companies choose to use a "stipend" approach to reimburse employees for phones and service plans. In this case a person would typically have only one phone. This is workable in some organizations, but raises compliance concerns in companies that require tight controls, monitoring, and message retention.

Each of these situations entails significant security considerations and the "right" answer will depend on the type of business and company in question.

One last note: Skype is a very interesting tool that has taken hold in many companies in a grass-roots, almost viral, manner to handle VoIP, IM, and desktop sharing/collaboration. This can be a challenging situation to manage. Skype now offers improved business management tools, but these cost money and many organizations are reluctant to take this conscious step when the "free" versions have long sufficed.

Online Webinars and Collaboration Tools

Collaboration tools are becoming common in business. With more and more employees working remotely, or distributed across multiple offices, it is necessary for them to share documents, work items, and research. In addition, with much work being outsourced, remotely engaging resources provides a far more cost-effective solution than travel, which is expensive and time-consuming. However, much of this information exchange and sharing is done on critical projects that often include enterprise intellectual property (IP), so the utmost care must be taken to maintain content control, audit tracking, and security in general.

Online collaboration in a Software as a Service (SaaS) model is becoming a very attractive option for small and medium enterprises (SME), as well as their larger counterparts. Even the government, including local, state, and federal, is rapidly adopting this easy-to-deploy and cost-effective service option. Only the Department of Defense (DoD) and their international counterparts are holding off because of security concerns—concerns that are very valid. The term *WebEx* has all but become the general term for webinars, but in reality there are many different WebEx alternatives in the market, which are often better. Go-to-Meeting, Microsoft LiveMeeting, Google Apps, Wimba (especially for the education vertical), ooVoo, and iLinc (especially when you want integrated video chat), Dimdim, Zoho, and even Skype all have specific advantages, depending on your business requirements. Having been in the SaaS industry for many years, I can say a few things candidly: First, you would be concerned, maybe horrified, if you knew about all the warts on each of the industry's players and in the industry as a whole. For example, the use of common passwords not tied to individual employees is widespread. Further complicating this issue is that, in numerous audits we've performed or been involved in over the years, it was often clear that many service providers don't have a easy way to address the exposure created by departing employees (clearly a common issue with enterprises as well). Second, even considering the concerns and risks, SaaS vendors in almost every case can deliver more reliable services in a more secure manner than most enterprises can, by developing their own solutions at reasonable level of operational and capital expense. With an unlimited amount of resources, including personnel, third-party contractors, and capital for software and hardware, an enterprise might produce a more reliable and secure solution that exceeds a SaaS provider's solution. If you are one of these rare entities, let us know if you have a job, and we will send you an inexhaustible list of employees who want to come work for you. On the other hand, if you are like most organizations in the world and have limited capital and operational resources, online collaboration can be a good solution for you.

The unfortunate reality with SaaS providers is that there is no single, common way to provide a security overlay, since each SaaS provider deploys its solution in a unique way.

Here is a guiding principle that will help you maneuver through evaluating each online collaboration solution: Ask for documentation about the service provider that details the areas you and your organization believe are important in helping you to make a decision about whose services to engage. If you're not sure what's important to your organization (that would be a red flag), then start with what your auditors typically ask you for. This list probably includes the following for each service provider you use:

- A copy of the service provider's security policy and any audits by third parties that have been performed. Prior-year reports are always good to review as well, since they will show the progress the service provider has made year over year.

- A detailed understanding of how authentication of users is handled and what audit reports the service provider can provide. Understand if they can integrate with your Active Directory, LDAP, or 2nd Factor Authentication system. This will save you a lot of pain in fulfilling audit reports in the future and simplify your user management process.

- A copy of the service provider's SAS70 Type II, a basic standard for auditing an organization, to be sure it has documented and practiced best practices that make operational sense and satisfy some basic opinions of the auditor. Anyone who has been through a SAS70 Type II knows that there are many weaknesses in the process no matter which audit firm you use. I do believe that the certification shows that a provider has reached a scale and level where it is servicing clients with enough clout to demand this commonly accepted audit. It also provides a basic review that you are unlikely to do on the provider yourself, and you can look for any sections that the report flags as areas for improvement. You should also look at sections in the report that you think are critical to making you comfortable with the provider. Keep in mind that the SAS70 Type II *does not* guarantee that the provider is performing business in the manner it has documented in its processes and procedures, nor does it guarantee that the provider has not changed its operation significantly since the last audit. It simply means that the SAS70 auditor has checked for documentation, and verbally validated with personnel that these documented processes have been completed. It is, as stated in the final review, an opinion from the auditor.

- If you perform business internationally, you should ask for region-specific compliance reports, such as ISO and privacy law compliance reports.

- A copy of the service provider's financials for the past two years. Many private companies will say they cannot provide this because they are privately held. Don't believe it. They might be reluctant to do so, but any provider that is viable and wants your business will provide this to you. On seeing them, though, you may find their financials don't look all that good, so you will need to determine if the risk of doing business with them is too high or if they have substantial enough backing from investors to execute their business plan.

- At least six reference clients, four that have been with the provider for more than two years, and two that have been taken on in the past six months. Request clients that are in the same industry and in general the same size as your organization.

Some additional common questions are:

- What is the provider's service roadmap and plan of record for the next 12 months?

- Where will your content transit and reside at rest (be stored)? This is important for multiple reasons, but mainly because few SaaS providers actually own the data center space where their equipment resides. Thus, when you ask for items like SAS70s, security policies, and other operational documents, you need to ask for those of the service provider's providers as well.

- Have there been any data breaches, exposure of one customer's data to another, or any other data compromise that was or was not reported?

- Ask for at least three references for customers that have departed the service provider in the past three months. This may be challenging to get, but well worth the effort. It will allow you to determine three primary things: First, why customers are leaving the service provider; second, if and when you leave the service provider, how well the service provider supports you in transferring your data, transferring your data; and third, the general professionalism of the organization.

- Size matters. Well, actually, it's scale that matters. We previously said that you should review the financials, but you should also review the future viability of the business. One or both of two things needs to happen with a SaaS provider: they need to reach a scale where they can efficiently invest in their infrastructure and support personnel and/or they need to have investors that have deep pockets and are willing to invest until they reach that scale. Finding investors, especially in this market, who are willing to invest for the long run is a big hurdle to overcome. In 2010, and probably for several years to come, there will be a number of small players in the sub-$15M range that will continue to scrape by, but their operation and capital investments will be strained. Be very careful when evaluating your provider and be comfortable that they not only can be innovative and feature-unique but also have available resources to continue to execute and provide the level of availability and security that your enterprise demands.

Implementations on the customer's premises can be slightly less complicated from a security perspective, as you can layer your access controls and existing security controls. Implementations of Microsoft SharePoint, Documentum, Alfresco, and IBM Tivoli range in scope significantly, and companies such as Oracle and Google claim to have products in this area as well. Each is unique, but relatively easy to protect in the scheme of business applications, assuming that you already have a layered security approach to your infrastructure.

FROM OUR CONTRIBUTORS

Dan Summa, CEO, Kindling

My experience running several online services companies has shown me that security is always a major focus. Over the past five years, it also has become a major consideration for customers when they're evaluating online SaaS companies.

Consider the amount of data handled by, and the level of confidentiality entrusted to, many SaaS providers: Salesforce.com with every lead and customer; banking applications that allow access not only to view your data but often to perform transactions; and remote data backup and archiving that includes email and IM. You rapidly begin to understand the magnitude of the damage a breach would inflict on an enterprise or individual.

Online collaboration and crowd sourcing is truly a monumental advancement considering that most collaboration tools today are limited to internal employees. While tools like SharePoint will advance document and information sharing within an enterprise, external SaaS solutions will enable idea, information, and experience sharing across large populations without their being employees of a single company.

Our application, Kindling, is used by organizations to provide a channel for their members to collaborate around ideas—arguably the most important IP a company owns. Fifteen years ago, could you imagine any organization trusting an outside provider with this IP? These days, an external vendor often has a heightened interest in security relative to the internal organization because if a SaaS vendor is careless with information and experiences a breach or data loss, that spells the end of the venture. Additionally, the SaaS vendor can spread the cost of security measures across multiple accounts, which an internal team cannot do.

When working with a vendor to facilitate collaboration within the enterprise, it's of course essential to choose a reputable and trustworthy partner.

Ray Harris, CEO, WebCast Group

As a provider of webinar and webcast services, we must be a trusted vendor that understands and respects both the security of our client's networks and the privacy of their data. SaaS webcast providers like ourselves gather user data in the form of registrations and then deliver rich media that enters corporate networks and private networks.

Privacy and data usage terms need to be clearly stated, or a company may find their webinar vendor is using their webinar viewer list in ways they never expected. For example, at this time both Cisco and GotoMeeting take the user registration data of their client's webinars and use that data to market their webinar services. Clearly, this practice could be perceived as a violation of privacy and a misuse of data. A user may sign up to watch a webinar in finance, for example, and within hours, or days, that same user is suddenly getting numerous emails from the webinar production company soliciting the user to try their webinar service.

Rich media is another very critical issue in the security of the multimedia enabled enterprise. Webinar and service providers routinely deliver slide shows and other HTML objects directly to the desks of workers inside corporate networks. In some cases, these users are first required to install a client-side application and in other cases, the user simply allows a Java or JavaScript program to run on their computers. The potential for harm is very great. Rich media can deliver great informational data but it can also deliver worms, client-side applications that track key strokes, applications that report data back to the main server, and much more.

It is critical that the IT departments running corporate networks keep browsers and operating systems updated. While this sounds like an over-simplification, the fact is that most attacks occur on older browsers and un-patched operating systems. Lastly, organizations need to select SaaS vendors that respect the client data and have clear guidelines stating that client data is never touched or used for any purpose other than the intended webcast and webinar usage.

Voice over IP

As you can imagine, voice communications, like any streams of data that include important content, are high-value targets. For example, the content of a voice call can include financial information for a public company, customer information, and personal information such as credit card info. A general consideration for the security of any communications technology is, what is the user base's expectation of confidentiality? In some cases, there may be no expectation that the content or conversation being exchanged is secure, and in other cases there may be a high degree of confidentiality expected. To make things easy, assume that the user base consists of HR, Research and Development (R&D), and the executive staff, and build toward their expectations.

IP telephony, or Voice over IP (VoIP), is one of the more complex communications systems to secure because of its many-to-many participant nature and its inside and outside the firewall connectivity requirements. In addition, to ensure low latency on the local and wide area network typically requires some level of quality of service (QoS) deployment to protect the voice quality of the call. When securing VoIP, integrity and availability are equally important for most cases, as is protection against misuse. Many breach and vector considerations must be accounted for, including:

- Integrity
  - Call interceptions (through man-in-the-middle attacks, session hijacking, or packet sniffers such as VOMIT)
  - Unauthorized access (to voicemail, call sessions, etc.)
  - Caller and IP identity spoofing
  - Toll fraud
  - Repudiation and logging
- Availability
  - Endpoint infection (virus, Trojan, malware)
  - Application layer attacks
  - Denial of service (DoS)

Threats to VoIP come in many flavors. They can be as simple as denying connectivity to more complex schemes, where the voice streams are intercepted and compiled into files that can be replayed. Interception of the VoIP stream is always a key concern. Voice Over Misconfigured IP Telephony, (VOMIT) is one of the most commonly used applications for capturing VoIP calls. Simply put, this tool allows a user to capture voice packets and reassemble them into audio files. Outside of physical protection of the infrastructure, which is impractical given the volume of calls that leave most enterprises, encryption is the most practical protection.

Another situation that comes in waves is penetration of the actual VoIP systems in ways that allow unauthorized users to originate calls. It seems we can go months with no enterprises having this issue and then have multiple enterprises compromised in the same month. For most large businesses that still incur toll charges, especially international toll charges, this can be a very expensive hack. Often these compromises are sold in a way that hundreds, if not thousands of calls are made before the situation is rectified. (This happens when people are sold minutes to make calls for free or at reduced rates. Often the purchaser is unaware that they are using stolen minutes.) Often, default administrative passwords are in place on the VoIP system from the initial install, after a reboot, or through troubleshooting, making this type of hack easier. Strong administration access controls are key.

Denial of service (DoS) is another major issue in VoIP, where it is often top of mind. An actual disruption of service can be created in many ways, all of which are real challenges, from flooding the network and slowing or blocking legitimate users, to sending a series of bad connections to a server, reducing resources. Layered security is the best approach to preventing this type of attack, combined with careful resource allocation and protection. If encryption is enabled, blocking unencrypted traffic becomes an easier approach for protecting the infrastructure from external attacks.

While there are many component standards in VoIP, the two primary standards are the International Telecommunication Union (ITU) H.323 and Session Initiation Protocol (SIP). In addition, Media Gateway Protocol (MGCP), is another common technique that implements H.323. These standards each allow an application or device to control a call session and to interact with the traditional switched telephone network.

The H.323 standard covers any device or application that uses H.323 to control the call session. Typically, this allows the device or application to interact with the switched-circuit network, or Plain Old Telephone (POT) network. The protocol includes call control, including establishment, maintenance, and termination through signaling, registration, synchronization, and packetization of media streams for both point-to-point and multipoint call sessions. The Session Initiation Protocol (SIP) is an ASCII-encoded application layer control protocol. Like H.323, SIP is used to establish, maintain, and terminate calls in both a point-to-point and multipoint call session; however, it is considered to be a more secure approach.

Another layer of protection recommended by most equipment vendors, including Cisco, is to separate VoIP traffic onto separate virtual local area network (VLAN) logical segments where the QoS and security controls can be applied. This allows the same physical infrastructure to be used while logically protecting it via a VLAN, ensuring confidential delivery of communications.

FROM OUR CONTRIBUTORS

Mark Kaish, SVP Technology Operations, COX Communications

Security for voice communications will continue to gain importance over the next 10 years as more consumers and businesses convert to VoIP. This will be driven by the attractiveness of the economics combined with the attractiveness associated with efficiencies of integrating common numbers and logic between landlines and mobile phones. Businesses and consumers today

Continued

FROM OUR CONTRIBUTORS   *(continued)*

typically rely on existing Local Area Networks (LANs) and computer systems to transport and manage the VoIP calls; this reliance will continue to increase over the upcoming years as well. The incremental risk introduced by threats to these infrastructure components being compromised by viruses or overrun with traffic such as Distributed Denial of Service (DDoS) is frequently underrated. Thus, investments in security to compensate for the increased risk are often not made. In addition, in most cases voice traffic is carried over the Internet where eavesdropping is a risk. Users often forget the potential implication of not encrypting voice communications where account numbers, medical information, PIN tones, and so forth can be intercepted across the public network.

These increased risks are often easily compensated for by integration of redundancy, call logic, and application of basic security applications such as antivirus software. More importantly, carriers recognize that security can be used to differentiate them from their competition and are applying more resources to protecting customers within the core network and/or are bundling security services with their transport services.

Mike Ferrari, Senior Director of Field Services, Allied Telesyn

Security breaches can seriously impact all parties involved in IP Video over public telecommunications networks—the user, the service provider, and the content owner. As a services director for a Triple Play equipment manufacturer, it's my job to ensure that my company recognizes these potential threat parameters and understands the best mitigation tactics.

With the rapid expansion of bandwidth availability in the access space over the past few years, video applications have exploded. Many of our customers operate as cable providers using Multicast IP Video from familiar content providers such as Disney, CNN, ESPN, and others. This is big business and the content providers will not tolerate security violations in either storage or transmission that allow unimpeded access to these services. Still, many other customers run IP Video conference applications that require maximum protection to ensure corporate trade secrets are not compromised. Many of the FTTH and xDSL connectivity endpoints involve customer premise equipment at the consumer's home as part of the network solution, and it is imperative that these "network elements" be locked down to both protect the user from the outside and protect the outside from the user. The network provider will ultimately be responsible for ensuring these threats are contained, and they will have to implement the best security practices that pertain to both the networking and IT domains. These are two diverse areas that require wide-ranging skill sets. As an equipment manufacturer, we must ensure that we supply providers with the necessary tools that are both cost effective and are very simple to use.

Video over IP

Video, in the scheme of Unified Communications and Collaboration (UCC), is an interesting variable. In its truest form it bridges the gap between those tangible, and extremely important, visual cues that happen in face-to-face interactions that cannot occur as effectively over audio, IM, or written communications. Visual cues are important, but another aspect to remember is that, when properly utilized by a participant or participants, video provides a higher level of engagement for all involved. If you consider for a moment that the average person can type 33–80 words per minute (wpm), read 250–400 wpm, and speak at 150–170 wpm, then there is no wonder that we are all bored in most non-face-to-face interactions with others, since the average human can comprehend verbal communications at rates in excess of 300 wpm. This obviously is compounded by the lack of presentation and social skills most people demonstrate when not face to face. The visual aspects of video, in addition to filling the visual cues we are starting to lack in other UCC, fill the gaps needed to keep our minds engaged in a presentation or in bidirectional communications. For these reasons, we believe video is a critical element in bridging the gap needed for us to continue to evolve as a technology-driven culture. Video, whether via video mail, broadcast, video on demand, bidirectional video conference, or multi-participant video conferences, allows our social fabric to continue to evolve, while leveraging the many advantages associated with not being physically present with each other at all times.

Video, in its many forms and delivery techniques, is a complex variable in the scheme of any IT infrastructure. However, with the introduction of Video over IP (VoIP) the problem has moved from separate network infrastructure such as coax to the IP network(s) that support all your business applications, and can no longer be ignored by network professionals within organizations and carriers.

With the currently available service options, video can be delivered in four primary forms:

- Video on demand (VoD)
- H.323 and/or SIP video conferencing
- Live streaming (such as broadcast IP TV, an event broadcast, or surveillance)
- A hybrid that has two or more functions as noted above

Each of these can be performed over IP networks, or over a closed dedicated infrastructure. In addition, all of these in part or whole can be delivered as a Customer Premises Solution, an SaaS model, or a hybrid of the two.

Based on the delivery mode of the video as mentioned above, you must define the origination and destination points for the video. Origination points can vary significantly, but include:

- **Stored source feed:** Primarily a video service that serves video on demand (VoD), although many stored source feeds can be scheduled to broadcast. Most often these are video servers or multimedia servers; however, they can also be served by specially-built applications.

- **Live source feed:** Anything that feeds video live from the origination to the destination can be considered a live source feed. These include webcams, video-enabled phones, high-end movie cameras, and video conference and telepresence systems.

Destination points have the broadest variance but fall into the following categories:

- Video to smart phones
- PCs, including ultra-small mobile computers
- Telepresence or video conference systems
- Display monitors, specifically those used for digital signage

Another major variable when considering the security of video content is what transports and networks it will transit from the origination to destination. In most scenarios, absent local origination and delivery over a LAN, the video stream will transit multiple networks. For example:

- Private or closed networks where the data always transits over a network that is secure and/or completely within the control of the party intending to protect the video content. Components often include:
  - Local area networks (LANs)
  - Multi-Protocol Label Switching (MPLS), Secure IP (IPSEC, SSL), Frame Relay, Asynchronous Transfer Mode (ATM), or private-line-based networks
  - Mobile networks where all remote users must access the content via a virtual private network (VPN) or secure client
- 3G/4G data cards
- 802-based networks and more

Lastly, you need to consider how secure the video content needs to be. At the end of the day, typically the more secure you make your data, the more limited the distribution will be and/or the more hoops a user, or IT group, will need to jump through in order to view the content. Video communications have and will continue to have continued adoption in corporate environments. Thus, the ability to restrict access and control distribution of video content is critical. Much like document and email content, video content must be protected and secure to ensure that its distribution and access are tightly controlled, and usage is logged.

FROM OUR CONTRIBUTORS

John Shaw, COO, VBrick Systems

In order to prepare for the security considerations of IP Video, one must anticipate how its adoption will evolve over the next few years. Business use of video, more than any other communications technology, is driven by consumerization—the expectation by employees, customers, and business partners that they can leverage the same type of communications and collaboration tools in their professional lives that they employ in their personal lives. Unified communications (UC), for example, was for many years a long discussed, but seldom delivered business goal. It was not until consumers experienced the truly integrated experience of devices like the iPhone that an equivalent level of seamless communications became an expectation in the workplace. Over the next several years these consumerization forces, and the business benefits and threats they portend, will only intensify.

Two-way and multi-party personal video delivered by applications such as Skype and the iPhone 4 will become a normal mode of business communication. For example, Microsoft's Office Communicator Suite and Avaya's Aurora UC environments already incorporate desktop video. Use of video conferencing will no longer be relegated to expensive video-equipped conferencing and telepresence rooms.

The overwhelming popularity of Internet-based video sharing sites is driving businesses to explore how they can create their own "Enterprise YouTubes." Employees will be equipped to create rich media content directly from their desktop—product training materials, HR updates, video newsletters—and share it with co-workers. Companies will be able to easily populate their websites or social media locales with compelling rich media material. In doing so, they can create "inbound marketing" campaigns that will motivate prospective customers to learn about the firms' products and services.

CEOs in large, distributed organizations have long sought to use the power and intimacy of broadcast video to communicate with employees. In the past, this often entailed building CEO studios, rolling in a satellite truck or an expensive video streaming service, and orchestrating highly staged events. Looking forward, live broadcast video will be used by executives across the organization to communicate in an ad hoc way to their sales teams, distributed product groups, or for company-wide meetings attended by tens of thousands of employees. Any video-equipped conference room or even desktop can become a virtual broadcast studio, and the company's LAN/WAN can be fully IP-video enabled. Employees will use chat to ask questions in real time, and the presenter can dynamically poll the attendees. Outside the firewall, firms

Continued

will use web-based media management portals combined with a Content Data Network to broadcast their message to customers, shareholders, and business partners.

The amazingly immersive character of telepresence systems will be further advanced by high resolution 1080p/60 and 2K/4K display formats, and 3D video. The cost of these systems will decline rapidly, making them accessible to more of the employee base.

These IP Video-based applications hold great promise for companies that plan for their adoption, and sizeable risk for firms who simply bar the door or conversely allow unfettered video to overrun their networks, content management repositories, and security systems.

Storage and Retention of User-Generated Content

Given how broad this category is, we felt we could not do it justice in a few paragraphs, so we are only going to lightly cover the topic in this book.

As with any type of communications, the government and industry are starting to ramp up consumer, employee, and investor protection. Today, government and industry mandates are widespread, including the Health Insurance Portability and Accountability Act (HIPAA), Payment Card Industry (PCI), SEC/ FINRA, federal mandates for retention of data for use in court, and state and federal privacy acts and laws, as well as numerous international equivalents. Some regulations are designed to protect the consumer or client, but many are also to protect the businesses and the industry; rarely do businesses see it that way, though. In general, data retention is seen as a liability to most businesses and at best an incremental expense.

Most regulations today are vague about the specific retention periods, which can range from the vague "best practices" and "industry practices" to as long as "forever."

Nick Mehta, CEO, LiveOfficeTBD

It's pretty interesting how data retention has evolved over the past 10 years, with changes in regulations and incredible technology advancements. But this is still a confusing and murky area for most organizations. In the absence of clear guidance, companies deal with the problem in very different ways, including:

■ Delete everything after 90 days.

- Have end-users categorize stuff manually and only keep business-relevant stuff more than 90 days.

- Just archive select users, like executive management or named custodians involved in a lawsuit.

- Keep all data for 3 years until an official and workable retention policy is defined.

- Retain data indefinitely since it's unclear what should be kept or deleted.

It's no one's fault, but it simply points to the complexity of matching business policies to the huge and growing volume of structured data and unstructured email communications. Inevitably, organizations must weigh the advantages of retaining information (in terms of its use to the business) with the liabilities of storing that information (e.g., storage costs, legal costs, and risks that the messages might come back to haunt you).

When it comes to answering the fundamental question: "How long should you keep electronic data and email messages around?" there is no one-size-fits-all policy. Regulatory issues aside, some key issues to consider are:

- What should you retain? Some companies choose to archive data for all users, while others may choose to archive selected users (e.g., those on legal hold or those in regulated roles) or selected messages.

- How long should you retain messages? Most companies retain information indefinitely, assuming that even if they deleted their copy, another copy likely exists somewhere. Some companies have a blanket retention period for all data (e.g., 7 years). Still others have granular retention policies by user or by message.

- At the end of the retention period, how do you dispose of data? You have to ensure no data on legal hold is being deleted. Further, you want to make this process as minimally-invasive as possible.

Your answers to these questions will help inform your decisions about what you need to archive, how long to retain these messages, and how to dispose of email after the retention period has expired. But, remember, the only thing worse than having no retention policy is actually having one but not enforcing it. If your policy is to delete all electronic data after one year, make sure you are in fact deleting *all* content after one year.

I continue to be surprised at how many organizations throughout the world make futile attempts to force fit their old strategies for paper document retention into the electronic world. For example, the following old world metaphors struggle to translate in the electronic world:

- Shredding: Although in the paper world, when you shred a document, you can often be sure that it no longer exists, in the electronic world, copies abound. Data is backed up and replicated for IT purposes—often to multiple sites. Users often make their own copies of data for convenience

Continued

purposes, storing it on laptop hard drives, USB sticks, and mobile devices. And email fundamentally is always "copied" since it has FROM and TO locations. So data destruction and retention policies need to evolve to the notion that data copies often always exist outside of your IT control.

■ Filing: Similarly, many organizations invested decades of time and energy into a Records Management or Document Management approach designed for the paper world. From "Banker Boxes" to filing cabinets to warehouses, companies and government bodies often have thousands or in some cases millions of paper documents on file. Yet, these organizations are now dealing with several orders of magnitude more documents (e.g., emails, instant messages, etc.) in the electronic world. The filing metaphor of a central department looking at each document and determining its role and value will not scale. Yet pushing this task on end users means more work for them and more risk for them to skirt the system. Given all of this, organizations are attempting to create automated approaches to categorizing and storing electronic data.

■ Search: When you have filing cabinets and warehouse boxes, you can use them to find the information you want. Yet much like Google versus Yahoo! on the Internet, a manual taxonomy doesn't scale for electronic data. Finding data becomes almost impossible in the electronic world without an effective search tool. As such, searching, and effective search tools specifically, has become a critical requirement in any data storage strategy.

No matter what, if you have the data, it's better to have it in one place where you can easily and cost-effectively search it for legal discovery, regulatory compliance, and other purposes (e.g., internal HR investigations). There are tools out there that can help manage the increased load of information. Don't go it alone and most importantly, don't blindly delete emails and data files that are seemingly inconsequential today. That "two minutes and done" message may be the one that saves you from a lawsuit down the road.

Justin Greene, CTO, SECCAS

Storage and retention of user-generated content in the Internet age is not as simple as it might seem. What sounds like a routine task presents a number of difficult technical challenges.

Users can access the Internet from almost anywhere: from work, home, mobile devices, and even from computers belonging to other people. It is not possible to effectively monitor all of the different points of access that an individual might use, so it is not possible to ensure that 100% all of their published content is even going through devices that are being monitored, much less captured.

In order to capture user-generated content, one must be able to recognize it as such. This is fairly straightforward for content that is published through private services that can be controlled, such as corporate email or corporate instant messaging services. In these cases the content can be captured on the server, and monitoring of the devices being used by the user is not necessary. However, capturing user-created content that is being published through third-party services, such as Instant Messenger services, blogging services, web-based email services, and social media websites can be difficult, if not impossible.

Some services offer archival functionality or APIs that can be leveraged to gain access to content so that it can be archived, but this requires prior knowledge that a user is using the service and often requires the user's credentials in order to access the content, which in turn requires the user's proactive participation in the capture process. Some content can be captured through the use of third-party surveillance software that is able to detect content being published to the various services and can then capture it en route to the service. This software, however, is effective on content for services of which it is aware. It may capture the major webmail providers, but it will not capture some small, obscure third-party web mail hosting service, or blogging service, or some new feature that was just made available on a known website.

Part of the issue is user education. Many users are often not educated with respect to what constitutes user-generated content. They may not understand that sending an email, or an Instant Message, or publishing a blog posting, or sending a tweet out on Twitter or even updating your status on a social media site are all forms of "publishing" information. For those who are in regulated industries, something as simple as updating a status on a social media site may be considered a "Public Appearance" (http://www.finra.org/industry/issues/advertising/p006118).

Businesses must walk a fine line between keeping their employees happy by allowing them to interact with their clients in the way that they and the client want, and staying compliant with whichever regulations govern their industry. Many businesses make the difficult decision to lock down all Internet access on workstations, networks, and mobile devices that they control and then to only allow users to publish content through services that the company knows that it is able to capture and archive.

Digital Rights Management and Content Protection

Content protection is a controversial subject. Historically, content distribution was controlled through the limitations of physical medium. Today, much content is stored and distributed on the web as opposed to at a brick and mortar store. This makes acquisition and distribution much more cost-effective and extremely easy to perform.

From Napster to other peer-to-peer networks, you can share almost any content today. Most content you purchase is subject to some form of legal protection that limits its use. Often these protections are based on federal and state laws that are not easily interpretable. Prior to the capability to distribute content on a wide scale through the Internet, many who purchased content such as a DVD or CD would copy that content on multiple devices for their personal use. In most cases, the content owners did not police this closely. It was widely known that people would share, trade, and even sometimes make copies of content for family or friends. Generally, it was cost prohibitive for content owners to police these because of the relatively low impact on the value of their content. However, with the advent of content sharing applications, and broad use of the Internet, the sharing of content started having a notable impact on various content industries, notably the music and movie industries. In response, they began stronger policing of content distribution, especially on the Internet, as well as creating standards that allowed them to better control content.

Content control can come in many forms. Digital Rights Management (DRM) is an example that allows content owners to encrypt content. DRM is one of many tools that content owners can use to inhibit unauthorized access and viewing. Others include watermarking and numerous proprietary solutions.

Digital Rights Management

What content owners want often varies significantly from what users want. Content owners need broad distribution of their content, but require control and restricted viewing and distribution. Because of that they may find Digital Rights Management (DRM) to be an attractive option.

Protecting content using DRM is relatively straightforward. In general, the following steps are used by most DRM systems:

1. Classify the content by determining the distribution and control attributes that each file or group of content (files) will have.

2. Post the content on a server or appliance that can be accessed by the intended user base. Access is thus available to users on an internal network, partner network, or the Internet.

3. A layer of access control is applied, so that when a user or group of users attempts to access the content, they are required to provide specific information that has been given to them or that the content owner desires or provides as a condition of purchasing the content.

4. Once the user has access to the content, it is made accessible within the defined controls (e.g., read, modify, distribute).

5. Rights may survive for a single transaction, for any period of time, or based on other defined criteria.

Because of this easily-defined process, and its effectiveness, DRM has become a widely accepted approach for securing content.

Watermarking

Watermarking is defined as "the process of embedding data into another object or signal." Watermarking can be used in many different ways. Some are visible to the end user, while others are hidden so that they may be used as evidence or searched for when content use or ownership is challenged. Most of us are aware that government documents, monetary currency, and high-quality papers have hidden watermarks that can only be viewed with a special light, exposed to a specific chemical, or in simpler applications, backlit by a strong light source.

Note that video watermarking is quite different from document watermarking. Watermarking within video is more complex, given the continuous changing of the usable area within a video frame. In a perfect world, the watermark image resides in an area of the video that will not restrict the viewing of the content.

UCC and UCC Compliance Requirements over the Next Decade

Unified Communications and Collaboration (UCC) will change significantly by 2020. In fact, from an end-user perspective, the most visual advances in technology will be presented via UCC interfaces and functionality. As discussed throughout this chapter, the changes will occur within four primary functionality areas: usability, workflow, integration with other media and business applications, and presence. There will be cosmetic changes as well, but we believe the interfaces of the future will be flexible enough to allow users to configure their own look, feel, and even primary feature sets. All of these changes, along with the resulting changes in user behavior, impact the way we apply security. Most importantly, the need for security to operate transparently for the end user, and efficiently for the security, compliance, and IT staff is and will continue to be paramount. Projects not being carried to completion because of applications introducing too much risk will not be the way of the future as it was in the past. Rather, IT security, from both a technology perspective and a personnel perspective, will adapt more readily to the needs of business. A well-designed and -implemented enterprise-wide security program will allow for use of a greater range of technology choices within an organization.

To understand what features and functions will change over time in the UCC industry, it is important to know who the industry technology players are. It's not hard to predict that Microsoft, Apple, and Google will be the clear winners in the UCC space. Apple is a major laggard at this time, and Google is just beginning to gain traction, and it is reasonable to assume that each can execute well, given their current focus. Recognizing again the ongoing blurring of personal and business applications, especially in the UCC space, Google and Apple will gain momentum, but Microsoft has some real long-term challenges ahead. However (and I know this because I have had close ties with Microsoft over the years), it is clear they recognize this threat. They have been dedicating significant resources to it and have assembled some of the brightest minds in the industry to stay competitive. This, combined with the power of integration Microsoft has with its other desktop business tools, will serve them well far into the future. There may be some disagreement with our assessment from industry titans that have their own forecast of the future, such as Cisco, Avaya, Siemens, IBM, and other players. However, it is unlikely there will be much more than novelty UCC adoption from these players.

FROM OUR CONTRIBUTORS

Steve O'Brien, SVP, USA.NET

The world of communications is rapidly changing around us, but few would argue that the technologies we use in our professional and social lives are quickly merging. However, users will expect the best features from each technology in both their personal and professional lives. If end users experience a particular capability, then in their view the technical feasibility has been proven. Unfortunately, economic, security, policy, and business considerations must always come into play for businesses and, thus, differences (often perceived as limitations) between consumer and business applications will exist.

In the new world where business applications are often provided in a Software as a Service (SaaS) model, some of these differences may actually be overcome. For example, cross-company communications and collaboration are often more achievable when the underlying application and data is provided In the Cloud (ITC) in a SaaS model. Today, in Salesforce.com, it is common for an organization to provide their external sales channel personnel access to their instance of Salesforce.com to input leads, generate quotes, and update customer information. Historically, in premise-based models it was rare to let external partners have access to internal systems. We see the same extensibility today with email, IM, and collaborative tools such as SharePoint, and anticipate this will continue to expand in federated models over the next 10 years.

2020 Revolution or Evolution?

A good juggler knows when he has enough balls in the air.
—Kevin Prince

In response to user demands and through proactive innovation, technology evolves as part of a natural cycle supporting our technology-driven lives and economy. Evolution in technology, as in human life, is natural. Just as in life, in the normal course of technology evolution, there is occasionally a huge acceleration and leap forward: a technology revolution. In this chapter we address some of the industry revolutions that have occurred, and those that we anticipate occurring over the next 10 years and beyond. Technology revolutions are important events in our lives because they typically represent a time when we are astounded and sometimes awed. Even those who are less impressed usually recognize the value of technology in our lives. Whether evolution or revolution, most of us in technology appreciate both the value of technology and also understand its disruptive potential in our lives. Information technology provides both the promise of improved efficiencies and the threat of technology reliance as technology continues to change; we can best be prepared for the threat created by our ongoing and increasing reliance on technology, and how to best protect it, by anticipating the logical, and sometimes unlikely.

This book generally focuses on the future of information security, but we felt that we should include a review its history as well. This chapter includes a lot of that history, specifically the history of changes we consider to be revolutionary.

IT Security Revolution

To date, with only a few exceptions, most technology advances within information security have been evolutionary rather than revolutionary. A few revolutionary advances have occurred and a few more will happen over the next 10 years. Given that we define revolution as a rapid and abnormal pace of evolution, you could say the late 1980s and the late 1990s in themselves were revolutionary times for IT security. However, we believe that during these times specific technologies drove advancement of the industry around them. Looking forward, if you consider for a moment that the ultimate goal of security is to ensure the integrity, confidentiality, availability, and activity auditability for an enterprise, you can envision a point in the near future when a truly revolutionary acceleration of capabilities will occur within IT security. This time the revolutionary event will be less about technology, and more about how to make existing technologies efficiently work together.

Let's start with where we are today. The following set of realities is accepted by most security experts:

- Security is a complex problem and is becoming more complex every day, as corporate network and business requirements continue to evolve. Very few security professionals, and even fewer IT professionals, argue against this point.

- Most security professionals accept we have most, if not all, the technology components needed to properly secure even the most complex corporate networks in place today.

- The main element missing in today's security deployments is how to consistently ensure that external human processes (those that automations aren't tasked to complete) are enforced and properly carried out in the day-to-day business.

- Last, and probably more contestable, is that absent technology and process failures, the core problem in IT security is that there is no consequence for doing bad things! There are minimal national and global resources applied to tracking down and prosecuting the bad guys. Unlike most crimes, there is no physical presence requirement for hacking and fraud. There is also, to date, limited loss of life.

In the end, the failures are our own. As a society, we lack the discipline to enforce the standards and best practices we establish and we simply don't prioritize IT security at the level it must reach to have fruitful impacts. Thus, the human and technology touch points are often IT security failures, not the technology. Technology typically operates properly, but the introduction of the human element, such as a user's failure to properly follow a defined process, a system or security admin misconfiguring a device or application, or an organization simply not properly leveraging the capabilities of a technology, often results in an IT or IT security failure. Of course, there is the occasion when a vendor oversold you on the capabilities of a solution, or the ease to properly implement it, in which case you will need to compensate for the difference between the expectation and the capability of the solution or accept the ongoing risk.

In the future, one anticipated revolution will occur when more end-to-end automation of data analysis across many systems is combined with automated learning of enterprise environments. Automated learning occurs as auto-detecting a new application when it's added, changed, moved, or deleted, continually testing it for vulnerabilities, and correlating activity data. To do this, many problems must be resolved, including how to calculate risk, value assets, automate more human processes to remove human errors, and integrate the technologies that exist today so that they properly and effectively work together. Today, most of these steps are performed or supplemented by security specialists manually configuring vulnerability scanners, Security Event and Incident Management (SEIM), and data analysis tools. Many of these tools have some level of elementary automated learning, but rarely is it leveraged by enterprises. The most obvious design flaw for IT security vendors is that the tools don't properly work well together, a situation caused by each vendor thinking they are the smartest group on the block. Enterprises struggle to patch multiple vendor solutions together and glean useful data from the abundance of data.

One common way enterprises compensate for these weaknesses is by engaging managed security service providers (MSSPs). This is not uncommon in the IT industry; in many scenarios, we all have seen where the implementation charges or ongoing management expenses for properly leveraging an enterprise application far exceed the expense of actually purchasing the initial hardware /software product. Third-party organizations, such as MSSPs, apply incremental value through their expertise in configuring and leveraging today's technologies, and analyzing the often high-volume and complex alerts generated by these technology components.

So taking into consideration that security is a complex problem and it's getting more complex every day, the questions is, can we also logically conclude that we, as an IT industry, are doing something wrong? The short answer is yes. If you're not a security vendor, allow us to let you in on one of the many IT security vendor secrets: the vendors participating in the IT industry live and die by competitive advantage, although admittedly that advantage is sometimes vague and hard to value. This is very common among high-tech startups and technology industry titans alike. These companies are for profit, and often funded by venture capitalists and financial institutes seeking aggressive returns for their investments. As such, no one player wants to share its technology, know-how, and trade secrets with others, since these are the competitive differentiators that separate one company from another. These attributes also explain why customers pay vendors for these services versus doing it themselves. This creates an anti-cooperative environment in which standards groups and cooperative initiatives rarely succeed. Companies allow individuals to participate in standards groups and cooperative initiatives for good external press; however, the actual value of the contributions by these groups is often watered down because of competitive concerns. There are a few exceptions, but most of the groups that have positive technology impacts are groups led by enterprise members, not vendor members, that push vendors to develop new features or processes.

In general, this landscape of limited cooperation results in slow changes to technologies, interoperability issues, and at worst, complete stagnation of technology evolution. This is especially true when funding is reduced, as happens during an economic downturn such as the one we're experiencing now. In reality, the problem is actually compounded because each time a vendor adds a new technology or makes a change to an existing technology, it reduces its ability to interact with other IT vendors' technologies (which often number in the hundreds), creating a domino effect. It's 2010 as we write this book, and I just loaded Internet Explorer 8. I spent an hour updating various drivers and applications so that they can interact with Internet Explorer. (Yes, even security guys use Microsoft applications such as IE from time to time to make sure their compatibility with external-facing applications is working . . . well, and to find vulnerabilities so we can give Microsoft a hard time.) So to say the least, with hundreds of application vendors constantly releasing new products and updates, each increasing the probability of some type of conflict between vendors and each introducing potential new weaknesses in your security environment, we have a problem, and the problem does constantly get worse. That said, the major software and appliance vendors have gotten better and better at working together; however, they have a long way to go. For example, I experienced a conflict between Internet Explorer 8, an HP printer, and a Logitech external camera. Microsoft, Logitech, and HP are not small mom and pop shops, yet I still had major issues. Problems of this sort are further complicated by the fact that most large enterprises use custom applications or, at a minimum, have done custom deployments of off-the-shelf software. The bottom line is demonstrated in Figure 6-1: as the number of systems and applications increase, so will the need to implement more security technologies and processes, and the unfortunate result is more complexity in your IT and IT security environment.

We've included two very simple illustrations in this section that we believe you will find to be useful. We also have a series of sample graphs, data, and reference links at www.tbd.com/samplegraphs that we will update and allow the user community to update as well. The reason we believe these simple charts are worthwhile is that most people don't often think about IT security unless that's their primary career. This lack of awareness requires us to use tools like these simple illustrations to bring clarity to non-security decision makers. In the elementary illustration shown in Figure 6-1, notice that as the number of systems and applications increases, the IT environment becomes more complex. In other words, the more systems and applications you have, the more work there is to do and the more complexity exists in making it all work together. By plugging in your own real data that tracks the number of systems, applications, and security initiatives, over time you will be able to demonstrate quantitatively in simple terms the increasing complexity that exists in your organization. This can help you prioritize future focus and spending, and perhaps help with budget approvals. Many security vendors may object to this chart because this is not how most of them see the world. Typically, vendors will explain that the more security you buy, the better your security gets. To a degree this is correct; however, the common relationship between security and IT is adversarial. To the average IT professional, the more security devices, applications, and policies you add, the more complex it is to manage your IT environment and to deliver a positive end user experience. Again, to a degree this is certainly true if security is not properly applied.

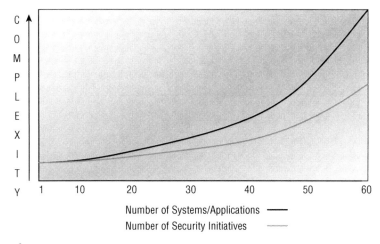

Figure 6-1

Why does the perception exist that IT becomes more complex the more you spend on security? The short answer is that security devices and applications do four things really well:

- They generate a lot of extremely useful information.
- They generate a lot of useless information.
- They generate a lot of wrong information (usually referred to as a *false positive*).
- They create additional complexity for the IT staff because it's hard to differentiate between important events and noise (false positives and informational events).

Because of these issues, the real cost of managing security is often underestimated, specifically because the operational cost for security and IT personnel is underestimated. Simply put, operational expenses will increase as both the number and complexity of security solutions increases, as well as when the IT infrastructure grows. Also overlooked is the increased operational expense of the IT staff needed, as they must comply with and manage the IT infrastructure within the more secure infrastructure that the IT security staff defines. Obviously compliance, regulatory requirements, and reporting further complicate operational aspects. Figure 6-2 shows a simple illustration that demonstrates these relationships.

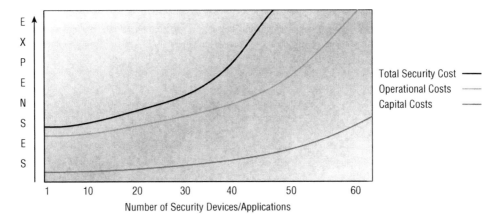

Figure 6-2

To recap, the more you spend on security, the more complexity you introduce, which not only drives up the cost of your capital but also exponentially drives up your security and IT operational expenses. The general rule of thumb is that the first 20 percent of your security spending in your overall security program will generate 90 percent of your protection. The last 80 percent of your security spending will only provide small incremental gains . . . and you never can be 100 percent secure. Keep this in mind and make sure that you optimize your basic investments before making incremental investments that could distract you. Constantly adding new security appliances or applications before you optimize what you already have is counterproductive and clearly not an effective way to manage either your capital or operational expenses.

The goal is obviously to spend the optimal level on security to create enough of a barrier to protect your environment against most security threats, while not exceeding a spending rate where your return per dollar spent to reduce risk becomes minimal. Don't get me wrong, if you have unlimited funding, spend away and provide a layered security environment with 24/7 expert staffing where you can sleep peacefully almost every night. But remember there is a balancing point where, as you add more and more security technology, the complexity and amount of information you must review outweigh the benefits, and worse is the increased probability that you will create an unfriendly user environment. Always remember that, in addition to maintaining a secure environment, your success is judged based largely on the user experience you are providing to your customers (i.e., employees, partners, customers, etc.). In any case, you must always recognize that, no matter how much you spend, there will be evolving threats that can beat the best security.

We first touched on the fact that the automation of the existing technologies we use will compensate for a lot of issues we already have within IT security. So, is there a solution to the complexity? Not entirely, at least not one that's realistic for us to implement in the short term. There is long-term hope, however. With vendor consolidation and inter-vendor partnerships, inter-vendor compatibility will get better over time. Also, the number of independent software and appliance manufacturers will consolidate. In addition, the continued development of technology, best practices, and as vendors gain more experience working together, it all will work better as well. Over the next 10 years, smaller enterprises that use more pedestrian applications will see the most benefit. Again, based on experience, even with enterprises using primarily off-the-shelf technology, the benefits will be offset by external threats evolving faster than the application vendors' own ability to improve security. For larger enterprises, organizations, and governments, these improvements are longer-term value propositions. In the interim we will see complexity increase. Also, within industries that use significant instances of proprietary and custom applications, security will be a major issue far into the future. The best course of action is to focus energies on optimizing the technologies you have in place. As you reach a point where you are confident that you have maximized the benefit of each technology you already have, then add the next logical layer to your security. Don't always focus on optimizing the technology itself as the first step. Implementing processes with checks and balances that confirm that your security is working in the way you've defined and implemented it (i.e., security scans, process checks, etc.) might be a better investment. Your environment will change, unfortunately sometimes without your knowing it, so making sure your previously implemented security is continuously operating effectively is critical. By starting with a baseline, and continually monitoring that baseline, you can measure your progress and also quickly identify counterproductive steps you may have mistakenly taken.

FROM OUR CONTRIBUTORS

Luis Fiallo, Managing Director for China Telecom Americas

It is unfortunately true that IT security is like insurance — companies often focus on the impact of breach and fraud relative to hard cash losses associated with regulatory penalties, loss of intellectual property, and productivity losses, but public exposure and PR fallout creates the largest potential for longer term revenue loss. On an international level, social aspects come into play as well. In much of Asia there is a high degree of trust and authority built into relationships. The value of trust and confidence in working with a company that has been attacked or is considered to lack appropriate levels of IT security diminishes the value of the relationship and company brand. Outside the companies that have been doing global business for extended periods, the need for IT security globally is often not understood, especially its role in protecting company goodwill.

While global threats pose a risk to anyone connected to the Internet, many companies in the U.S. have seen a higher proportion of attacks and threats due to the high visibility of U.S. companies on the Internet and their web presence. As international firms from emerging regions of the world continue to expand globally, they too will become targets of Internet-based attacks. In addition, as more and more populations of the world join the Internet, the target base for fraud and compromised systems will increase. The continued lack of cross-country cooperation in controlling fraud and security exposure in terms of legal and regulatory compliance will continue to be an obstacle in conducting international trade.

The Missing Deterrent

While this book covers primarily technology, skills, processes, and best practices that have and can improve the overall landscape of IT security, we would be remiss if we didn't cover one additional key element that impacts the industry but is rarely addressed. International law and penalty is a core element missing within the arsenal of the IT security industry that haunts us. It's simply one issue that most of us individually, and even as a group, have limited control of outside the United States. We can petition our government, which in return must engage the governments of other countries. However, unless the level of threat increases to a point where it is having a widespread, national impact or threatens lives, little will be done. In some cases, nothing can be done regardless of the impact because of the lack of cooperation from other governments.

The action the U.S. government has taken in the past 10 years can be classified into a few broad categories:

- Improving the focus and security of the U.S. government's networks. Although many might disagree with this, we must accept that recognition of a problem is a good first step.

- Improving awareness that the U.S. government is doing something.

- Increasing use of commercial products to reduce the cost of IT for the government (which in most cases unfortunately makes the government less secure).

- Increasing compliance requirements related to the protection of personal information.

With minimal exception, there has been limited action to increase the pain and risk to the bad guys that reside outside the United States and nations friendly to the United States.

In almost every aspect of our lives, we are guided first by what's right and wrong, and then by laws and regulations. In other parts of the world, the standards of right and wrong are often different than in the United States, and certainly the laws and regulations are significantly different or nonexistent when it comes to Internet regulations. Beyond a few countries that have mature laws, the global environment begins to deteriorate. As everyone knows, there are even state-endorsed and -sponsored cyber-crime activities. Combine this and the quickly advancing for-profit marketplace with malware and hacking and you have a very hostile environment for anyone connected to the public Internet . . . which is just about everyone.

FROM OUR CONTRIBUTORS

Jim Tiller, Vice President, Security North America, BT

There is a fundamental lack of meaningful deterrents for those willing to commit cyber-attacks against companies, organizations, and governments. In almost every aspect of our lives we are guided by a number influences, such as ethics helping us to evaluate right from wrong, culture and socially acceptable behavior, and, of course law. Each one of these basic aspects have individual, group, local, regional, and global manifestations.

When we look at the actions of cyber-criminals and the like launching attacks against others on the Internet, we must also look at some of the factors that drive these actions to understand why effective deterrents have yet to fully materialize.

We must acknowledge that there is separation between the attacker and the victim. For typical hackers using the Internet, their victim is simply a computer, not a human or someone they can harm. Given that they do not equate

Continued

their actions to common criminal activities, they fail to fully resonate with the implications of their actions, distorting their own moral and ethical framework. Moreover, the abstraction that exists in the attack also provides a sense of anonymity and freedom from capture, undermining applicable laws.

Motivation is a considerable factor, and there is a direct correlation between the level of motivation and the effectiveness of deterrents. Deterrents act as a risk to the hacker (what if they were discovered and caught?), and the degree of their motivation has a substantial influence on their risk appetite. The greater the motivation, the more risk they are willing to take. Additionally, motivation is inexorably tied to how hackers rationalize their actions, the means used to justify their misbehavior. Characteristics of justification can range from vandalism to acts of patriotism, but many of today's drivers are based on monetary gain.

Moreover, motivation and rationalization can be further impacted by culture and socially acceptable behavior. These can exist as physical or virtual communities of like-minded individuals, or reflect the mantra of state. Manifestos at the group or even country level will greatly affect the interpretation of what is acceptable and the degree of risk concerning capture.

Ultimately, these factors will drive the creation of deterrents. It's worth noting that deterrents come in two very basic forms: security controls and law. Clearly, security controls are methods employed to pose a barrier to the attacker to make it more difficult by requiring more investment by the hacker and by raising the potential of discovery, both of which contribute to the hacker's evaluation of the risk they're facing. Security controls of this nature do exist.

Conversely, deterrents based on law are far more questionable and, based on the increasing volume, sophistication, and impact of threats in the last few years, they cannot be seen as effective. The dominating causes for this are a combination of several factors.

First of all, not all laws are equal and we cannot assume they are comprehensive; in fact, they might not even exist at all. Most countries don't have laws related to cyber-crime. Of course, in some circumstances this is further exacerbated by non-extradition laws, making these countries havens for hackers. Nevertheless, for those few countries that do have laws of this nature, they are typically radically different from one another in their definition of what constitutes a crime and how those definitions are interpreted in the courts of law.

This creates an interesting and gaping loophole that hackers squeeze through. Cyber-attacks are, for the most part, not restricted by geography—they can be performed from virtually anywhere and against anyone. If by some miraculous means the hackers are caught, in nearly all cases the local laws apply, not necessarily the laws governing the location of the victim.

The root of the challenge is that there is currently no global harmonization of cyber-laws, which unfortunately is unlikely to occur. Each country is acting based on their position, politics, and own government structure, which is rarely fully compatible with those of other countries or with their processes for creating, defining, and enforcing laws. Therefore, there is a fundamental gap between the ability to facilitate comprehensive and aligned laws between very different countries and the fact that hackers are using a virtual environment that knows no such boundaries. Clearly, the global confusion and the inept politics inhibiting meaningful progress is not only completely devoid of deterrence, but actually manifests as encouragement based on the knowledge that the likelihood of capture is miniscule—greatly lowering a hacker's risk appetite.

This aspect leads us to the second factor—enforcement, or the lack thereof. Assuming a meaningful law exists and that the perpetrator is acting in a region where that law is applicable, there are still many barriers to enforcement. Most notably lacking is the ability to effectively detect the existence of illegal activity. Of course when cyber-criminals activities are discovered, a great deal of money and time is needed to ensure that the threat is accurately identified, evidence is collected, and that ultimately a case is built. The level of investment and effort greatly decreases the range of criminals that will attract the attention of law enforcement. If the capture and prosecution is not high profile enough or will not garner fines to justify the investment needed, it simply falls to the bottom of the pile.

These two factors eventually contribute to the last factor, which is to deal with the slow, reactive nature of enforcement, the scope of prosecution, and publicizing the results. For law to be a meaningful deterrent, criminals have to understand and be informed of the implications of their actions. This alone raises several notable points that impede deterrence.

Technically speaking, an extraordinarily small percentage of attacks result in someone being captured and prosecuted. Of that group, far fewer are publicized. When reports do finally hit the newsstand, many show that the investigation had taken years and the attackers may have been technically sophisticated but made stupid mistakes that led to their discovery and ultimate capture. Hackers reading such a report are reaffirmed in their belief that getting caught is highly unlikely, and they will seek to avoid making stupid mistakes. Whether their conclusion about the likelihood of being caught is entirely true or not is irrelevant; it's what they believe and hence undermines any deterrence that was intended.

It's important that we acknowledge that deterrents, specifically those within the scope of law and enforcement, are founded on the physiological interpretation of their effectiveness ultimately impacting a criminal's risk appetite. Unfortunately, due to the lack of harmonization, clarity in definition, commonality in legal interpretations, and the fundamentals of enforcement weaknesses, today's laws, enforcement tactics, and results are simply not meaningful deterrents.

Security in 20/20 Hindsight

Now, let's take a step back. For those new to the security industry, or those simply looking for a factual review of that industry, this section provides some history and explains how the authors see each technology evolving. Because we have limited space, we'll highlight only a few technologies that marked high points for advancing the security industry. The following technologies made our short list:

- Intrusion detection systems/intrusion protection systems/data loss prevention (DLP)
- Anti-spam and anti-virus technology
- Identity management/network access control/single sign-on
- Mobility/wireless/ultra-mobile
- SaaS/cloud computing
- Penetration testing/vulnerability testing/risk assessments

And of course, we should consider how all this might come together and actually work in the real world.

FROM OUR CONTRIBUTORS

Counse Broders, Industry Analyst

Money. The Internet economy is making it easier to become rich in a faster way, with the global reach of services allowing an entrepreneur the ability to be obscure one day, and a global phenomenon the next. It's this faster speed that entices criminals as well. As more of our economy runs on digits, more thieves look to pilfer it.

Communication goes to the heart of commerce: without it deals are not done, goods do not move, and people don't get paid. Ensuring a secure communication medium is critical. Just as we need policemen driving down the street to add a sense of security to our physical environment, there is a need for protection online.

Intrusion Detection Systems, Intrusion Protection Systems, and Data Loss Prevention in 20/20 Hindsight

The goal of intrusion detection is to monitor network assets to detect anomalous behavior and misuse at a point in the network that provides the most visibility.

The evolution of intrusion detection systems (IDSs) goes back further than you might expect. The concept of IDS has been around for nearly 30 years, but in the late nineties we experienced a dramatic rise in interest and adoption of the technology into enterprise information security infrastructures. We believe, but are open to being corrected, that it began in 1980, with James Anderson's paper, "Computer Security Threat Monitoring and Surveillance."[1] Since then, several pivotal advancements in IDS technology have taken intrusion detection to its current state. Anderson's paper, which was written for a government organization, introduced the foundational concept that audit trails contained vital information that could provide more value for tracking misuse and for understanding user behavior than any other source. This theory evolved first as host-based intrusion detection and then into network-based intrusion detection systems (IDS).

Network intrusion detection systems (NID/NIDS) are typically network appliances, or occasionally software running on servers, that collect data from the network or networks to which they are connected and generate alerts when security activities occur. NIDS monitor the data traffic transiting a network point or a series of network points. Often NIDS are considered "packet-sniffers" since they collect data at a packet level from a connection point in the network without interfering with the dataflow. Often that collected data is retained, or included in the alert so that it can be further analyzed or retained for forensics purposes. Once the data is collected, it is run through a series of subprocesses that perform analysis against static and dynamic rules. Most NIDSs still compare the captured data to a signature database consisting of profiles of known attack patterns. In addition to signature-based NIDSs, or alternatively, anomalous activity detection is an additional new way to detect malicious behavior. In essence, NIDS creates a baseline of the network and when anything changes from the baseline, it considers the event an anomaly and generates an alert for further analysis. NIDSs have historically been incapable of operating effectively in the following environments:

- VLAN networks
- Switched networks
- Encrypted networks
- High-speed networks (anything over 10 gigabits)
- Closed networks (where constant signature updates could not be received)

However, in recent years, each of these limitations has been overcome.

Network-based IDSs were, in our minds, a clear catalyst in the advancement of the security industry. While the technology created a solution that provided a tremendous value to the industry, it also created an awareness of the complexities in actually monitoring activities on an enterprise network. From signature based technologies to adaptive learning technologies, the endless scenarios that could be formulated that represented an attack became the mantra of the multitude of startups, each of which proposed that their way of dealing with the threats within IT security was uniquely theirs.

Now that we've completely mapped out all the potential risks and scenarios in which attackers might attempt to offend our corporate networks, or the tools have such advanced artificial intelligence (AI) that they can adapt and learn every nuance of our infrastructure, we can completely automate blocking of traffic through network- and host-based intrusion defense systems (NIPSs and HIPSs). That was a sarcastic statement if you didn't catch it. Don't get us wrong, there is great value in IPSs and they do reduce workloads; however, they are not the catchall nor are they revolutionary—rather they were developed through a natural evolution of IDSs. This difference, the ability for IPSs to block traffic versus simply alerting you to what occurred, as is the case with IDSs, is valuable. They provide great value in blocking obvious, and sometimes very offensive, attacks that the standard firewall historically cannot detect.

The current evolution in IPS is data loss prevention (DLP). DLP comes in many flavors, ranging from what appear to be enhanced IPS and content filtering to more advanced systems that proactively analyze content that is deployed throughout the IT infrastructure—including servers, desktops, laptops, and mobile devices. Candidly, this is where the first approaches to IT security should have been applied. The laptop that the sales guy lost may have some things important to the sales guy on it, maybe even a couple corporate presentations and a few emails back and forth to prospects and clients. However, the loss from a corporate perspective is simply a nuisance, not a serious threat that could result in creating a bad PR event or loss of proprietary information, nor did it breach any compliance regulations. Without knowing specifically what is on that computer and that no real damage will be done, however, you might have a few sleepless nights. Now imagine the peace of mind you would have by knowing what content resides on every machine in the environment and being able to identify, prioritize, and establish rules, and both control and take action on the results on an ongoing basis. That is the promise of DLP.

We've addressed the future of IDS, IPS, DLP, and firewalls previously in this section, but we believe that these technologies will continue to merge into Unified Threat Management (UTM) platforms, where the distinction between functionalities that exist today will continue to merge. Over time, the defensive nature of destinations (systems and applications) will be managed as a single point rather than applying the technology defenses as a incremental layer of external security on a separate device.

FROM OUR CONTRIBUTORS

Don Gray, Chief Security Strategist, Solutionary

Transforming the overwhelming amount of data produced by intrusion detection systems into meaningful, actionable intelligence makes them one of the most effective tools for identifying threats as they occur. Future IDS/IPS technologies will integrate additional contextual information about the systems they protect, correlating behavioral, reputational, and vulnerability intelligence to identify threats.

Since its declared death in 2003 by then Gartner Analyst Richard Stiennon, IDSs continue to be a staple in most security programs and implementations. At the time, Gartner identified the following shortcomings with IDS and the budding Intrusion Prevention Systems (IPS) technologies:

- An inability to monitor traffic at transmission rates greater than 600 megabits per second.[2]
- A resource taxing incident-response process.
- False positives and negatives.
- An increased burden on the IS organization by requiring full-time monitoring. (24 hours a day, seven days a week, 365 days a year.)

Since then, the first problem has proved to be surmountable with the creation of optimized software and adoption of specialized hardware. The tug-of-war between our ability to increase network throughput and our ability to monitor the information flowing on that network will continue to escalate, but it's not anticipated that one side of the equation will overwhelm the other in any meaningful way.

But what about Gartner's other three points?

Integrating asset information and user identification into IDS/IPS solutions allows security analysts to quickly understand and react to the information provided, thereby mitigating the taxing incident-response process. IDS/IPS output has been transformed from arcane alerts into actionable intelligence.

The adoption of richer, protocol and context-aware detection mechanisms, which map to the organizations' security policies, have mitigated false positives and negatives. In addition, the correlation of asset information, as well as both passive and active system profiling and vulnerability information, has significantly reduced false positives, ensuring that only on-target threats are considered for further analysis and validation.

False negatives continue to be an issue with most IDS/IPS technologies. These technologies aren't good at identifying threats that are outside of their scope of knowledge. Statistical analysis of monitored throughput can help identify new threats, but only if they result in enough of a change in traffic levels to trip preset trigger points.

Continued

FROM OUR CONTRIBUTORS *(continued)*

The monitoring burden has been addressed by the marketplace through the availability of cost-effective Managed Security Services (MSS) and improved packaged Security Information and Event Management (SIEM) products. This doesn't eliminate the need for human analysis and validation of alerts raised by IDS/IPS technologies. Instead, it makes analysis and validation more efficient and effective, resulting in reduced costs.

So the reality is, although mitigated, these issues still exist. How then can the continued use of these flawed technologies be explained? The answer boils down to the fact that even with all of these limitations and burdens, IDS/IPS technologies continue to be among the most effective tools for identifying threats as they occur.

Also, as predicted (but less well remembered) by Gartner and others, IDS/IPS has been integrated into traditional firewalls by vendors like Cisco and Checkpoint, and the Universal Threat Management (UTM) market has flourished in small and medium-sized businesses and is utilized by enterprises for their Small Office/Home Office (SOHO) needs. In addition, IDS/IPS technologies have been extended to address application security specific threats with the additional contextual knowledge of the application design and structure.

One area of concern with IDS/IPS in the future is the widespread adoption and implementation of IPv6. Although more sophisticated organizations have already experimented with and implemented IPv6, until widespread adoption occurs, the full impact of the dynamic addressing, re-addressing, and security encapsulation (encryption) will not be known. It is anticipated that the use of encryption will continue to rise and will eventually constitute the majority of network traffic.

It is also anticipated that the future of most security technologies, including IDS/IPS, will involve gathering and integrating more contextual information about the expected normal operation and behavior of the network devices, system platforms, applications, and users being monitored for intrusions.

In this respect, intrusion detection becomes less about specific IDS/IPS technologies and more about the integration and correlation of contextual, procedural, behavioral, and reputational information.

Much like threat management in the physical world, effective information security intrusion detection and prevention requires defensive measures to be implemented to reduce the number of attack vectors and attack surface areas, the definition of normal, expected functioning of the infrastructure functions (devices, platforms, and applications) and expected actions of the users; the reputation of the users (are they known bad-actors?); an understanding of the target's vulnerabilities; and the ability to gather and correlate this information into actionable intelligence.

The best available IDS/IPS technology, when implemented without all other measures being in place, will provide limited value to the organization, regardless of the security analyst's knowledge and experience.

---

[2]Gartner Information Security Hype Cycle Declares Intrusion Detection Systems a Market Failure. June 11, 2003. (http://www.gartner.com/5_about/press_releases/pr11june 2003c.jsp)

Identity Management/Network Access Control/Single Sign-on

First, we'll take a shot at defining what the key components of the broad category of Access Control are:

- *Identity management* in simple terms is the management of a user's identity. Within the enterprise, identity management systems consist of a combination of user directories, system directories, access control systems, and a set of policies that allow for interaction between these data sets. It includes the maintenance of the systems and users (additions, changes, deletions) and generally offers single sign-on so that the user only has to log in to the LAN or a local authoritative system once to gain access to multiple resources. User management and user provisioning are required capabilities for any identity management system.

- *Access control* is a system that enables an authority (typically to include the IT security group and HR) to control access to areas and resources in a given IT environment. The business driver is to be able to limit access of unauthorized users, thus providing the ability to secure important, confidential, or sensitive information. A fundamental requirement is also to be able to track users that access the information and what they do with the content (e.g., read, change, delete, download, etc.).

- *Network access control* (NAC) is a system that enables an organization to control who is allowed to connect to a network, both locally and remotely. Again, the business driver is to be able to limit access of unauthorized users, thus providing the ability to secure important, confidential, or sensitive information that resides on the protected network or network segment. A fundamental requirement for all access control, including NAC, is to be able to track users that access the information and what they do with the content (i.e. read, change, delete, download, etc).

- *Single sign-on* (SSO) is a property of access control of multiple, related, but independent, software systems. With this property, a user logs in once and gains access to all systems without being prompted to log in again at each of them. Single sign-off is the reverse property, whereby a single action of signing out terminates access to multiple software systems. As different applications and resources support different authentication mechanisms, single sign-on has to internally translate between different credentials and what is used for initial authentication.

Many attempts have been made by large vendors such as Sun and Oracle to buy into the identity management market, but given their lack of DNA, the solutions often become heavily focused on their own application solutions. In most application development companies, the DNA, or a core focus on security from the planning process through general release, is lacking. The solution is straightforward. Let one of the major embedded NAC vendors (we hate to say it, but this would be someone like Microsoft with Active Directory or even a major LDAP vendor) buy one of the more evolved single sign-on vendors and call it a day.

Mobility/Wireless/Ultra-Mobile

There clearly have been several revolutions within mobility, but two of the most notable are, first, the original cell phone, now evolved many times over and, second, the ability to transfer data, as data, over the wireless networks, which also has evolved many times now. Simply being able to work away from your desk is the principle change for most businesses. In all cases, security has not been a high priority, with perhaps the exception of the RIM BlackBerry.

Mobility creates many issues for organizations. They range from basic asset management to employee productivity . . . and, of course, security. One of the biggest challenges is ownership of the mobile asset—specifically smart phones and mobile devices. Often, the device is owned by the employee. Thus, control of the device when it is used for both personal and professional purposes becomes controversial. The BlackBerry has great control capabilities built into its management console, but few enterprises use them. In reality, there are many third-party centralized management consoles for smart phones that cover almost all major brands.

Over the next 10 years mobility will become easier to manage and secure. Asset and cost management are major business issues today, but will simplify over time due to commoditization of usage cost, and common applets will be created for all the major PDA and cell phone manufacturers that will allow tracking. Security, too, will become easier to manage with secure communications becoming commercially viable. All of these issues should be lesser business issues as we leave this decade. That said, the continued utilization by employees of one device for both business and personal use will create new issues. While we don't believe it will stick, the move to usage-based plans for data by carriers could also create new challenges.

SaaS and Cloud Computing

Software as a Service (SaaS) and In the Cloud (ITC)-based services seek to provide customers a higher quality of service at a lower cost than they can reach by providing these services themselves. We have all heard it many times over from vendors: "We want to let you focus on your core business, while we take care of X", where X is whatever the vendor is trying to sell. SaaS, ITC, and a few other creative names all represent the latest attempts to wrap managed services into a new name. To call these services revolutionary, we would need to compare the current crop to those in the days of client servers when many business applications were housed, managed, and provided as a remote managed service. While calling them revolutionary might be going too far, some of the new SaaS services are much more efficient, flexible, and certainly more reliable than any of their predecessors. One of the most successful examples is Salesforce.com. They succeeded, and continue to succeed, for many reasons, including ease of use and the attractive total cost of ownership (TCO) compared to deploying your own solution. They continue to succeed based on their willingness to allow others to build applications around Salesforce.com.

Relative to security, SaaS/ITC solutions create unique challenges for security personnel. While recently many of these solutions allowed for easy integration of your own authentication system, there are still challenges. Again, securing SaaS and ITC solutions is unique to each solution, so we felt providing an online area for this section with real-world use cases would be the most effective way to convey information. Check `www.tbd.com/saassecurity`.

We should mention before we leave the subject that one of the key functions you should build is an automated process that pulls the authentication logs of your SaaS/ITC application and compares them to your authentication logs. Any delta is a big red flag.

FROM OUR CONTRIBUTORS

Chris Richter, CISM, CISSP, VP and General Manager of Security Products and Services, Savvis

It's generally accepted that cloud computing is considered the next major revolution in IT. The way enterprises plan their IT infrastructure purchases, projects, data, and application development is being impacted profoundly in ways we could not have foreseen just a few years ago. It should be pointed out, however, that at least one prognosticator, Nicholas Carr, made a compelling prediction in an article appearing in the Spring 2005 issue of the MIT Sloan Management Review, entitled "The End of Corporate Computing." In this article, Carr put forth his belief that IT today looks much like electric power generation 100 years ago, where each company purchased and maintained its own generator; and like the private generator, private data centers will give way to large-scale, centralized utilities, which one can argue is cloud computing. I've seen first hand plenty of evidence of this transformation, as each of the many IT executives I've spoken with over the past year is seriously considering cloud computing as part of its two-to-five year planning process. The broad impact of this "mile-wide tidal wave" also encompasses all players in the business of IT security, including security product developers and manufacturers, managed security service providers (MSSPs), compliance auditors, professional security services firms, and security training organizations.

Continued

FROM OUR CONTRIBUTORS *(continued)*

Before we get into the ways the security industry is affected by this shift, let's review briefly the three standard cloud architectures, and the four deployment models.

Cloud architectures:

■ **Software as a Service (SaaS)** services enable enterprises to use a service provider's cloud-based application services. Good examples of this are Qualys, Inc.'s QualysGuard vulnerability scanning services, and Google Inc.'s Google Apps offerings.

■ **Platform as a Service (PaaS)** services provide application authoring tools and runtime environments without hardware investment. Development providers include services from Engine Yard, and Google Inc.'s Google App Engine.

■ **Infrastructure as a Service (IaaS)** services can be defined as, in the most basic sense, a virtualized IT infrastructure that makes use of a combination of shared and/or dedicated resources. Typifying the lineup of IaaS providers are Savvis Inc., Terremark Inc., and AT&T Inc.

Deployment models:

■ **Private Clouds** are delivered and managed by either an enterprise or by its service provider, and are always deployed in a single-tenant model.

■ **Public Clouds** are delivered and managed by service providers, and can offer single- or multi-tenant models.

■ **Hybrid Clouds** are a mixture of public and private delivery models and are typically delivered and managed by service providers.

■ **Community Clouds** are shared by several companies or organizations that have a common mission or interest. This model may be managed by a private organization or an external service provider.

The NIST Cloud Model is shown in the following figure.

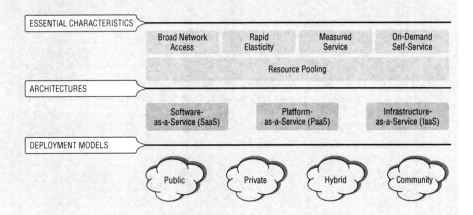

The challenge that cloud computing presents to the IT security industry is how to adapt products and services that have been developed, priced, and sold to enterprises with dedicated IT infrastructures, to a new model that is vastly different.

For example, security hardware vendors are actively looking for ways to develop versions of their traditional, standalone products that actually run on a virtual machine, i.e., as a *virtual appliance.* Yet others are modifying their hardware appliances—by increasing their capacity and functionality—such that they can integrate with cloud architectures designed to support multiple enterprises.

Product design considerations are but one aspect of adapting to the cloud. Another is pricing, which is viewed as something of a coming storm for many CFOs who wonder how this new paradigm will impact revenue and profitability. One of the promises of cloud computing is that it is less expensive for an enterprise than purchasing dedicated infrastructure. This expectation is based partly on the concept that, in a cloud computing environment, an enterprise is using a pool of resources that is shared by other companies; and partly on the premise that in a true utility billing model, one should pay only for what they use. As a result, many security hardware and software vendors are reviewing pricing models which involve payment based on utilization of their products. As most hardware and software vendors currently base their sales forecasts on sales of individual appliance units or licenses, shifting to a utility model is requiring a complete rethinking of their revenue models.

For Managed Security Services Providers (MSSPs), the impact of cloud computing will vary. For SaaS-based MSSPs, their delivery model has been around for several years, and only recently has been pulled under the umbrella-definition of cloud computing. But as more security hardware and software vendors offer their products in a SaaS delivery model, the security SaaS market will continue to grow. Alternately, MSSPs who deliver security monitoring and management for traditional IT infrastructures are now trying to adapt their services to manage virtual security appliances, and multi-tenant security infrastructures. The challenge for MSSPs who cater to IaaS-based public-cloud customers, for example, will be to demonstrate that they can securely access a single customer's cloud environment, without compromising the confidentiality, integrity, and availability of either the cloud-hosting provider, or other tenants', IT assets. MSSPs will also find challenges in managing specific instances of virtualized or shared security devices that are already provided by, and built into, a cloud-hosting provider's infrastructure. In such cases, the cloud-hosting provider itself may act as the exclusive MSSP.

The implications of cloud computing for security and compliance auditors and consultants are also substantial. For IaaS, multi-tenant cloud environments, auditors most closely examine the cloud-hosting-provider's services, facilities, technologies used, and policies to validate, among other things, that

■ a provider's customers cannot physically access another customer's environment;

Continued

FROM OUR CONTRIBUTORS   *(continued)*

- logical access rules limit a customer to only their own data, and appropriate privileges are established and controlled;
- one customer cannot consume an inappropriate amount of resources on a shared platform;
- audit and logging trails can be uniquely associated with a given customer, and more specifically, with an individual's unique ID;
- the provider's policies allow for timely forensic investigations in the event of a compromise.

Cloud-computing environments present the same, and in some cases more complex, threat and risk scenarios as traditional IT environments. Most audit control requirements, and the controls themselves, have been developed for physical infrastructure, so their application to cloud-based and virtual infrastructure components is not always clear cut.

Rapid change entails inherent risks and rewards. Cloud computing brings with it a new plane of security issues and vulnerabilities, which itself is spawning security innovation and new ways of measuring risk and costs of risk mitigation. A transformation is coming in the way IT security as a business is structured, and the way in which IT consumes security products.

Douglas Barbin, CPA, CISSP, CFE, GCFA, PCI-QSA, Director, Assurance and Compliance Services, SAS 70 Solutions, Inc.

One of the biggest impacts of the current wave of cloud computing has been that business relationships are starting to become more complex. Service (or cloud) provider relationships were traditionally one-to-many (i.e. between a provider and its shared customers). Now, a SaaS provider may host an application at an Infrastructure-as-a-Service (IaaS) provider who may also have another managed service provider (MSP) performing maintenance and upgrades. This expansion will continue on to 2020 include sub-service providers that span continents. In these scenarios, how does a company understand where their data is, not to mention who is responsible for what part of security? The answer starts with contracts and service-level agreements, but is actually much more complex.

In 2020, having security requirements included as part of service-level agreements will not be enough. The ultimate end user will need to have a clear set of control requirements with assigned ownership for each logical and functional area of security. These requirements and owners will then need to map to contracts such that there are no gaps in security responsibilities. The hope is that in ten years this will not be a manual process that includes contract review and fancy Excel work. The expectation is that the more that providers share information through technology vehicles such as APIs developed by `cloudaudit .org`, the more quickly this piecing together of security requirements can be done both during the sales process as well as two years into the contract.

> Most security literature preaches fear and concern with cloud computing, citing lack of control and transparency as the highest concerns. I would argue that most cloud providers actually maintain a higher level of security than an enterprise if for no other reason than the clear fact that they have more to lose. In 2020, transparency will not be optional for cloud providers and that the leading cloud providers will provide easy access to the information which will help their clients sleep better at night.

Testing Your Information Protection: Penetration Test/Vulnerability Test/Risk Assessments

Whether you are tasked with a role in IT security or you are simply managing your own personal systems, you will find the evolution of the IT security industry to be interesting. However, it's the day-to-day improvement of your own unique IT security environment that is the critical measure of success that impacts you and your career. A lot of experience—both the authors' and our contributors'—is behind how we define the starting point for improving your IT security. Most of what follows in this section is documented more completely in many other books and web sources than it is here. There are many books written on how to tactically improve your security. While we would love to dedicate this whole section, or for that matter a whole book to how to tactically improve your security, that is not the purpose of this book. However, we felt it necessary to provide some practical guidance within the scheme of our historical review and our projections. As you read this, please make sure that you refer to the website at www.tbd.com to get up-to-date information and best practices from experts around the world. Now, to priority number one: prioritization.

When considering how to improve the security you already have in place, you must evaluate what resources you can bring to bear. Let's step back to one of the generally accepted points that most security professionals agree on: *we have all the technology components today needed to secure the average enterprise environment; we simply need to make them work together*. One of the first steps you must take when considering where to start after you understand the resources you have is to document the value of the IT assets within the overall enterprise. When possible, you should automate the system inventory collection and updating so as to keep all the information current as systems are added, moved, changed, and removed from use. You should also understand where content resides and what the business rules are for the use of that content.

There are several automated programs, both commercial and open source, that will scan servers and PCs for content. Many DLP systems have content scanners built in as a core feature. Content classification can be very broad or very specific depending on the unique business requirements of the enterprise. Here are some examples of content classification:

- Personally identifiable information (PII)
  - Social Security numbers
  - Driver's license numbers
  - Home addresses
  - Telephone numbers

- Health information (usually best defined under HIPAA regulations)
  - Diagnoses
  - Subscriptions and medicines
  - Surgery or corrective care

- Intellectual property
  - Customer list(s)
  - Price list(s)
  - Nonpublic product information
  - Partner and distribution list
  - Employee information
  - Research and development (R&D) strategy and projects

Often these programs are very flexible and allow you to:

- Search for variations in data (e.g. a telephone number using a ".", "-" or "( )").

- Perform conditional searches that help you properly prioritize searches. For example, Social Security numbers may be allowed on the HR server but no other company equipment.

- Take action on any security policy-breaking content, such as by sending a notice to a user, encrypting it, or moving it to another location.

In all cases, you should start with understanding the most critical assets of the enterprise and what the compliance requirements are for the content.

Now let's envision one of the possible revolutions in security that simply puts together many of the existing security applications we have today. Remember, our theory is not that new technologies need to be created, rather we as an industry must make the products we already have work more efficiently together. So imagine if you will:

- an agent or system that frequently scans each device and application on your network and provides the asset value based on what content is on each system

- an application that then

    a. takes action to protect the identified content that is important to a enterprise and

    b. scores the output of the results based on business rules that you have established within the scoring application for each system.

So, from a practical perspective, let's use a simple example of an enterprise being concerned about the risk to the business if it failed to meet the regulatory requirement to protect Social Security information. This is important since now most states require businesses and organizations to protect Social Security numbers.

The security agent or external security device scans each system that connects to or is present in the enterprise's IT environment. A business rule is created that says that any system within the IT environment that contains a Social Security number is considered a critical asset. The security application identifies four servers within the Human Resources Group that have each employee's Social Security number. No surprise. However, it also identifies 98 laptops that have one or more Social Security numbers on them. Research reveals that all 98 laptops fall into one or multiple of the three classifications:

- **Class 1:** Each of 73 laptops have the user's or a family member's Social Security number on it for personal use. At this point, you have some business decisions to make, but the simplest is that since the organization is at compliance risk should a user's Social Security number be lost while stored on a company asset (i.e., the laptop) you don't allow employees to store Social Security numbers on company assets unless there is an approved business reason.

- **Class 2:** Thirteen laptops have fake Social Security numbers that are used within presentations or documents to illustrate some business process where a Social Security number was utilized. There is no risk to the business, since the Social Security numbers aren't real. Yet, you don't want to see this false alert each time the security application runs and generates results. So, the easiest result is to provide everyone with one or two common fake Social Security numbers and then create a rule within the security application to ignore those fake Social Security numbers.

- **Class 3:** Twelve laptops have employees' or customers' Social Security numbers on them. This would probably be a big surprise, so the security team just got points from the business units. However, 3 of the 12 laptops had legitimate reasons to have the data. The remainder had the data removed. At this point, you could build a rule that identifies that the three laptops have legitimate use and mark them green continuously or simply have the systems ignored going forward. There are reasons to continue to scan the laptops, however, because you might create new rules that require a scan for credit cards, and thus these systems won't be accidentally missed because of a bad rule.

Take the preceding classification capability one step further and when Social Security numbers are found, whether or not they are allowed, they must be encrypted (except the few that you allow for samples as identified in class 2 in the preceding list). Further expand the rules so that if there are three failed logins on a PC, that PC is put in locked state that only an admin can release. Also, add a phone home feature that allows you perform remote functions on the PC and to potentially track it down. This will provide you with significant confidence that you can recover or delete confidential data and it will provide general asset protection. Obviously similar rules could be applied to any content such as healthcare information, credit card numbers, personal information, and the like.

The information you decide to protect in this way will be the foundation from which you can build an effective security program. This information also enables you to build a strategy for protecting the content. We will address how it fits into the overall plan after we identify the weaknesses in the security layers and IT infrastructure where the content resides.

Weaknesses in an IT infrastructure are often very easy to identify. There are open source and commercial products and services for identifying weaknesses. Penetration testing, vulnerability assessments, and IT security risk assessments are all very different, and there is no common definition for these used between vendors. What one vendor calls a penetration test may be a simple scan, while another vendor's IT security risk assessment may use the same very basic scan. This leaves the customers to interpret the various vendor proposals. In general, all three of these engagements are attempting to identify weaknesses within the IT security structure and provide a report so the customer can take action to reduce threats to their data and IT infrastructure. At a basic level, each should provide an inventory of IT assets and business processes, threats, and vulnerabilities in order to establish a foundation for developing an appropriate IT security program. Understanding these variables in order to understand risk is the key to determining the level of protection.

All organizations should have a full IT risk assessment program, so we will focus on the broadest and most comprehensive analysis, which, if done properly, includes a vulnerability scan as well as a penetration test. The specific scope of an IT risk analysis is difficult to define because it takes the widest view of not only your IT systems but also your business processes. It should include a vulnerability scan, testing of applications (penetration test), and it should minimally include a set of variables that allow you to understand the IT risks within your infrastructure and those that are most likely to impact your business. The end product of an IT risk analysis should provide:

- An inventory of all your IT assets (systems and applications)
- A list of business processes and applications that have dependence on existing IT assets
- A report showing you vulnerabilities of existing IT assets

- An assessment of the probabilities of threats occurring to existing IT assets (there are many methodologies to scoring)

- A business view of the impact in the event of a system or process failure or breach if one were to occur

- A description of the countermeasures recommended to reduce the risks to an acceptable level for the business

- A process for keeping the risk assessment up-to-date as personnel, business requirements, and the infrastructure changes

Risk assessments are difficult to perform because they take into consideration both technology and business aspects of an organization. Achieving consensus on the basic questions a risk assessment should ask is important. Some general guidelines for conducting an effective risk analysis include:

1. **Business process asset review:** A business process asset review should be performed to identify, at a minimum, those business processes and business applications that are critical to ongoing operations of the business. These business processes typically rely on underlying IT infrastructure.

2. **Information asset review:** An information asset review then needs to be performed to identify, at a minimum, those information assets that are critical to ongoing operations or which contain confidential or critical data. The end result for the inventory assessment should include a prioritization and ownership list for each asset.

3. **Business impact analysis:** Combining the data from the business process asset review and the information asset review allows you to see what business processes rely on IT assets. The purpose of the business impact analysis is to document the potential impact of loss of the IT assets. Consideration should be given to operational (including brand impact), financial, regulatory, and legal impacts.

4. **Vulnerability analysis:** A vulnerability analysis is used to identify weaknesses and vulnerabilities associated with IT assets. The vulnerability analysis should identify specific vulnerabilities related to IT assets identified in the IT asset review, as well as where those vulnerabilities exist. A ranking in severity for each vulnerability should be a standard part of the output.

5. **Threat analysis:** A threat analysis should be conducted to identify threats that could result in intentional or accidental destruction, modification, or release of data, computer, or telecommunication resources.

6. **Risk analysis:** A risk analysis is a collective review of the vulnerabilities and threats to all identified assets to determine the likelihood and impact. This analysis forms the foundation for security program planning.

The initial revolution was the advent of scanning technologies, but the next revolution will not be in technology, rather it will be in adherence to standardized policies that drive processes through automation.

FROM OUR CONTRIBUTORS

Dirk Anderson, Managing Director, Coalfire Systems

The sad truth is the vast majority of companies and organizations that engage our services continue to have incomplete knowledge of what sensitive data they are collecting or storing, much less where that data might reside. Penetration and vulnerability testing identify potential gaps in the security program which can be exploited by an attacker. However, there is limited, if any, value to those test results unless the organization understands the value and location of sensitive data and critical systems.

Only a few organizations have formalized and actually implemented data classification processes to identify what types of data they should be monitoring, or are defining what the appropriate levels of protection are for the different types of data. A compounding factor is that where process flow diagrams exist at all, they are generally created during the design or planning phase of a project, are usually outdated by the time the project is complete, and are seldom updated afterwards. The same is generally true of system inventories and network diagrams. As a result, in almost a hundred percent of cases where we begin the risk assessment process, we identify highly sensitive or business-critical data that is inadequately protected from a confidentiality, integrity, or availability perspective. (Note: the "almost" is only there at the insistence of our lawyers.)

The old business adage of "you can't manage what you can't measure" applies to information security as much as it does to any other business process, and therein lies the rub. Even today the majority of business managers erroneously put the emphasis on the "technology" in information technology, when the truth is it's the "information" that really matters to them. Too often management and the actual information owners are unaware of their role in risk management and simply expect that their IT staff has some psychic knowledge of what information is sensitive to the business, and the expectations for protecting that data.

The net result is twofold. First, and as already noted, sensitive or critical data is frequently left under- or unprotected because business management is unaware of its value or location. Second, less valuable data and infrastructure is *over* protected, resulting in unnecessary complexity and costs to the business.

So, while vulnerability and penetration testing serve a critical role in measuring control effectiveness, most organizations would garner much higher value at the beginning by starting with a less technical evaluation and focusing on real information security risk management.

Note

1. This paper is available at: `http://csrc.nist.gov/publications/history/ande80.pdf`

Security as a Business Now and Then

Life is like riding a bicycle. To keep your balance you must keep moving.
— Albert Einstein

Momentum in any industry is critical, but it is rarely industry-wide; rather it's driven within a broader base of companies by a few key players who have great success, while the majority of their peers simply survive, if that—most startup companies fail. Within an industry, momentum is rarely created out of marketing hype alone. Sometimes success is created by a unique product or service, often by user need and demand for a product or service, or occasionally it is born out of necessity. Regardless of how an industry is formed, a lack of momentum typically leads to consolidation and high failure rates of participating companies, resulting in less investment, slower innovation, and fewer jobs. Sometimes lack of momentum comes from a market's maturing over time. The IT security industry operates under the same rules as all industries, although at times it may not seem that is the case. Some would say that the IT security industry is a sham that should not exist because security should be built into IT products. While it's true that security should be built into IT applications, it isn't. Look at the IT industry as a whole, and ask yourself: "In how many other areas can you buy a product that is missing many of the key features a user demands?" You purchase desktops, laptops, servers, and applications, and they include only basic elements of security, yet everyone understands that users and enterprises require security. From conversations with thousands of business professionals over the years, including many hundreds of executives, it's clear they feel that the biggest shortcoming of most IT products is the lack of embedded security. If you consider IT security to be the band-aid for the shortcomings of the IT industry, you can't blame the innovators for finding a business opportunity within the gap created by not having security embedded within IT products. We are, after all, a capitalist country.

Significant and heated arguments exist around IT security. Many argue that if you push the vendors hard enough or you don't purchase vendor products until they step up and incorporate security into their solutions, you would and could save a lot of time and money—and certainly benefit the overall IT industry. Then there is reality: We doubt many businesses could afford to wait years for this to occur, and in reality it would take decades. The likelihood that application vendors and network and service providers will fix even the most obvious security flaws within my lifetime are slim. Thus, the need for IT security was born from an obvious need and will continue to survive as a standalone discipline, albeit in an evolving form, for the next 20 to 30 years because the needs and shortcomings it addresses will continue to exist. So, let's focus on the interim and how each of us can have an impact on improving the IT world.

The Purpose of IT

The purpose of information technology (IT) is to enable business. The purpose of security, business continuity, and governance is to enable IT. The specific purpose of security is to protect and maintain the integrity of data, while the specific purpose of business continuity is to enable your business to continue to operate in adverse and unusual situations. The purpose of governance and compliance is to ensure that you have the proper controls in place and have access to the right data to make business decisions; with this data you can properly perform your business in a confident manner and your employees and customers are protected against misdeeds and unconscionable actions. The business of security, whether in a business that provides security services or within an IT or IT security group inside an organization, plays an important role in life, and is highly valuable to the business's success.

An effective security, business continuity, and governance program allows an organization to:

- Effectively secure its data and business transactions, providing confidence to the business that the integrity of their data has not been compromised
- Ensure the availability of the applications that are fundamental to the business
- Govern the business processes, IT infrastructure, and meet compliance requirements

In a perfect world, the needs of the business are properly balanced with the capabilities of their IT. However, there is typically an imbalance and the needs and expectations of the business exceed the capabilities of IT because of inadequate funding, lack of expertise, or more often than not the unrealistic expectations of the business.

FROM OUR CONTRIBUTORS

Eric Shepcaro, Chief Executive Officer, Telx

Information technology involves many things, including the design of systems and architecture, management of databases, the communication architecture for processing and communicating information, and most importantly, the management of the information. According to Gartner, corporations globally will spend $3.4 trillion on information technology in 2010. Today, IT has become central to running and managing a corporation and must sit at the executive leadership table as corporate strategies are determined and tactics are implemented. Information and IT is now used by corporations in a predictive mode to determine customers' buying behaviors through visualization tools, how best to sell and market to them with such tools as Salesforce and Google AdWords, how best to deliver product to them through an end-to-end automated supply chain, and how to determine return on investments with real-time analytics. And because personal data and corporate data now run through all of these processes and systems, security must be a critical initiative of every IT organization and corporation.

Evolving Purpose into Action

IT and IT security professionals certainly have access to more tools, information, and experience today than our predecessors did. Today's technology provides all the pieces needed to create a truly effective security, business continuity, and governance program, but we need to be able to bring into focus the complete picture and create a roadmap to get there. We have what we need to provide the correct elements, processes, and controls to allow us to manage changes as they are introduced into our realm of control, yet rarely does an organization perform the magic of putting it all together.

Most security programs fail for three simple reasons: lack of goal setting, failure to follow a defined plan, and because the elements of the program are not prioritized correctly. To address these problems, we believe you must establish a plan and stay focused in the face of the many distractions around you.

Why is goal setting so rarely a key consideration in an IT security program? We have found that in general, with some clear exceptions, security professionals lack planning and project management skills. Often this is caused by the need for immediate action, or rather reaction, to the surrounding chaotic environment in which they operate. Because security is, by its nature, a state of mind rather than an actual destination to be reached, most professionals go about defining their security programs by following their instincts and reacting to events and immediate business demands rather than proactively planning. Practical experience has proven that this is not a good approach, regardless of whether you're talking about security or any other task in your career or personal life. Goal setting is a critical element of success.

FROM OUR CONTRIBUTORS

Steve Addison, VP of Business Development, Cosaint

Voltaire was right when he wrote, "The perfect is the enemy of the good."

Unrealistic goals are probably the most common problem that we come across when we talk to IT and security staff who've tried unsuccessfully to establish security awareness training programs. Most of the time, it's not because they didn't understand the security aspects, or because they didn't have clear goals in mind. Mostly, they failed to take into account critical cultural and management factors in their organization, and didn't combine their own efforts with the efforts of other groups.

Probably the problem that we hear about most frequently is the failure to involve other groups in the project at an early stage. All too often, an IT, security, or compliance group will create their own program without talking to the HR or training departments. Then, when they try to launch the program, they find that HR won't support it by managing the student lists, or that the training they're expecting to provide to new staff won't be allocated any time during the new hire (onboarding) process. And not involving business unit managers in the early stages reduces the chance that they'll support the program by allocating time for existing staff to take the training. An awareness training program must satisfy the needs of multiple stakeholders, so the involvement of all key groups from an early stage in the planning process is vital to success.

Another mistake is to consider the project goal to be the launch of the program to staff and to develop a project plan and — more importantly, a budget — on this basis. This is far from optimal. Organizations experience staff turnover, training required by compliance has to be completed each year, and new threats may emerge. So the work has only just started when the ribbon is cut. If a program is to be sustainable in the long term, not only must the initial costs be acceptable, but the ongoing costs (both monetary and in terms of administrative labor) must also be reasonable.

A further problem — less common, but almost inevitably fatal to a program's success — is ignoring business factors when setting project goals. Security staff may earnestly believe that all staff require at least 40 hours of security education each year, but business managers faced with tight budgets are unlikely to agree and might offer just 45 minutes! Failing to recognize the realities of business and factor these into the initial project goals can doom a project from the start.

Last, but far from least, security awareness programs (like most technology projects) can be prone to 'gold plating' during the planning stages. A simple web-based training program could easily become a Hollywood-scale multi-media development project without strict management of the requirements.

Setting realistic goals is the first — and most critical — step to creating a successful security awareness training program.

The Map to Success

At one time or another, most of us have decided that we should strive to be healthier than we are. We fall into two populations: some people commit to a program of exercise and/or diet with a defined plan, while others just tell themselves that they will do a few things to improve their health. Those who commit to a plan constantly measure their success and adjust their goals. They must constantly update that plan in order to adapt to internal and external variables such as age, injuries, availability of suitable foods, work hours, and so on. So not only must you have a plan that provides actions that lead to you becoming healthier, but you must also constantly adapt it based on changes. While a plan does not always result in success, committing to a well thought out plan with defined goals and activities to get there will increase your chances for success. Rarely, if ever, do people without a plan succeed.

The concepts just discussed obviously apply not only to your health goals, but to many things in life. Creating goals, and the associated plans to reach those goals, for the way we will secure IT environments, with timelines, will benefit each of us. The process of goal setting must include input and sign-off from the business. This allows the business to be part of the process and establish a vested interest. Some of the goal setting processes used within this chapter are general industry best practices to establish reasonable goals, while other elements of the goal setting process must be unique to your industry, your company, and to your IT environment and special business requirements. Layering security without prioritizing your goals (e.g., protecting high value assets, conforming to an industry or governmental compliance requirement, etc.) will simply waste a lot of valuable resources, including your time. Like your health, security has a lot to do with your state of mind. Like your health, security is not a destination to be reached, rather it's an ongoing process with interim milestones and goals that you must constantly monitor, change, adapt, and update. More importantly, with a list of goals, you always know you're making progress as you accomplish each goal, rather than being in constant reactionary mode. This certainly makes a good foundation for a positive attitude for the IT and IT security staff, but it also allows you to demonstrate to the business your ongoing contributions.

Secondly, and closely related, is creating a plan and following it. Even if you can establish a goal or set of goals, without mapping out a plan to achieve those goals the end result will be, at best, inefficient. Creating a *realistic* plan that properly weighs priorities and impacts in a way that allows progress in small steps also allows you and your team to feel fulfillment in the process of securing the organizations you are responsible for. We can tell you that, while setting a goal of having the "best security in the industry" sounds great at first, after a few months or years, when you look back, you'll feel like you've accomplished very little, and when your management looks at your goal to success ratio, you'll start to realize how unrealistic that goal was. We will address this in Chapter 9, but to formulate goals and create a plan, you must predict the future landscape of the industry and properly establish priorities within your plan.

The Relationship: Security and Luck

One of the best quotes we've ever read is "luck is when opportunity meets preparedness." It is also a great quote because it is true for both individuals and companies. The quote also de-emphasizes the weight of chance and applies action and responsibility to the concept of luck. How many businesses miss a company-making opportunity because they failed to prepare or didn't react quickly to an opportunity in a marketplace when it arose? The company saw the opportunity, discussed it, maybe even put it on the roadmap for later development, but never took action. The security industry in itself is made up of companies that saw, sometimes even predicted, an opportunity that was available because security had not been built into the base functionality of some product or application. Each of these "opportunities" were then made more valuable to business because of the general complexities of Information Technology (IT).

I'd love to say that if you work hard and are prepared, effectively leverage every resource and budget dollar you have, and have business buy-in, your job would be safe if a major compromise occurred, but history has shown that the IT security staff is the low man on the totem pole when assigning blame occurs. Significant career risk is present in almost any corporate role; however, the risk is compounded when the entire business's success is based upon protection of the company's crown jewels. Unfortunately for us in IT security, many things are considered the crown jewels; to list a few: customer list, R&D intellectual property, employee information, company communications and financials. In today's highly regulated market, the ability to be compliant in itself can be a crown jewel. While IT security is a rewarding career, like many unpleasant career realities, it's a job that often has many more risks than monetary rewards.

Luck, and even pure chance, are rampant in the day-to-day life of IT security. While we all see and remember the big front page headlines of corporations being hacked, losing tapes or computers that have employee or consumer data on them, unintentionally exposing data, having their websites defaced, suffering large scale malware breakouts, and so forth, the reality is that few companies with IT infrastructures connected to public networks are compromised. Don't get me wrong, more companies have malware and issues than any of us will probably ever know; however, the underlying problems will probably not have a big impact on the corporations. Unfortunately, this is where luck and preparedness come in again. You can't take the chance that you will be one of the many lucky ones that isn't targeted or that an impacting event won't come your way. You need to stay diligent and prepared so that if, make that *when*, you are threatened, you protect your environment, or at minimum you can show diligent efforts to meet or exceed industry efforts.

Security: An Industry or a Feature of IT?

Let's address two questions we commonly hear: Is the IT security industry really a separate industry or is it just a subset of IT? Is security a true stand-alone, for profit business or will it become a feature within IT products and services in the future? Let's take the easy subject first: Should security businesses such as security products, security professional services, and security services be stand-alone industries? The short answer is no. The IT security industry is part of the IT industry. You could also successfully argue that compliance has come to the center stage and that IT security is now a subset of IT governance, risk management, and compliance (GRC). Security is much like availability, an important attribute and requirement within IT, but not a standalone industry. Also, as mentioned previously in this chapter, if the application, product, and carriers had security built into the core of their products and services, there would be no need for separate and distinct devices and applications that only perform security functions, which would eliminate the question of a separate IT security industry. (These types of solutions are often referred to as "point solutions.")

> **NOTE** A point solution is a solution of one type, typically for one problem, rather than for a broad spectrum of problems. For example, if the end systems (PCs, servers, and mobile devices) were secure, and the carriers could perform basic protection from denial of service (DOS) attacks, it can be argued that network security devices (e.g., firewalls, intrusion protection systems [IPS], gateway antivirus, and so forth) would not be needed. Security at endpoint would truly enable a perimeterless networking architecture, assuming some level of flow control by the carrier where your network accessibility is protected.

Over time, there will be many changes that impact the classification of IT security, one of which is how tightly IT security and physical security become intertwined. There have been different instances during the past 10 years, where physical security products, such as biometrics and radio-frequency ID (RFID), have been integrated within IT security products, applications, and solutions. The result is much like what occurred when voice and data were integrated into single access links and Voice over IP (VoIP) and Video over IP (VID) began transiting the local area network (LAN) and IP-based wide area network (WAN): personnel needed to expand their expertise to better understand voice and video and take on more responsibilities. In this world of convergence, personnel need to understand the complexities introduced when putting latency sensitive voice and video over the data network. The integration of physical and IT security brings up some extremely interesting opportunities and challenges for business. Integrating presence to include physical presence alone is a great variable to be able to include in security logic. Consider that an employee, or group of employees, is required to physically be on-site to access a certain database. This requirement could be driven by data privacy laws, Department of Defense mandates, or a myriad of other business requirements. Now imagine logic that requires the employee to have physically checked in through security (e.g., an employee card, a biometrics scan, or an RFID tracker). This is a powerful combination that could potentially protect against a perimeter compromise, an individual employee's access being compromised or lost, or a combination of IT security failures. This direction of the industry continues to evolve, and we expect further integration efforts will benefit us significantly over the next 10 years, but this will not be the core driver of industry consolidation.

The harder question is if the IT security industry is a separate industry or just a subset of IT. At the heart of today's problems, and over the next 10 years, is that security is not built in as a feature within most of our key business applications. The reality is the application vendors, product vendors, and carriers are not good at embedding security within their products and services. That has led both of us, and probably many of you, to lifetime careers in the IT security industry, and there appears to be no end in sight. While there is always the possibility that the software vendors and network providers might wake up tomorrow and embed security within their products and services, but we would bet that generally across the IT industry it won't be in our lifetime. Also, if one class of vendor were to embed security and the other didn't, you would still need compensating measures to supplement for the weakest link. For example, if the carriers not only protected your network connection from distributed denial of service (DDOS) attacks but also from viruses, malware, hackers, and other external threats, while the internal systems had no protection, you would have major security holes. Rarely does any enterprise's IT infrastructure live on an island unto itself. For example, contractors, partner connections, wireless access points, mobile devices that leave and return to connect to the internal network, and so forth are requirements in the business world today. Each of these individually could be secured, but you would still have an overall security problem. Cosmetically, whether IT security is an industry, part of IT, or part of compliance really doesn't matter. The need for dedicated IT security experts will exist long into the future.

FROM OUR CONTRIBUTORS

Don DeBolt, Director of Intelligence, CA

Today's business threats are omnipresent and enabled significantly through the use of technology. Organized and state-sponsored crime is a reality and these commercially backed actors are weaponizing technology to obtain their goals. Residence within your company or residence on your device enables them to target your data or launch attacks in pursuit of others' data.

Security vendors have identified a number of business opportunities by filling the gaps left by the evolution from central to distributed systems. However, the model that has evolved is similar to that of a doctor treating the symptoms rather than the disease. Technology vendors are in a unique position to architect security into their products and treat the disease, while security vendors typically only treat the symptoms.

Data is what we are trying to protect, and unfortunately it is still very difficult to isolate data from executable code. Distributed platforms and robust user experiences require data and code to be mixed, thus perpetuating this classic IT security challenge. Control over the executable code and separation of that code from data is the holy grail of IT security. Unfortunately, this typically takes draconian measures to perform and most of these measures reduce overall functionality or require new hardware paradigms to enforce. Businesses and people are typically not ready for this level of change and as a result they continue to put their data at risk.

I look toward the "app-paradigm" with anticipation and hope. The ability to remove super-user control and the ability to audit the programming code allowed to run on the end device addresses some of the fundamental flaws in IT today. The applications that do run are still at risk of exploitation, but the level of control demonstrated by this paradigm provides security professionals the chance to once again gain control of their environment. This, however, places a greater security burden on the technology vendor rather than the security vendor or the security professional.

Over the course of the next decade we will see an explosion of mobile and embedded devices. The technology vendors that succeed must view security as a valuable differentiator and architect it into their offerings. The corporations that succeed will be those that place a premium on security. These companies will empower their IT and IT security professionals to choose the technology platforms providing the company with the most control over their environment. Failure to move in this direction will mean job security for the security vendors, but will only serve to perpetuate the treat-the-symptom model in use today.

Continued

FROM OUR CONTRIBUTORS *(continued)*

Dave Meizlik, Director of Product Marketing and Communications for Websense, Inc.

Security is not and never will be a feature of IT largely because security doesn't drive business. Sure, security will always be managed as an IT function, and the ever-diligent security team will make an earnest and valiant effort to ensure both employees and corporate assets are protected. The bottom line, however, is that security will not trump business return when making IT investment decisions. Whether or not to migrate your CRM solution to the cloud is, today, only marginally impacted by the security implications, and likely to be even less so tomorrow as markets continue to accelerate. In actuality, CRM migration is driven nearly entirely by two factors: availability and cost reduction.

Threats and risks will always be present, and as long as businesses remain profitable, those threats will be considered acceptable. Companies know this very well, and so too do the vendors. Vendors build products to deliver value, not to provide security (with the obvious exception of security product vendors). How secure are Microsoft products, yet how successful are they? How secure are Adobe products, yet how successful are they? While an organization might base its decision on what vendor solution to purchase in part on its security, such a decision will invariably be balanced against the revenue-bearing advantages of the competing solutions.

With that cynical outlook, you might ask, "Then does security matter?" Of course it does. The more appropriate question is, "How much does it matter?" And the answer is "not enough to make it a feature of IT".

Consolidation of the IT Security Industry

A more specific question, which is probably more appropriate, is: of the 300+ vendors classified in the IT security industry, how many are really companies rather than features of a product? Not many. If you look at all the desktop applications for security, they should all be in one agent. If you look at all the gateway security applications, they should all be on one single inline product. We are seeing consolidation, especially in the financially strained markets of today, for example, the Unified Threat Management (UTM) devices. Of course, the same could be said about most industries. However, sometime in the future, probably more than 10 years, there will be a significant consolidation with only a few major players left focused exclusively on IT security. We don't anticipate that the security industry itself will dissolve for far longer than that, more like 20 to 30 or more years, maybe never. Many of the problems within IT lie not in the fact that products are poorly designed but in that they must be integrated to work together with other products. When you have two products designed by two different vendors and then put together in a unique environment, problems, specifically security problems, will result.

When we started in this industry in the late 1980s, neither of us anticipated that we'd still have our lives consumed by one discipline in the IT industry. Yet today, over 20 years later, here we are, both still focused on securing the networks and products that are built without the most basic features that would natively provide protection against known and unknown threats.

So, what are the business areas within the security industry? There are many, but we would propose they all can be categorized into four broad areas:

- Security products, which are manufactured and sold in the IT industry to compensate for inherent product and network weaknesses

- Managed security services where commercial products and proprietary solutions are packaged to include the automation and people who perform management of security products on behalf of their customers

- Professional services abound in every industry, and given the complexity of security, will always be required within the IT industry.

- Media and analyst is another category. There are a large number of reporters, freelancers, and analysts that exclusively focus on the security industry.

The IT security product industry is a very crowded space. There are a few large and hundreds of smaller players in this subcategory of the security industry. In 2008, 63 of the fastest growing 5000 companies in the United States were focused primarily on IT security,[1] with the lowest growth of these companies being 63 percent annual growth. The largest players are McAfee and Symantec, and there are some broader IT players such as Cisco, Juniper, 3Com, and Nortel.

FROM OUR CONTRIBUTORS

Mark D McLaughlin, President and CEO, VeriSign

In technology, you sometimes hear developers and product people talk about "elegance." It is a form of praise for code or a solution that solves a problem in a very simple way. Simplicity is good because it means efficiency and ease of use. Simplicity, though, is harder to come by these days in the security space because of the ever-increasing intricate connections and networking that continue to break down the defendable IT boundaries that are used to thwart security threats. It's a real conundrum and one of the reasons there was an explosion of standalone security companies founded in the last decade. These companies tended to focus on one problem that could best be described today as a feature of a solution. However, because they focused on one or a few specific threats, they have been able to build elegant products and services to target the threat. The problem, though, is that also over the last decade, customers have been reasonably demanding more security

Continued

services in less software and appliances as the network has become amorphous and potential threats grow with each new connection or device on the network.

Naturally, over time, large security providers have emerged because they are able to aggregate many security solutions onto a single platform. This is a threat to many smaller security providers as they see their services become features bundled into unified threat management platforms. On the other hand, the large security providers run up against a problem of their own: how to focus on the alarming rate of new threats in a cost effective way, and how to integrate new services into their platforms when multiple services running together create their own unintended vulnerabilities.

The result of these trends over time will be a winnowing out of the smaller security providers to leave those that are solving large problems in elegant ways, and the acquisition of these players by the larger firms. That means there will be healthy competition in the security space for a long time and enough promise of return on investment to continue focused venture funding on companies that promise more than a feature.

Maria Lewis Kussmaul, CFA, Founding Partner, Head of Information Security Investment Banking, America's Growth Capital

Nearly 90 information security mergers and acquisitions (M&A) transactions have been announced year-to-date in 2010, with volume, valuations, and median transaction size all running ahead of last year's pace. Powered by powerful global trends, IT security continues to be among the most active sectors in the M&A landscape — and America's Growth Capital, with 45 information security transactions advised on since 2003, is among the most active financial advisors to the sector.

IT security has several unique characteristics that make it a stand-out among IT sectors. Cyber-threats and governance/compliance requirements fuel spending, even in a budget-constrained economy. Enterprises' preference for best-in-class solutions keeps innovation and profit margins high, particularly relative to less dynamic IT sectors where change can be measured in vendor-promoted product releases flush with often inconsequential features of low incremental value. In an environment where the perpetrators are as clever and innovative as their pursuers, feature enhancement or product substitution in IT security solutions is often quickly reactive, remedial, and remunerative.

While the IT security sector produces precious few new platform-caliber companies (i.e. those capable of supporting fold-in feature integration around a need substantial enough to fuel a company to self-sustaining growth and profitability), it spawns ample high value security M&A targets providing security solutions, product lines, feature sets, and enhancements to existing IT applications, networks, products, and services. IT security consolidation is also driven by the requirement that all IT product vendors, service providers, and platform- or infrastructure-as-a-service hosts, whatever their specialization from CAD/CAM to consumer, have "security inside." Hence the field of prospective acquirers is larger than for any other IT sector, as these would-be strategic partners seek to augment their development and marketing staffs with security DNA, their core technologies with security IP, and their top lines with potentially high growth security-related sales. As hard as it is for enterprises to staff security operations personnel, it is equally, and perhaps even more, difficult for IT developers to attract and retain security expertise fluent in the feature/functionality of their product set or services solutions. Often, the only way to attain critical mass in security competency is to buy a security vendor.

Finally, each time IT evolves, security must evolve with it — and it does so often as an afterthought. Despite well-documented security lapses in enterprise application development, we are largely perpetuating the problem as those same applications or their equivalents are being hosted for SaaS, virtualized, or becoming cloud based. Thus another wave of IT security innovation via startups and M&A will inevitably ensue to fill the gaps. Whether the M&A catalyst is cat and mouse technology leap-frogging between hackers and defenders, emergent next generation computing, transport or application security requirements, or new regulations, policies, or best practices stimulating IT security purchases, acquirers often find it is better to buy than build — which puts a gleam in an investment banker's eye.

Buying Security: Defining the Value

All of us are also, in some way, consumers of IT security products and services. How you buy, implement, and manage a security solution is critical in its long-term return on investment (ROI) and total cost of ownership (TCO). Looking at it from a purchaser's perspective, the products and services for IT security can be classified into the following categories:

- Software as a Service (SaaS)
- Managed services
- Professional services
- Licenses
- Commercial product
- Open source product

In the 1990s and into the early 2000s, many companies floundered on how to justify their IT security products and services to the buyers. That's always an indicator that an industry is either (1) early to a marketplace or (2) a marketplace doesn't exist for their product or service. Fortunately for many of us, it is the former and it just takes time for the market to mature. That's not to discount the fact that many products failed because they never really provided any value in solving a buyer's problem, or the product solved it in a more complex way than buyers were willing to accept. How are most security companies successful? Many companies are often successful on the simple spin and marketing value of FUD (Fear, Uncertainty, and Doubt). It's a strategy that, when spun wisely, can be very effective. It is no coincidence that this is the title of Bruce Schneier's 2005 book.

The contemporary view is that FUD doesn't sell and the gut feeling of a CSO doesn't create security budgets for IT organizations. Rather, the market has matured and the compelling elements to justify a purchase are focused on fulfilling compliance requirements and using some acceptable mathematical equation that's tied to industry stats or metrics. For example, you can say that you have a solid justification for a purchase if you can justify one (or a combination) of these:

- Probability of breach
- Value of asset
- Risk of loss/breach
- Impact of loss/breach
- Compliance requirements

In a financially strained market where every budget dollar is scrutinized, there is little room for subjectivity and gut feel. Today, only critical projects are funded.

In reality, the one common element that has always been the key to success between a vendor and a customer and to a smaller degree vice versa is . . . trust. Trust can be created in many ways, but technical prowess and customer references are often two core elements.

FROM OUR CONTRIBUTORS

Thomas Dunbar, SVP, Global IT Chief Security Officer, XL Global Services, a member of XL Group plc

There are many variables that come into play when an enterprise evaluates which security products to acquire and which security vendors to use. At the core, one must first understand what the specific business requirements are that need to be fulfilled. Often within IT security, the key question is what risk is the business attempting to reduce or mitigate, or in today's compliance driven environment, what is the regulatory requirement that must be met. This is complex for organizations doing work in a single geography and even more complicated for multi-nationals where business owners have different local needs and regulatory requirements vary significantly. Regardless of the driver, or geographical influence, we must always consider cost and reward of any IT project. Frequently, IT security staff must go back to the business and request adjustments to the business requirements in order to best meet or establish realistic expectations for the project. This can be painful, as we all know. However, business requirements sometimes cannot be met within the capabilities of technology or within the defined budgets, and it is best to address these issues up front. During this process, solutions can sometimes be found that leverage existing technologies or simply incorporate processes that allow for risk reduction with a lower investment. This can be a painful, cyclical process for all involved, but this level setting helps all parties win in the end.

Once you understand the business influences, you must evaluate a variety of technical elements including end user and business process impacts, compatibility, ability to expand with business needs, and risk reduction effectiveness. As noted, evaluation of technologies and security services you already have may be the best and most cost effective way to deploy a solution. Discussions with peer CISOs reveal that it happens extremely frequently that new business problems, evolving threats, and perceived risks can be countered through leveraging technology that is already in place. With the auto-updating capabilities of many IT and IT security solutions in the market today, the solution to mitigate the new risk is often already deployed before the business owners even ask about the problem. Frequently headlines trail the risk, and a good security organization will have responded to a threat in advance of the business's awareness. However, given today's zero-day threats and the ability for reporters to post articles online within minutes, it's clearly not always the case.

Finally, assuming that you lack the technology or services to meet the business need, you must implement new processes, and/or select new technologies and vendors. Beyond technical capabilities, you must feel comfortable not only with the technology, but also the vendor's viability as a business and their ability to provide ongoing support.

Budgets and Prioritizations

The business of security is affected by numerous factors such as IT and IT security budgets, regulatory changes, technology changes, customer pressures, and industry threats. Any combination of these factors can greatly increase or decrease the need for chief security officers (CSO) and/or chief information officers (CIO) to apply security measures. To state the obvious, the level of effectiveness for an enterprise's security typically increases when security spending increases not only because of the amount of security being applied individually to an enterprise but also because innovations are simultaneously being funded in the marketplace, and as security spending decreases, the innovation funding decreases. Fortunately for those of us in the security industry, the increases are typically significant, while the decreases are typically moderated by the fact that security needs and regulatory requirements are constantly increasing.

Over the next 10 years, we project that IT security budgets will continue to increase, driven primarily by regulatory requirements and the increase of global threats. That may seem self-serving given that we are both in the security industry; however, there seem to be no mitigating factors that would influence IT security spending in any other way. Also, given our backgrounds, we believe there are many vectors that hackers and malware developers still have not explored and that are very difficult to protect against without enterprises making incremental spending commitments. We are truly on a tipping point where IT and automation will take steps forward in making mankind more efficient and more productive, but with that step comes incremental risk both to the economy and to our way of life. Many of these steps are to eliminate the influence of human error, but in reality people will always be designing, coding, and implementing most of the automation. Thus, the human influence will always be present, at least within the next 10 years.

FROM OUR CONTRIBUTORS

Rich Nespola, Chairman of the Board and Chief Executive Officer, TMNG Global

In 2010, after more than a year of scaling back capital-intensive IT projects, most IT security organizations in the communications market are now ramping up their budgets in the key areas of identity and access management (IAM) and data loss prevention (DLP). Having worked with leading communications companies for 20 years, TMNG Global has observed the sector's focus on security rise and fall over time. But in today's environment, as consumers and businesses demand data delivery at any time, to any location, on any device, the need for customer and data authentication and the potential for data loss are of paramount importance to service providers.

Further, with open networks and collaborative business models, security experts must be concerned not only about the security of their own environment, but also that of their collaboration partners, as it is the weakest link in the chain that is the most likely to be compromised.

The telecommunications ecosystem has experienced dynamic change in recent years with the proliferation of powerful mobile devices, the expansion of broadband and IP services, more collaborative business models, and new direct and alternative distribution channels. In this complex ecosystem, the movement from voice-centric to data-centric offerings challenges the provider's ability to provide data security. Historically, in a voice-centric environment with less complex business models, network firewalls achieved acceptable results. The proliferation of data and its rapid distribution based on new competitive paradigms has caused the traditional way of safeguarding data to change dramatically.

As TMNG Global works with its clients to develop new business models and more efficient operating environments, security across hardware, software, and devices is a critical issue. It is also of utmost importance to regulators, who have mandates to protect business and consumer data within the province of their privacy laws.

In this brief synopsis the conclusion is very simple — vigilance is mission-critical and traditional methods to ensure network and data security, on- and off-site, are challenged as never before. As communications providers develop their IT strategies and establish their budgets, the economies of scale through collaboration with communications partners must be employed to provide security at all points in the ecosystem.

Venture Capital and Investment in IT Security

The two most important aspects of how IT security will evolve over the next 10 years are (1) what will the spending rate be, as we just discussed, and (2) what investments will be made in technological and process advancements. There are three primary investment vehicles that fuel most technology innovation:

- Individuals who invest their own time and money to create and bootstrap a company

- Research & development funding by government and not-for-profit entities

- Venture capitalists (VC), who fund companies to develop products before revenue, up to profitability, and during growth

Individuals, typically the founder or founding employees, who fund early stage companies are becoming rarer and rarer within IT security. The reason is that the time from initial development to when the individual can either assume they can reach scale in order to attract a venture capitalist or attract the attention for someone to acquire them is getting longer and longer. This is actually fairly true across most technology innovation categories today. Over the past 10 years, it was reasonable to assume that if you could show a rough proof of concept you could get VC funding. Thus, an individual might be able to bootstrap a company for $200K and certainly less than $1 million in expenses. Then, the VC would step in and fund the company through a point where the individual could recover his investment, plus hopefully significantly more. Unfortunately, VCs are being far more conservative these days or putting terms on the table that significantly reduce the upside for the original individual investor. This conservatism results in most startup companies needing to be able to self-fund anywhere from, on the low side $500K, to upwards of $5M before they can receive substantial VC funding. There is a class of investors called "angel investors" that help fill the gap between founders and VCs. Angel investors are typically not a formal group of repeat investors, but rather friends and family or high net worth individuals looking to take on more risk in return for a higher return. We hear mixed messages from startups; some claim that over the years many angel investors have been hurt by the failure rate of high-tech startup companies and angel funding is becoming more and more difficult to arrange. On the flip side, we also hear and see many new high tech startups finding angel funding pretty easily. In all cases, everyone agrees that any investments today, at any stage, are scrutinized more than in the past.

Research and development (R&D) funding has been significantly reduced over the years and few programs outlay significant amounts for noncommercial investments that can be used to fund the startup of a company. Often, fee-oriented R&D is reserved for large corporations, specialty feature creation for revenue-generating companies, and universities. While there are a few programs still in existence, they are highly competitive and rarely represent startup funding.

The VCs post-2008 are significantly different than the VCs previously. They are typically larger, more conservative, and can demand far more attractive terms for their business than in years past. There has been significant consolidation within this industry as well. Some of the consolidation was associated with the general financial turmoil of the market, but in general many closed because of poor performance in their underlying portfolios. As a result, the VCs are dependent and graded more often on the performance of their portfolios versus living off management fees, which they often received regardless of performance. So now, each investment is stringently reviewed not only by individual analysts, but by committees of partners. Early stage, pre-revenue, companies are very difficult to analyze and represent high risk to investors. The trend, even for those investing in early stage companies, is to start with small funding amounts until a company can prove their business plan and ability to execute.

FROM OUR CONTRIBUTORS

David Cowan, Partner, Bessemer Venture

Every new Internet phenomenon introduces vulnerabilities that hackers will exploit. For each hypergrowth online market — email, e-commerce, music sharing, banking, trading, dating, casinos, VoIP, social networks — demand grows just as fast for the security mechanisms that only young, nimble startups can innovate. So naturally, venture investors look for opportunities to fund those startups poised to dominate each of these new markets. But how do venture capitalists (VCs) select which teams to fund among the hundreds seeking VC at any time?

- **Follow the hackers:** To anticipate demand for security solutions, follow the activities of the hackers, or other bad players in the ecosystem, over the years, their objectives and tactics have shifted. Some sought fun and glory by defacing enterprise websites, some sought personal satisfaction from damaging their employers, some sought to profit from spam, phishing, DOS extortion, and ID theft; others pursued nationalistic goals by spying on or attacking their enemies' computers. Venture investors need to anticipate the demand for security by mapping out the current vectors of attack.

- **Identify the right business model:** Security startups have sold software tools (RSA circa 1990), server software (Checkpoint 1994), encryption services (VeriSign 1995), client applications (Symantec 1996), hardware appliances (Nokia 1997), consumer hardware devices (SecurID 1998), consulting services (@Stake, 1999), semi-conductors (Cavium 2000), data analytics (Counterpane 2001), free browser plug-ins (McAfee SiteAdvisor 2005) and ad-supported tools (SpiceWorks 2006). For each type of security threat, there is an ideal way for the customer and the vendor to package the solution. For example, the anti-spam service providers Postini, MessageLabs, and FrontBridge all outperformed dozens of anti-spam software competitors, because enterprises found it much easier and cheaper to implement the services. Many effective security technologies (e.g. biometric devices) fail to dominate their markets because they are too difficult or expensive to implement. Furthermore, as threats age and the large, public vendors with vast distribution networks offer solutions, it becomes increasingly difficult for startups to serve those markets.

- **Back the experts:** Experience counts for a lot in data security. The field is driven by many counter-intuitive principles that demand architects and product managers steeped in its special nuances. For example:

  - Public scrutiny makes transparent security more effective than stealth security, and it makes old security protocols more effective than new ones.

  - Unwieldy products that deflect 99.99% of attackers are less effective than simple solutions that repel 86% of the attackers.

  - No security solution is 100% effective (so never say that it is).

  - Static security products will be defeated, so always deliver the solution as a service with on-going improvements.

So what do these rules mean for the prospect of raising VC for IT security startups today?

During the years 1997 to 2004, hackers targeted more and more enterprise resources, such as web home pages, phone circuit use, and credit card databases. Enterprises needed solution suites that they naturally bought from large integrators like Cisco, Symantec, and MacAfee. Yet these integrators

Continued

needed best-of-breed technology to compete and so they gobbled up start-ups, yielding good investment returns.

At some point, the integrators had suites so extensive that they no longer felt the need to keep acquiring new teams. The threats and solutions were both so complex that to win new sales, integration and service trumped efficacy. In addition, by 2005 the hackers had largely turned their attention toward the more profitable consumer attacks and, more recently, to national-istic hacks. As a result, the integrators stopped buying startups, and the flow of venture capital toward IT security has largely dried up.

The security startups most likely to raise venture capital today address threats to consumer financial data, social network profiles, ISP infrastructure (e.g., IPv6, DNS) and, increasingly, homeland security.

Rob Ward, Managing Director, Meritech Capital

The security sector will remain a robust area of investment for venture capital-ists for some time to come. While the industry has matured, the ever-changing methods of attack on the part of bad actors means constant innovation is required. At the same time, businesses are increasingly connected and usually conducting ever more mission-critical transactions over the Internet — which means the cost of failure is rapidly rising.

But what are the characteristics of the security companies that will be most attractive to venture capitalists in the foreseeable future?

- **Broad-based platform:** Too many security startups are merely prod-ucts or features masquerading as companies, and consequently can't sustain their initial promising growth rates. Particularly in the current economic environment, companies are under increasing pressure to do more with smaller budgets. A broader suite of applications means a lower total cost of ownership and a better, more practical admin-istrative and operational experience. As with any maturing industry, the successful security startups of tomorrow will need a broad-based solution to displace larger incumbents, and will benefit from the abil-ity to land on and expand from several discrete pain points within an enterprise.

- **Flexibility and depth of delivery form factor:** SaaS and virtualiza-tion are changing the rules about how new technology is delivered to enterprises, and security is no exception. But the unusual require-ments of the security market mean that a hybrid approach will become the new standard. Successful startups in this industry will stretch the security bromide of "defense in depth" to incorporate additional network and corporate elements, so that a robust solution will reside both in the cloud and on premise, and be lightweight and distrib-uted but also networked, and will benefit from community-based intelligence.

■ **Solving the big, difficult, unsolved problems:** The next big opportunities in the security industry lie in the exploding markets like social networking and social commerce; smart meters, smart grids, and energy infrastructure; and cloud services. Even existing markets harbor large opportunities — such as the ability to effectively deliver real-time authentication without using PII. Governments will increasingly continue to require better cyber-security solutions. So long as there is technology innovation there will be the concomitant need for security innovation.

Notes

1. Inc.com's list of the 5000 fastest growing private companies in America is available at `http://www.inc.com/inc5000/2008/lists/security-companies.html?o=0&c=200821870`.

   Inc.com's list of the 5000 fastest growing security companies in America is available at `http://www.inc.com/inc5000/2008/lists/top100-industry-security.html?sort=listrank&order=&o=50`.

Impact of the Economy over the Next 10 Years

The world's financial ecosystem is a fragile, intertwined fabric of trust, confidence, and economics sprinkled with a lot of faith. This means any significant impact on our willingness to accept the way the system works could be easily shaken.

—Doug Howard

It is amazing in many ways that billions of people have reached an agreement that certain financial instruments can be used in global commerce. If you think about the fact that countries can print currency on otherwise valueless paper and coinage that has no valuable metal content, it may give you pause as to how our commerce system really works. Global commerce is based on the trust and confidence that a valueless representation of an underlying worth will be accepted in fair trade for other valuable items. Think for a moment of the countries with hyperinflation and the impact it had on people. One moment a house is valued at $50k, then, with little more than a change in confidence and trust, the value of the currency drops so that a $50k house doubles or triples in value. Now apply that to automobiles and other major consumer goods. Worse, apply it to day-to-day necessities and consider the effect on the population of any country where people already live at or below the poverty level. The examples are typically limited to countries where the government has made bad decisions and flooded the market with currency or the global economic system recognized some new risk specific to that country. Does it sound like the United States could be quickly approaching a profile that matches this description? Some think so, but fortunately most do not. In 2010, inflation in the United States is sitting at a 44-year low, but inflation is still a concern, while countries such as Brazil and China are seeing significant inflation already.

Once, the core value of these monetary instruments was tied to the gold reserves of a country. Somewhat silly if you think about it; however, at least they were tied to some tangible asset that could be used to define the value of an item. Now, the valueless representation of a tangible good is dependent exclusively on the confidence of a government system to maintain the worth of its currency. Yeah, okay, you're thinking, "Why am I reading basic Economics 101 in an IT-security-oriented book?" The answer is simple: a large part of the trust we put in our government, and the global economic system, is based on our trust that we all have easy and reliable access to being able to make a financial transaction in a timely fashion. Now imagine that:

- A global system virus is released and all the core credit card systems for Visa, MasterCard, Discovery, and/or American Express are compromised, or

- Credit card processing companies (known as core processors) are compromised, or

- The ATM networks for banks are disabled

Any of the above may result in actions corresponding to those that happened after 9-11 with the airline industry. In order to maintain integrity and reduce the overall risk to the entire financial system, you shut it down until you can bring confidence back into the system that transactions being processed are valid. Now I don't want to provide props for the credit card industry, but let's be honest . . . the *global* financial engine really is tied to credit cards today, especially for the average consumer and many businesses. Now if this shutdown of our financial system lasted 24 hours, it would be really bad, but the world would survive. Every ATM machine in the world couldn't be filled fast enough to keep up with the demand for cash. Imagine if you are traveling during this time. Personally, given the amount of time that each of the two of us travel, we might starve before getting back home . . . hopefully someone would show pity on us and the millions of other cashless travelers in some way. Now what happens if the shutdown is longer than, say, 72 hours? How about a week? A month?

No matter the outage period, the confidence of consumers worldwide will be shaken. The result will be that people will take out cash reserves as soon as they can. People will store hordes of cash under their mattresses or some other local place they can easily access it. People will stockpile food and water to last for longer periods. Far-fetched? Not really. When people feel that their ability to obtain the goods and services that are essential in their daily lives is threatened, they panic. Just go to a grocery store when there is the threat of snow cover in a state further south than New Jersey on the East Coast: Panic . . . pure and simple panic that people won't have access to basic essentials. Now, imagine the world without the ability to perform financial transactions. During this global financial outage, the confidence of the world's population will be shaken. If the population goes hours, days, weeks, or more without being able to buy goods, they will lose confidence in the systems and prepare better for the next event.

It's been proven over and over that consumer confidence is the single most important driver in the global financial system. Simply look at the impact of the recession that was painfully felt in 2008 and then the nagging hangover thereafter. While there are plenty of fundamental failures in the U.S. financial systems that led to the collapse, the reality is the American people could have, and have in the past, ignored many of the underlying facts and continued to spend (and it may have gotten worse or self-corrected). The lack of jobs did not result in reduction in spending. Instead, fear drove people to hunker down and as a result revenues of companies fell and investment into funds was reduced. As a result of that, jobs were lost and people defaulted on loans . . . and the financial dominos continued to tumble. We are not trying to simplify the financial crisis that the United States and the global markets experienced, nor are we financial experts, rather we are trying to drive home the single point that the U.S. and global financial markets are fragile. More importantly, we want to highlight the relationship between consumer emotion and the domino effect that can occur should consumer confidence quickly weaken.

So why is this fragility so important? Simply put, there are hundreds if not thousands of scenarios where confidence—yours, ours, and consumers' in general—in the world's financial systems could be shaken by the failure of IT security. If the financial systems fail or confidence is reduced, even if it's not related to a technological event, the impact will be destructive to the world's economies. Recessions, depressions, inflation, stock market crashes, real estate values, commodity prices, and so forth all have an impact on employment rates, salaries, and IT security spending in general. So, in every way we must be aware of how the financial wellness, or sickness, of our world is affected by IT security. These intertwined relationships must be balanced, but as security personnel we must use these times of financial restraint to optimize the resources and expenses already in place. We as security experts must make sure that the systems we are trusted to protect succeed and that we do not fail, which in many cases could lead to very real disasters for our companies, our country, and the global economy.

Economic Recession

Let's start with the obvious. Economic recessions impact IT spending, security IT spending, business continuity, and many other related infrastructure expenditures. That's already been proven countless times in the past. So while the risk of not being able to secure a business's IT infrastructure, or that some businesses may cease to exist because they cannot meet basic compliance requirements, is scary, the really concerning fact is that even reasonably secure companies are still at high risk as well. As previously noted in this book, without constant analysis and adaptation of your security infrastructure, it weakens quickly. Lack of funding for IT, and specifically information security, has a rapidly deteriorating effect on the viability of a system.

A severe byproduct of the economic downturn is also the negative impacts to the workforce across the nation, or across the world as we saw in 2009. Often jobs are lost, houses are foreclosed on, families are broken apart, and the basic emotional need to feel secure is lost across a population as a whole. The desperation spreads. The willingness to do anything to survive and provide for yourself and those who depend on you becomes overwhelming. For those of us with children, can you imagine not being able to afford the basic essentials in life such as food and shelter? It's heartbreaking just to consider. The American dream has usually included leaving your children financially better off than you. Most of you, by the mere fact you purchased this book, probably aren't in such a desperate situation, nor are we, but I truly can imagine it and it's frightening. The rest of this chapter considers how rapidly the U.S. economic downturn impacted less fortunate countries such as India, China, and other countries dependent on us purchasing their goods and services to keep their populations employed.

What If?

Since we are doing a lot of imagining, let's do a "what if" exercise.

It's hard to imagine, I know, that anyone in the world would have ill will toward the U.S. or the Western world. Just kidding! In reality, no one living in the United States or Western world today can doubt that there are bad guys who want to cause us harm. It's not hard to imagine that some of the IT workers and developers outside of the United States and Western world countries who worked on our widest deployed software—such as those produced by Microsoft, IBM, Oracle, and other giants of the industry—might know a few secrets about how to compromise these applications and systems. (And don't forget services companies whose employees might be located outside of the Western world and have direct access to those systems.) Yes there are quality checks, yes there are policies, yes some things are caught . . . but no amount of checksums will catch everything, a situation that is obvious from a count of the simple vulnerabilities that are produced with no apparent malice on a daily basis.

Now imagine these employees are laid off and have no opportunity to provide for the basic needs of their families, or that they are still employed but are afraid for their jobs because personnel around them are being laid off. Now Joe Bad Guy comes along and offers $5,000 or $10,000 in exchange for some information or a small task. This is a year's pay in many countries, maybe more. Conditions are also far worse in many countries for the unemployed. So would you starve to death or go without a warm place to sleep if someone offered you an alternative?

Can you say you would take the high road if someone offered you the ability to feed your children when you saw no other hope? It's hard for many of us to imagine such a situation, but if you've been to some of the less fortunate areas within the United States or to a developing country, you would recognize that on a global basis, choices like this happen every day.

NOTE We've both traveled to less developed countries than those visited by most folks on vacation. We both readily agree that even with our survival instincts, we would have difficulty just surviving, let alone trying to provide for a family in these environments without a source of income.

As we expand our global workforce and the reaches of our IT infrastructure, we must recognize the risk of such influences. There are also many other factors at play as well. Think of how many spies have been "turned" based on seemingly small financial gain. Think of how many religious and ideological influences have impacted the world. I use the international employee example, but U.S. personnel are no less susceptible when faced with survival and protection of their families.

The reality is that 9-11 was a physical attack against the United States, but a virtual attack on our infrastructure systems would have no less of a financial impact. Imagine if our power grids went offline. Imagine if our transportation IT infrastructure were compromised. Imagine if an airline's IT systems or those of the FAA were impacted. All these systems are heavily automated and sensitive to IT security compromises. Many of these scenarios end in the loss of human life.

We don't offer these scenarios to instill fear, uncertainty, and doubt in the social fabric of our lives. They aren't scenarios that the bad guys haven't thought of or aren't already working on. You bought this book, so you probably already have the same concerns or the basis to formulate the same concerns. We are simply conveying our opinions and concerns about the fragile state of our IT infrastructure. We aren't implying you shouldn't be a global company or use offshore resources, rather that you should be aware of the risks that might impact your business and you personally.

Economic Booms

Economic booms typically create more need for IT, information security, and business continuity, resulting in increased spending; however, the rapidly changing demands on IT infrastructure often leave teams scrambling to keep up with basic capacity needs. Economic booms often lead to throwing lots of technology at problems without optimizing each investment or properly leveraging the capabilities of a product or service. This often leads to an architecture diagram that looks really good hanging on the wall, or a capabilities matrix that looks very impressive to the boss, but the practical implementation is lacking. If you ever have the luxury of a economic boom resulting in a large budget with unlimited restrictions, go back to Chapter 6 and make sure you optimize and prioritize all your investments. Focus on spending that first leverages the technologies you have, such as staffing and services, and then move to additional technology. That is, of course, after you've given yourself a well-deserved raise for all the money you could have wasted buying a suite of security products you would never had gotten around to implementing.

Our 10-year forecast unfortunately doesn't include a financial boom, but the above applies as we leave 2010 behind and begin our recovery. Optimization of dollars in IT will be with us for a long time into the future.

Hyperinflation

Hyperinflation, high inflation, or simply rapid and consistent inflation puts lots of strain on IT. Imagine for a minute that the vendors, especially service vendors, you now use and with which you have signed multiyear contracts with, have their costs increase by 10 percent, 20 percent, or 50 percent? Why would that occur? Well, inflation drives up the cost of goods, personnel costs through salaries, benefits and healthcare, travel costs, third-party vendors which they rely on, new capital expenditures and so forth. In reality, most healthy companies operate with a 10 to 30 percent profit, most on the lower end. In most long-term contracts, the fees the vendors charge are locked to a flat rate or have only minor annual increases that are typically capped at a low rate. Vendors selling products are less susceptible to this, as they can increase their product prices, assuming, of course, the inflation impacts their competitors.

While the United States currently is at a 44-year low for inflation, close to deflation in fact, most economists voice strong concern that, with the amount of money the government has introduced into the economy (as have many countries), we have a high risk of inflation. At the same time, within IT we have more and more solutions moving into managed services, Software as a Service (SaaS), and In the Cloud (ITC) models. This is great for the industry and for consumers of IT solutions, as it provides optional ways of buying needed products and IT solutions. It does, however, introduce great financial risks to the service providers that few industry participants have considered. This risk—where prices for vendors are locked in with customers in long-term contracts, but their costs are under the influence of high inflation—is a real risk. Most customers and vendors alike have operated where the cost of IT has constantly decreased over the past 10 years. Every enterprise wants to be able to control costs and have predictability over the terms of their contracts, but they also don't want vendors to fail.

The vendors will come back and beg for relief, but your business will also be under the same pressures and looking everywhere to reduce costs and leverage existing capital while trying to stabilize your cost structure. Few companies are or will be immune to inflation. For those of you that are services vendors, you must be aware of this in your business models and, where possible, introduce the concept of adding "inflation adjustment" clauses to your contracts. For consumers of IT services, you obviously realize it's a competitive world and you don't need to accept such terms in most situations in today's environment. Therefore, this is a scenario where the only and best solution is for inflation never to become a problem.

Skill Shortages

We are currently in a time when American jobs are under constant threat because of the economic climate following the 2009 recession, as well as simultaneous pressures from lower-cost offshore labor. The salary equality between countries also has a long way to go. Over time salaries will stabilize on a global basis, but that time period is likely measured in decades, maybe even a century or more. The next 10 years for most geographies and specialty IT jobs, including security, will be marked by increased demand and increased salaries. However, this will be tempered with a global workforce that will become highly competitive. It is unlikely in our lifetimes, assuming continued economic recovery, that the supply of qualified personnel in the Middle East and Asia—specifically India, China, Singapore, and the Philippines—will exceed employment demand globally. As we write this, an English-speaking college graduate with approximately five years experience in advanced programming/development skills will get paid $8–12k annually in most developing Asian countries and $8–24k annually in India. The comparison would be $50k+ annually in the United States. While it's true that there are some efficiencies lost, and certainly some risk introduced, when outsourcing and especially outsourcing outside your host nation, the gains are obvious. Global companies, and even U.S.-centric companies, must compete with an expanding number of global competitors that come to the United States.

Another Terrorist Attack

Discussion of a terrorist attack might seem to be slightly out of place in this chapter and at this point in the book; however, next to loss of life, the long lasting impact is the stress it causes to our financial systems. When fear is fanned, many reactions are possible. Removing yourself from harm's way is one natural reaction, and the global travel and hospitality industries were taken to their knees as people feared the thought of getting on a plane, train, or even attending a major event after 9-11.

Imagine an attack that occurs in multiple public spaces, such as malls or parks, and the impact of people not purchasing consumer products and services at the same rates they currently do. Unfortunately, now after 9-11, we all have a baseline to see the impacts of such events. The reality is that the United States, and the rest of the world, rebounded quickly after 9-11 as the realization hit that the threat of further immediate attacks was unlikely. If there had been a series of attacks prolonged over several months, the impact to the United States would have been significantly more painful in both the short- and long-term. Extend these attacks to a few other nations and the global economy also begins to crumble.

Another serious threat is to the continuous flow of natural resources that the United States needs—specifically oil. If the continuity of these resources is interrupted, there are serious consequences. The Strategic Petroleum Reserve (SPR) is an emergency fuel store of oil maintained by the U.S. Department of Energy. It was created in 1975 when the United States realized the global supply could be cut off. According to the U.S. Department of Energy's latest numbers from December 27th, 2009, the Strategic Petroleum Reserve (SPR) currently has enough capacity to support the U.S.'s needs for just over one month. If you take into consideration oil that can be provided from the United States as a supplement, the United States would have enough oil for just less than two months. Unfortunately, the primary source for oil, and the routes it must transit, are more geographically convenient for the terrorist organizations.

We have come to realize how limited at the time were the resources of the terrorists outside of the primary terrorist networks, specifically the Middle East. While the actions taken immediately after the attacks now seem to be based on limited, and sometimes incorrect, information, the reality is no one knew what their resources were. Not taking any action would have been detrimental as well. Unfortunately, a byproduct of the Western world's reaction to the attacks, and specifically a reaction to the United States, is a broader and deeper level of hatred toward us. This unfortunately will likely lead to more financial resources being funneled to terrorist organizations that seek to harm our interests and those of our partners in the world. While we believe physical targets and human lives are still primary targets for terrorist organizations, we, like many others believe that more and more cyber-threats will come from state-sponsored and terrorist organizations.

The Outlook

Globally, IT security jobs will continue to grow in demand, as will the need for IT jobs. As described throughout the book, it is unlikely that product and software companies will integrate security within the core of their products at any level that impacts the need for external security products, services, and professional services, as such Chief Information Security Officers (CISOs) and security staffs, will continue to thrive. There will be some changes and we will see the need for these roles to continue to evolve in ways that leverage more project management, business climate, and global risk and compliance (GRC) skills.

Regionally, the United States will still have a healthy market for these careers far beyond the next 10 years. There will be pressures to find efficiencies with leveraging offshore IT resources just as there is today, and as a company's workforce becomes more global in nature the jobs will follow a similar distribution pattern. One hopes that the jobs go to the most qualified people and not the least expensive people. We suspect that with security there will be reluctance, in most cases, to move the function offshore for U.S.-headquartered companies. However, the more global and distributed a workforce and the more centralized IT is in a geography outside the United States, the more likely it is that the security function will also be moved outside the United States.

Within India there will be IT growth, but there will be significant competition from developing Asian countries, as well as from South America and Europe, where the workforces are becoming more IT literate and English is being taught as a secondary language through all levels of education. While there are still many challenges in outsourcing, more and more of them are being overcome through being overcome as we apply the experiences of the past 10 years with both failed and successful attempts.

China will certainly become an IT development hub for the United States, however, in what way it is hard to forecast as of yet. If China continues to develop at the rate it is today, and as it is forecasted to grow as the economy recovers, there will be significant consumption of the resources produced by China within China. It will also take many years for the cultures of China and the Western worlds to merge in ways that business transactions take place with ease. China has the advantage of being able to learn some things from India in regard to what works with the United States and what doesn't, but the cultural differences between China and India are so different that it is unlikely this will be of significant value. The same applies to U.S. companies that have done business in India; this will prove to be of little value in trying to transfer the experience to China.

The final variables to mention are the incentives and penalties being imposed by governments to discourage the use of non-national work resources. In 2009, the Obama administration ran on an election platform based on keeping U.S. jobs and penalizing U.S. companies that took U.S. jobs offshore. While this is always encouraging, if done without great consideration the end result will be simply making U.S. companies uncompetitive with their global counterparts. At worst, it forces companies to move their headquarters to friendlier countries.

That sounds like an extreme reaction by businesses until you consider the benefits Bermuda and other near shore countries offer because of their beneficial tax laws for businesses that have significant capital assets. Businesses are run by people; thus, the desire to survive is strong. This business requirement to seek the most cost-effective resources, including people, will define where jobs will reside over the next 10 to 50 years. In a global environment, key jobs such as security can reside anywhere the skills meet the business requirements.

Eleven (Maybe Not So Crazy) Scenarios That Could Happen

In three words I can sum up everything I've learned about life. It goes on.
—Robert Frost

Stories enhance our lives through creativity, imagination, knowledge transfer, and sometimes a simple recounting of history. We've also found that often the world around us is more entertaining than those stories that have sprung from our imaginations. In this chapter, we attempt to blend reality with imagination to predict events that might impact us over the next 10 years. While some of these ideas are based on, let's say some rather large assumptions and mythical projections, a lot could happen in the future that would surprise us. Whether you agree or disagree with these scenarios, they demonstrate the fragility of technology, our lives, and the world in which we live. These scenarios are built to provide a spark for you to consider how your business might address identical or similar events through countermeasure planning and preparation. Sometimes simply writing down a few straw-man action plans that address a given scenario will give you a basis for a quicker reaction to an event, and thus a competitive advantage for your business.

Situation One: Which Way Do I Go?

It's today, and the world is humming along. People are happily getting their Starbucks, the stock market is up, no major traffic jams, the wife and kids are healthy and well. Around the world the normal activity of commerce is occurring:

Location Profile 1: Four hundred eighty nautical miles southwest of Japan the heavy oil tanker *Constellation* is headed in from its transpacific trip. The ship is on autopilot with the various course corrections being made by the computer as wind, currents, and other influences of Mother Nature move the ship around. The crew is relaxed, doing their normal daily activities.

Location Profile 2: Several time zones away in the Northern Pacific, the ships fishing for king crab are returning to check the pots they set. After only 4 hours of rest for the crew, they are anxious to see the catch. Ice is everywhere, and the swells are at 12 feet. The slightest miscalculations can lead to the loss of tens or hundreds of thousands of dollars in equipment and cargo, and even the loss of life. Have you ever watched *World's Most Deadly Catch* on the National Geographic channel? You get the picture.

Location Profile 3: At Camp Lejeune, the Marine base on the eastern coast of North Carolina, a Marine task group is doing live fire testing with their new arsenal of guided missiles and flight support coordination systems. The Weapons Training Battalion exercise includes helicopters and the 10th Marine Regiment Artillery as well as 1st Battalion 2nd Marines ground troops and tanks, and air support. This follows an earlier recognizance exercise, which was led by the 2nd Marine Special Operations Battalion. Everyone is alert and aware of the dangers in a live fire exercise.

Location Profile 4: Over Iraq an Unmanned Aerial Vehicle (UAV) is taking live video and feeding it back to various military operational centers. Within the data stream is the Key Length Value (KLV) metadata that provide telemetry information from the onboard GPS unit. The pilot, in an undisclosed remote and safe location, sees the video and KLV data with a 100 ms delay and adjusts his flight based on points of interest.

Location Profile 5: All over the world. Each year, there are over 20 million manned flights, so on any given day there are almost 55 thousand recorded flights. Across the globe, thousands of commercial, private, and military aircraft, both manned and unmanned, are in the air as on any other typical day of our lives.

Now imagine that a large portion of the Global Positioning System (GPS) goes down. In each of the situations detailed in the Location Profiles just listed, failure of GPS could result in severe events such as loss of life or large-scale destruction of property; at minimum, each location would suffer loss of productivity and significant inconvenience.

How could GPS go down? GPS is a system with numerous backup components, but they are mostly controlled by common and/or connected systems. At this time, because of the necessity for automation, the need for cost effective management, systems updating, and general feeding of the control infrastructure and systems, the GPS network is connected to the public networks, and that is a weakness. Historically, many control networks, those that manage and provide controls for Department of Defense (DoD), utilities, and other highly sensitive networks, were in a closed network with no public Internet connections. While there are protected gateways and multiple layers of security, one small, seemingly innocent event could bring it down.

Imagine this scenario: The core management infrastructure for GPS just had a virus introduced by a contractor who let his child download an apparently harmless game onto his work computer because their home computer failed over the weekend. Sure, the management infrastructure is protected by a multi-tier security infrastructure, and policy prohibits the contractor from connecting his computer to the network, but the program he completed over the weekend was loaded on a memory stick and, because the program he wrote was uncompiled, the virus wrote itself into the software code. The Trojan could impact only a small population of systems in the world that had actual uncompiled software code. Worse, since the virus simply wrote a series of delayed commands stitched into the normal commands of the code that only activated on a rare combination of events, quality assurance testing of the application after it was compiled didn't catch the Trojan. Since the Trojan was in the compiled code, no antivirus software or malware caught it.

Because the contractor was a U.S. citizen, working on-site most of the time, and the application he wrote was only for a reporting module, the application had not been run through an in-depth software security review.

Six months later, the Trojan activates based on the rare combination of events the software normally monitors, and systematically targets all systems using the administrative password that it will sniff on the local system when the next administrator logs on. In the closed system, most of the admin logins and passwords are the same on multiple systems. Now with administrative password and root access to the entire Microsoft-based domain, it begins to copy any nonexecutable files in an attempt to capture personal information from within whichever network it may have infected. Fortunately, the core GPS Command and Control network is mostly self-contained and the Trojan doesn't find a way to connect outside the network. However, the secondary command of the Trojan instructs it to delete all system files and reboot . . . down goes the Command and Control network for the Global Positioning System and 40 percent of the world's GPS-based technology is no longer receiving coordinate information.

In 2010 GPS is a consumer luxury, but it's already a necessity in many businesses. Flash forward 5 years and most private vehicles now have GPS. Flash forward 10 years and every transport system is controlled through automation with only cursory human overview. Flash forward 20+ years and part of the population now has personal self-navigating transportation.

Our reliance on GPS increases every day, and even if you dismiss the fact that these systems, like any other in the world, can be compromised, you need to consider the Global Positioning System is at risk of failures and blackouts. In May 2010, Colonel Dave Buckman, command lead for position, navigation, and timing for the Air Force Space Command, stated boldly over Twitter that "the GPS will not go down," in response to a Government Accountability Office (GOA) report suggesting the high risk associated with a degradation in GPS performance.

In mid-2009 a federal watchdog agency warned the U.S. Congress that, as a direct result of underinvestment by the U.S. Air Force, the GPS infrastructure is at high risk of failure. According to the previously mentioned GOA report, "In recent years, the Air Force has struggled to successfully build GPS satellites within cost and schedule goals" as part of a $2 billion modernization program.

Buckman agreed with GOA that there was a risk of performance issues; however, the Air Force Space Command was indeed working to prevent any disruptions.

"We definitely need to keep this in perspective. Since 1995, GPS has never failed to exceed performance standards," Buckman argued.

In addition, the Obama Administration announced earlier this year that it will move forward with plans to shut down LORAN-C, a ground station that is the only backup for the current GPS system. At the time of publication, the U.S. Air Force was scrambling to find an alternative backup to GPS.

We all know that our lives, and our technologies, are becoming more and more dependent on GPS every day. Location-based services are intertwined with most mobile applications, and most are now completely reliant on getting from point A to point B through real-time mapping services. Over time, alternative GPS systems will be launched by other governments and by the private sector; however, for now we are primarily dependent on the U.S. government for our GPS. Therefore, let's keep our fingers crossed that the proper funding is supplied to maintain it; otherwise, our transportation systems could come to a chaotic halt. The best advice is to make sure safeguards are in place for when the GPS system goes down. Make sure that the transition from technology controls for telemetry input to human controls and input can happen in a controlled and predictable fashion without GPS. Fortunately, Starbucks is on every corner, so at least we will be able to find our $5 coffee fix while they fix the GPS system when it fails.

Situation Two: Is the Network Down?

September 11, 2001 was a sad and eye-opening day. I can honestly say that I had never thought about a terrorist using a plane as a supermissile to take lives, destroy landmarks, and make a worldwide emotional and economical impact. Since that time, I have thought how injudicious these terrorists really are. In Chapter 1, I wrote about the period of time when hackers would compromise a website and all they would do is post their picture or modify the home page with profanity or other messages. I thought, "Wow, you had that level of access, and all you wanted to do was be known." This is now how I feel about the terrorists of 9/11. While the World Trade Center buildings, Pentagon, and White House are lofty targets to be sure, all the terrorists got out of that is emotional impact. If they really wanted to bring the United States to its knees, other targets would have been far more advantageous.

Imagine destroying (with planes or anything else), the major nexus points for the telecommunications of nearly all of the United States. These nexus points aren't just the Internet; they include all any data network (private or public) Internet, fax, mobile phone, and nearly every other communication method we rely on. Stock trades get processed through these lines. Credit card transactions are performed. Literally everything that makes our world go around happens though the complex telecommunications network that criss-crosses this country. Without it, we would be back to the stone age, temporarily or permanently, depending on several factors, including government and military involvement, social order, and a host of other things.

What few realize is that there are a handful of locations called "carrier hotels" where all these lines, cables, microwave dishes, fiber-optic cables, carriers, telecommunication providers, exchanges, and everything else all meet up. Carrier hotels are collocation facilities that are usually vendor neutral, where one provider can hand off service to another provider. The locations of these carrier hotels are well known to anyone in the telecommunications industry and are usually identified by their actual street address. For example, the largest and most utilized carrier hotel on the west coast is "One Wilshire," the address in Los Angeles, California of the building (see Figure 9-1).

Figure 9-1

In the 1980s, deregulation was looming and Pacific Bell banned competitors from mounting microwave antennas on their building. As a result, competitor and long-distance provider MCI mounted its own microwave station on one of the tallest buildings in Los Angeles, One Wilshire. And so began One Wilshire's importance as a telecommunications site.

These buildings have what are known as *meet me rooms*. A meet me room is a physical location where connections, peering points, and links are made. They are usually full of cages and racks separating one entity from another. Cables are everywhere, oftentimes under the floor, in "risers," or are on horizontal ladders near the ceiling. Figure 9-2 shows two views of a meet me room.

Figure 9-2

Said to be the most interconnected space in the world and the most expensive real estate in North America, the meet me room is the heart of One Wilshire. Here the primary fiber optic cables are routed, split, and shared. Because of the presence of so many telecommunication providers and companies in this room and the ability to freely interconnect between them, rackspace here becomes extremely valuable. For comparison, the average price for office space in downtown Los Angeles is $1.75 per square foot per month. At the meet me room, $250 per square foot would be a bargain.

Over 1800 known conduits contain the fiber optic cables that flow through One Wilshire's stairwells and vertical utility corridors, called risers (see Figure 9-3). Cable connects the commercial tenants on floors 5 through 29 to the 4th floor meet me room, and to a wireless meet me room constructed on the 30th floor.

As you can imagine, there is a lot of cable entering and exiting this building. As a result, the impact of local road construction could be devastating. Whenever a permit is pulled by a city contractor for any underground repairs outside One Wilshire, the various telecommunication companies with cable in the area come out and paint the cable routes on the asphalt, creating a visible graphic of the complexity of what lies just under the surface, as shown in Figure 9-4. This is known as a "Surface Cable Map."

Figure 9-3

Figure 9-4

The main fiber-optic cables connecting One Wilshire to the world enter the building from under the street through closets in the walls of the building's parking garage, as shown in Figure 9-5. Given the importance of the building to the global communications network, access to the parking garage is controlled, and the building is said to be monitored continuously by federal security officials.

Figure 9-5

These carrier hotels are not easy to move or replace. The physical cable routed there, the cooling requirements of the computer telecommunications equipment, humidity controls, fire suppression, and a host of other factors evolve at these carrier hotels, making them some of our country's most valuable locations. One very unique requirement of a location like this is power consumption.

In the event of a blackout, the building's five generators will automatically start. It takes the generators three seconds to engage and stabilize. During this brief period, the entire building runs on batteries. There are 11,000 gallons of diesel stored on-site, enough to run the generators for 24 hours before being refueled. It isn't difficult to spot a telco hotel from the sky either. (See Figure 9-6.)

Figure 9-6

The existence of telco hotels in the region around One Wilshire is indicated by the presence of new and extensive cooling units on the roofs of adjacent buildings, many of which were nearly vacant until the telco companies moved in.[1]

An attack on a site such as One Wilshire would be extremely disruptive to businesses all across the world. Combining that with a coordinated attack against other critical carrier hotels would be cataclysmic. As I mentioned before, there are only a handful of these nexus points; a few of the prime targets are as follows:

60 Hudson Street, New York City, New York

60 Hudson Street is a major telecommunications facility and an historic landmark located in Lower Manhattan, New York City, not far from where the World Trade Center buildings used to be. During the heyday of the telegraph, 60 Hudson, then known as the Western Union Building, was a premier nexus of worldwide communications (see Figure 9-7). After Western Union moved its headquarters to New Jersey, the building was converted into a carrier hotel where over 100 telecommunications companies have offices and can interchange telecommunications traffic through a meet me room. It is a premier nexus of world-wide communications.

Figure 9-7

In 2006, a New York City panel approved the storage of nearly 2000 gallons (7500 liters) of diesel fuel on six floors of the building, part of some 80,000 gallons (300,000 liters) of fuel oil stored in the building.

The strategic location of 60 Hudson St. is widely utilized within the industry by such customers as AT&T, Bell Canada, British Telecom, China Netcom, China Telecom, Level 3, SBC, Time Warner Telecom, and Verizon.

900 North Franklin Street, Chicago, IL 60610

900 North Franklin, shown in Figure 9-8, is located in the heart of downtown Chicago and sits on top of dual OC48-BLSR4 SONET rings as well as many other telecommunication lines. These SONET rings provide the carrier hotel with Tier 1 connectivity to numerous network carriers.

Figure 9-8

56 Marietta, Atlanta, Georgia

56 Marietta is a 160,000 sq. ft. fully dedicated carrier hotel/interconnect facility that is home to the Southeast's largest concentration of telecommunication companies. 56 Marietta is usually over 90 percent occupied with 60+ carriers and over 100 telecommunications-related companies.

There are a few other carrier hotels that hold this same level of criticality if destroyed. Some companies rely solely upon a single facility for all their telecommunications. Companies that are well prepared for disaster and most telecommunication providers have redundant lines that can stay online if a single location is destroyed. However, the weak point in this scheme is that these providers have their alternate lines through one of the other major centers. That is why a coordinated attack against all the major carrier hotels would be a very effective attack indeed. There are probably only six to eight locations that would have to be targeted to cause a major telecommunications blackout that would be very difficult to recover from. Recovery (if possible) would be measured in terms of weeks, and more likely months.

A coordinated, lethal attack against these critical locations would literally shut down the United States and many parts of the world. Creative attackers could use planes, dirty bombs, or any number of other methods. Probably an Oklahoma City bombing–style attack would be the most simple and effective to successfully execute. Fires combined with the explosive material stored in these buildings is a recipe for a destructive magnitude that is difficult to comprehend. I don't think it is possible for anyone to imagine the full impact of an attack like this. Needless to say, it would be immeasurably more devastating than 9/11.

Situation Three: Snip the Wires

What if someone wanted to have the same impact as destroying carrier hotels, but didn't want to have to coordinate the bombing of all these targets? Well, as it turns out, there is an easier way to get the same effect, and all you need is a pair of bolt cutters (Figure 9-9). But first, a little background.

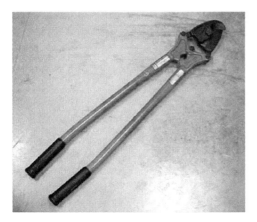

Figure 9-9

In 1988, a reclusive Denver billionaire named Philip Anschutz acquired Southern Pacific from Santa Fe Industries, after the Interstate Commerce Commission ruled that the 1983 merger of the Atchison, Topeka and Santa Fe Railroad with Southern Pacific was anticompetitive.

SP Telecom was established in San Francisco in 1988 as a subsidiary of Southern Pacific Transportation Co. It was founded to construct telecommunications lines along Southern Pacific's 15,000 miles of railroad right-of-way. Anschutz had the vision to not only make this part of his company a subsidiary, but in 1992, he negotiated an easement agreement with Southern Pacific to lay fiber-optic cable along 11,700 miles of its track as well (Figure 9-10). (I should probably note that SP Telecom was not the first successful telecommunications spin-off from Southern Pacific. Earlier, the railroad company had created and sold another subsidiary that later became Sprint Corp.) In 1995, Anschutz acquired the Dallas-based firm Qwest Communications Corp and they made their headquarters in Denver, Colorado.[2]

Figure 9-10

The company developed a train engine, shown in Figure 9-11, that would dig up the ground next to the rails and bury fiber-optic cable, all while traveling down the track.

Figure 9-11

What you see is a two-dimensional image as if looking down on the earth. So naturally, all of the fiber lines are safely underground and their exact locations probably not easily identifiable right? Wrong. What happens when those train tracks come to a body of water or a larger river? They build a bridge. In the case of the fiber-optic networks, these cables become exposed and are suspended over the river or lake. All it would take is someone with some bolt cutters to walk up to these exposed lines and "snip." While this doesn't have the long-lasting effects destroying a carrier hotel does, a similar outage could be created, disrupting telecommunication for a matter of days at least.

So where are these critical fiber points? I am not going to tell you. But ask yourself how difficult it would be to overlay a fiber map, railroad map, and geography map (specifically with river and lakes). Could it be that easy?

Situation Four: The Pandemic

"Ladies and gentlemen, thanks for joining us today. In just a moment we will close the cabin doors. We ask that each of you quickly store your luggage and find your seats so that we may depart on time," came from the overhead speakers. The passengers stored their luggage and with some frustration and adjustments each bag found a home in the overheads or under the seats of the plane. A full flight, as is normal these days. This flight, on January 11, 2013, a Boeing 757 scheduled to fly from Washington DC to Los Angeles, is carrying 279 passengers.

Patrick looked to his right and introduced himself, "Are you on your way home, or is home DC?"

An elderly gentleman in a business suit turned and responded, "Actually I live in Orange County, but this was the best flight I could get from Cairo. Yourself?"

"I've flown in from London. I live in LA."

"Seems that we both had quite a trip."

"Indeed, I was in Asia the past few weeks and then India . . . Hong Kong, Singapore, and Korea," replied Patrick looking a bit tired from his travels.

"Seems we passed each other at some point during your travels. I was in Hong Kong as well. I was in Cairo as I mentioned, but also South Africa earlier." Replied the gentleman, "I'm George."

"Nice to meet a fellow traveler. I'm Patrick."

These fellow travelers spoke on occasion. They watched a movie, and like most of the other travelers who had connected through IAD, visited the restroom a couple times during this trip.

Of the 279 travelers, 78 of them connected in DC from 8 other countries and 53 passengers will connect to 23 cities in the U.S. and 4 international locations. Each passenger will come in close contact with, on average, 12 people over the next 24 hours and close vicinity with 44 people during the same period. So, in summary:

- 53 people will come into contact with over 2300 people, as follows:
- 38 people will come into contact with 44 people each in 23 U.S. cities resulting in direct or casual exposure to over 1672 people.
- 15 people will come into contact with 44 people each in four international locations, resulting in contact with over 660 people through direct or casual contact.
- 226 people will come into contact with 44 people each in Southern California, resulting in direct or casual contact with over 9944 people.

So in total, over 279 people and their direct contacts will have casual or direct contact with the 12,276 passengers from the flight spanning over five countries in three continents in less than 24 hours. Now, throw in a passenger that is infectious, not demonstrating any severe symptoms as of yet, who rode in the economy section with a disease that can be exchanged through airborne means. Jin Lee had been visiting Ireland for 2 days from South Korea prior to the flight. He now was going to LA to visit his brother he had not seen for 10 years. Unfortunately, and to Jin's surprise, he had been exposed to an infectious disease released by a North Korean terrorist group on a parking shuttle when he parked his car back in South Korea. This designer infectious disease was created to wreak havoc on the world's population and spread through both airborne and physical contact. The original plan had been to infect a group of host North Korean volunteers and send them out into the world; however, it was anticipated this might be difficult given the international climate and suspicions towards North Korean citizens. As such, they simply paid a relative in South Korea to "spill a bottle of water" on the shuttle, implying to this innocent South Korean relative that it was simply a signal to another passenger they needed to get across the border, not that they were releasing a global pandemic. Not knowing the truth, the person unwittingly infected himself and 18 other passengers on the shuttle. The average disease takes 24 hours to 4 days before symptoms are obvious. This disease was designed to take 5–7 days for outward symptoms, but was infectious from day 2 through death. Worse, the initial symptoms are flu-like, but after 7–10 days, the brain swells until the infected person dies. The disease, a modified version of the flu, had characteristics that caused rapid mutations.

Now, consider the compounding effect that occurs when each of the 12,276 people directly or indirectly exposed to our original passengers come into contact with others around the world. (This doesn't take into account the other passengers at the original source location, the parking shuttle, where 18 passengers and a driver were exposed to the pathogen and have been infecting others.) With some general assumptions, you can calculate that within 5 days several million people would have casual contact with a network of people downstream of our original Washington DC to Los Angeles travelers.

The immediate reaction of any government to an outbreak this widespread and serious would to be to quarantine the population. To what extreme the quarantine is applied is the question. How long will it last? Will they find a quick cure or will it take an extended period? Will the disease mutate (as proposed in this scenario)? Will more diseases be released in other locations? Will more than one disease with similar symptoms be released and confuse the situation? How much will our confidence be shaken and our fears run rampant? How will people safely get basic necessities such as food?

Regardless of the answers to these questions, the Internet and our corporate networks will be challenged to adapt to the changes. First, simple changes such as enabling mobility will be a high priority. Simple things such as purchasing laptops for employees that historically had desktops or enabling their personal computers to connect to the corporate network will be challenging. Printers, scanners, mobile phones, or call forwarding controls from corporate will all be needed. New access bandwidth and connectivity for voice and data will be required to support the increased load. Do most employees even have Internet access at home today? Most of us in technology jobs would say yes, but how about other industries? Beyond most white collar work, how will manufacturing and services business operate? Revenues will fall and personnel will be let go . . . the downward spiral of businesses will hit hard and fast.

A natural pandemic occurs on average 3–4 times per century as compared to epidemics which occur each year. Typically, it takes researchers 6–9 months to create a vaccine for a mutation in the disease. Through natural or engineered mutations, during the time between vaccines, large population fatalities could occur if the disease is not contained.

The common flu impacts 5–20 percent of the U.S. population each year, with an estimated $10 billion financial impact. Given the amount of press it received, we all probably remember the threat of the bird flu that started in 2005 and is still present. Avian flu, or H1N1 flu, was identified in Hong Kong in 1997. The global media picked up the story when 1.5 million birds were killed in Hong Kong in an attempt to contain the disease. The flu then spread to other animals, including humans. A major concern was the fact that it typically takes researchers 6–9 months to create a vaccine for a mutation in a disease and mutations often happen quickly when a disease jumps from one species to another. The CDC projected an infected passenger flying from Asia to Denver, through contact on the plane and then those individuals spreading out to their destinations, could create a nationwide pandemic in the United States within 48 hours. The flu's mortality rate was 60 percent for those infected. Fortunately, the flu has not, to date, had the widespread impact that was originally anticipated as it did not spread in a predictable flu-like fashion.

As security and business continuity professionals, a little planning with senior management to anticipate these types of naturally occurring pandemics, and the threat of human-introduced pandemics, is a good investment of company resources and time.

Situation Five: Cyber-Hijacking, Blackmail, and Ransom

Imagine getting a call where the person on the other end of the phone tells you that if you do not do everything they say, they will kill you. They go on to tell you that they have gained access to your newly installed pacemaker and will turn it off or send an electrical current that could kill you if you do not comply with their demands. Not possible?

In July 2009, the United States Food and Drug Administration (FDA) approved the use of pacemakers that allow doctors to monitor the conditions of patients over the Internet. In July of 2009, Carol Kasyjanski (age 61) became the first American recipient of the wireless pacemaker.[3] Dr. Steven Greenberg, her doctor and director of St. Francis's Arrhythmia and Pacemaker Center, said that the new wireless technology will likely become the new standard in pacemakers as well as other medical devices.

This wireless pacemaker, shown in Figure 9-12, is made by St. Jude Medical Inc. although there are many patents for wireless medical devices of one kind or another.

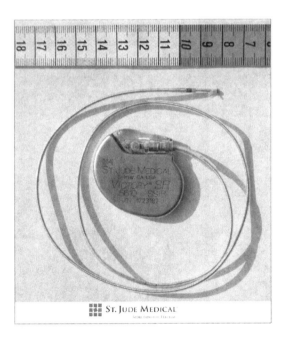

Figure 9-12

There are more than three million people worldwide with pacemakers and 600,000 more are implanted each year. But these aren't the only medical devices going high tech. Millions of patients benefit from implantable medical devices that treat chronic ailments such as diabetes, cardiac arrhythmia, and even Parkinson's disease with various combinations of electrical therapy and drug infusion. The most modern of these devices utilize radio communications for diagnostic and therapeutic functions, which allow doctors to remotely monitor patients' vital signs via the Internet. Previously, medical professionals would use regular clinical checkups. Now with just their web browser, they can get real-time updates on patients. George Wood, a 73-year-old Midland, Canada man, is the first to have implanted a defibrillator that can be remotely controlled over the Internet.

A recent study released by Kevin Fu, Assistant Professor at the University of Massachusetts Amherst, entitled "Implantable Medical Devices: Security and Privacy for Pervasive, Wireless Healthcare" states the following:

> *The rapid convergence of medical devices with wireless communication and Internet connectivity gives rise to an increased risk to security and privacy. Such devices must now defend against *intentional* malfunctions caused by malevolence. Our interdisciplinary research team used a software radio to test in vitro the security and privacy of a real implantable cardioverter defibrillator. Our findings demonstrate a variety of threats to patient privacy and device safety. For instance, an unauthenticated wireless command causes a shock that is known to induce a fatal heart rhythm.*[4]

Will it be possible in the future for hackers to compromise systems and simply stop your heart or inject drugs that could kill you?

What about more standard equipment that hospitals and doctors' offices use? For over a decade, many medical equipment manufacturers have used remote control and monitoring software. These systems are used in nearly every hospital and medical office worldwide. These systems were designed to perform system diagnostics and automatically report back to the manufacturer when problems occur. Some of these systems include software that allows someone across the Internet to take control of the system and reprogram it if necessary.

The Healthcare Information Portability and Accountability Act (HIPAA) does not do anything to protect these systems, but all protocols, access points, and systems are designed in compliance with these regulations.

Some of these devices utilize third-party remote access software modules. Over time, bugs and software vulnerabilities are found in these programs. Usually, these software programs are left unpatched, exposed, and vulnerable for years. Exploiting these known vulnerabilities is one method of gaining control of these systems.

The majority of these systems are designed to monitor the battery life, power consumptions, and other base-level features of the devices. These systems offer the ability to remotely turn off, turn on, power cycle, check temperature, remotely control, and manage I/O devices. While the capabilities available through remote control may have been limited in years past, manufacturers, vendors, suppliers, doctors, and other medical professionals want access to these devices 24/7 from anywhere, which means Internet access.

If a cyber-criminal were able to access these systems, a myriad of possibilities unfold. An inaccurate diagnosis may occur. One patient's records could be altered or swapped for those of another patient. Critical alarms could be disabled. Unneeded and harmful or potentially lethal drugs could be prescribed.

What if cyber-criminals used this as a method of attack against politicians or their family members? What about high net worth individuals being targeted for ransom or other exploitation? What other types of manipulation tactics could be employed when you have this type of control?

Situation Six: The Facebook Killer

For many people, social networking services such as Facebook have become the primary method by which friends, family, and associates keep up on each other's lives and socialize with one another. This has led to a drastic reduction in telephone conversations as well as in-person get-togethers. I know of people who literally go days and even weeks with only communicating through social networking mediums.

Jill's friends and family began to worry about her after they haven't heard from her in several days. Jill had recently graduated from college and began looking for a job. She lived in a one-bedroom apartment by herself, broke up with her boyfriend just prior to graduation, and had been dating heavily ever since. Normally, Jill kept in touch with friends and family via Facebook, making several posts a day. Since the advent of Facebook, Jill had little need to keep in touch via the phone any longer. Her friends and family were used to her common posts and felt like they were keeping up with her life better since she began using Facebook in her sophomore year. They knew she was busy dating and looking for a job, but it was very rare to not get several posts each day from her and for the last two days, there had been none. Members of her family began calling her, but she didn't answer. She lived in another city so they called the police. The police arrived at her apartment to find no one was there. A missing persons report was filed and the police began to investigate.

In the apartment, her luggage was still there, despite her recent Facebook posts regarding an interview that would take her away for a couple of days. Perhaps she had returned or had taken a smaller bag for clothes. There was no sign of the things her family said she would never go anywhere without, including her purse, laptop, and mobile phone. Her posts did not indicate where exactly she was going or whom she would be with. They never mentioned the names of the companies she was having interviews with, although investigators found a job application on her desk. She also mentioned several times going out but never with whom. She did name a few common hang-out places that she often went. The investigators took pictures of Jill to those locations. Patrons and employees certainly recognized her, but none of them recalled her being there in the last week or so. They contacted the company where she had filled out an application. They stated that they had set up an interview with her the previous week, but she never showed up. This was very unlike "prompt and reliable" Jill, her family told the investigators.

Her family provided all the communications they had received from her prior to her disappearance. The investigators began reviewing the Facebook posts for the previous several weeks, looking for clues as to what happened. One tech-savvy investigator noticed a difference in the way her most recent posts look as compared to historical posts. In more recent posts, she had only two spaces between sentences and her older posts had only one space. Additionally, Jill used to word "too" properly before, but in her final posts used the word "to" where it should have been "too." The investigator decided to look into this further. He learned of a "textual analysis" expert who claimed it was possible to do analysis of textual writings just like one does handwriting analysis. The expert ran all the text samples they could find through the computer. Sure enough, they found that the text that was posted the week before she disappeared has a very different text signature than prior posts. The investigator began to believe that someone else made the posts on her behalf.

The investigators used her Facebook profile to identify all her friends and contacts that live near her. They began to interview each one, but none saw her a week or more before her family determined she was missing, and all had strong alibis. They interviewed recent dates, friends she spent time with, and her previous boyfriend, all of whom knew nothing about what happened to her. Just as the investigators were about to give up with no new leads to go on, the same tech-savvy investigator decided to take the text samples from the last week of her Facebook posts, and run them against all of her Facebook friends' posts. Almost immediately a match was made. It was her old boyfriend Tom.

They questioned Tom. He had a strong alibi for the time Jill went missing. He was with friends, family, or coworkers pretty much constantly for at least a week prior to Jill going missing. Jill's mother got a call from someone who said they had found a phone and she was the first contact in the contact list and they wanted to return it to its owner. Jill's mom learned it was Jill's phone that had been found near a dumpster only a few miles from Jill's apartment. The police took the phone as evidence. The phone had been wiped clean of prints. Investigators saw the posts made to Facebook from the smart phone. They also saw a series of photos that were taken, one of which is identified as being near Tom's place of employment.

They bring Tom in for questioning. After hours of interrogation, he admitted he had abducted Jill and tells investigators where they can find the body.

He admits he used her phone and laptop to falsify Facebook posts to throw investigators off his track.

Situation Seven: Is It Getting Hot?

We all understand that certain events are completely outside the control of man. Numerous movies and documentaries have been written about earthquakes, meteoroid strikes, tidal waves, a polar shift, alien invasions, and the unnatural mutations of many creatures. As time passes, inherently the risk to the Earth being impacted by celestial events increases because of the simple laws of probability. In 2012, a new 11-year solar cycle will occur once again. According to NASA, during the later part of each cycle there is typically an increase in intensity and activity levels. In addition, there are more anomalous fluctuations with extreme lower or higher intensity levels. Some scientist projected that this cycle will represent an 8000-year high for solar flare intensity. Coincidentally, or maybe not, one of the prophesied doomsdays is to occur on December 21, 2012. Is this prophecy, which is based on the fact that the Mayan calendar is not documented beyond this point in time, actually based on factual science? Did this ancient Mayan civilization understand that the sun's magnetism undergoes polarity changes every 11 years or so?

What will happen with increased solar flare activity? First, the sun has always generated solar flares. However, during the time of the 11-year solar maximum, when the sun is most active, an explosive solar flare with the energy of 100 billion Hiroshima-sized atomic bombs may occur. Although these larger flares will occur nearly 100 million miles away, they will cause problems here on Earth.

The predictions of damage resulting from these large flares vary, but to summarize, scientists forecast several resulting events:

1. Solar flares come in many forms, one of which is the X-ray flare. X-ray flares travel at the speed of light; thus, we get little warning when one will hit the Earth; at the speed of light, an X-ray can reach the Earth in around 8 minutes. We are somewhat protected by the ionosphere, the outermost layer of the Earth's atmosphere absorbs much of the X-ray's power. The result, however, is that the ionosphere becomes more charged, thus blocking many radio waves, especially high-frequency waves.

    NASA states the following about X-rays:

    along with energetic ultraviolet radiation, they heat the Earth's outer atmosphere, causing it to expand. This increases the drag on Earth-orbiting satellites, reducing their lifetime in orbit. Also, both intense radio emission from flares and these changes in the atmosphere can degrade the precision of Global Positioning System (GPS) measurements.

2. A more severe event might be produced on the sun: a coronal mass ejection (CME). While a CME does not travel at the speed of light, the first effects can hit the Earth within several hours, although in general they take 3–5 days to reach the Earth. Also, their effects on Earth and our local orbit can be more impactful than X-ray flares. A benign result is the aurora light shows, typical seen close to the Earth's poles. A more severe impact is the radiation levels external of the Earth's magnetosphere where unprotected spacecraft, astronauts, and satellites might be impacted. Another result is the expansion of the Earth's atmosphere because of solar winds. In this scenario, satellites could lose orbit because of an expanding atmosphere.

3. In rare situations, currents at ground level on Earth can increase as well. A real-world example occurred on March 13, 1989, when six million people lost power in the Quebec region of Canada after a huge increase in solar activity caused a surge from ground-induced currents. Quebec was paralyzed for 9 hours while engineers worked on a solution to the problem. Sweden has been impacted similarly as well. The probability of impact is increasing as well, given that as part of a natural cycle, 5 percent of the magnetic field of the Earth is being lost each decade. As the magnetic field decreases, the impact of solar flares and CMEs will increase as we are less protected.

So why should we care? Most concerns in IT security are based on the ability of outside influences, such as hackers, to compromise our IT infrastructure. Would the world be impacted if we lost 10 percent, 25 percent, 50 percent or 100 percent of our satellite communications? Would you be impacted? NASA states that:

There are over 936 operating satellites in space, worth an estimated $200 billion to replace. They account for nearly $225 billion in revenue for the international telecommunications industry every year.

They are protected by NOAA's staff of 50 space weather forecasters on a reduced annual (FY05) budget of $5 million.

Worse, how would your business be impacted if you were without power, and those around you were also out of power? The reality is that the North American, specifically the United States's, power grids operate at near peak capacity. The impact of a CME could easily be a nationwide power outage. In one geographic area you would have large-scale outages, while in other regions there would be no impact. As NASA reports:

"From a public policy perspective, it is quite significant that we have begun the extremely challenging task of assessing space weather impacts in a quantitative

way," said Daniel Baker, professor and director of the Laboratory for Atmospheric and Space Physics at the University of Colorado in Boulder. Baker chaired the panel that prepared the report.

"Whether it is terrestrial catastrophes or extreme space weather incidents, the results can be devastating to modern societies that depend in a myriad of ways on advanced technological systems," said Baker.

Further analysis, specific to the United States, shows that given the continued technology advancements and reliance on the our national power grid to support electronics, an outage, especially an extended outage, could result in significant loss of life, disruption of critical transportation, and significant impacts to government services. Most developed countries would be similarly impacted. Figure 9-13 shows the areas that would most probably be impacted.

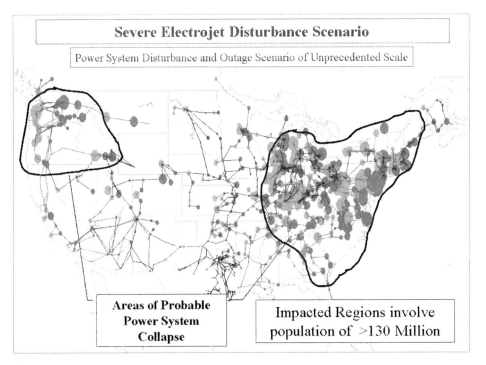

Figure 9-13

Source: http://www.nasa.gov/images/content/299632main_sun_hazards_lg.jpg

In 2006 NASA predicted the 24th solar cycle, peaking in 2012, to have significant activity and intensity; however, those predictions have not come true. For now, the good news is most scientists agree that 2012 is unlikely to be a major earth-impacting solar cycle. The one thing to keep in mind of course is that predicting the sun's activities is much like predicting the weather. Therefore, I think that should give each of us a little pause as we pass through 2012.

As security professionals, we are also responsible for the continuity of our IT infrastructure and protecting it from man-made and natural catastrophes. Preparation for this type of event will help separate good IT security professionals from great ones. While you can't prepare for all scenarios, you should understand the risk and preventative measures that can be taken. Often you will find that common threats, especially natural ones, have some of the same basic preventative measures.

See the following sources for more information about the issues raised in this section:

- The Solar Flare Theory Educational Web Pages (NASA's Goddard Space Flight Center): `http://hesperia.gsfc.nasa.gov/sftheory/index.htm`

- 2012: Beginning of the End or Why the World Won't End?: `http://www.nasa.gov/topics/earth/features/2012.html`

Situation Eight: Which Way Is Up

Continuing on the theme of 2012, let's look at the scenario called polar shift. In this event, the polarity of the poles shifts. In other words, north becomes south and south becomes north. There is also historical proof that, on average, the earth has had a polar shift every 300,000 years; it's been 780,000 years since the last one. Other variables include a 1 degree per decade polar shift and a 5 percent per decade reduction in the Earth's magnetic field. How the shifting of the Earth's poles actually occurs is heavily debated. How long it takes for the shift to occur ranges from instantaneously with mass devastation to occurring over thousands of years with only the magnetic references changing, not a physical movement of the Earth's tectonic plates. A geomagnetic shift is different than a polar shift and is believed to happen rarely, the last one occurring 800 million+ years ago. A geomagnetic shift is when the Earth's physical polar regions shift.

The scientific counterarguments are equally compelling that a polar shift isn't occurring December of 2012. For example, if it has been 780,000 years since the last polar shift and the average is 300,000 year, aren't we overdue? Based on averages, obviously yes; however, scientists believe there have been other periods where shifts did not occur for as much as 4 million years. The actual pole location, which is now in Canada, is believed to constantly shift, and thus what some are pointing to as the beginning of a major shift is actually normal. How about the reduced magnetic field? Again, there's compelling data that this should be happening; however, the magnetic field is actually at a high relative to the past 1000 years, and in fact it is higher than the average. The magnetic field apparently fluctuates quite a bit.

How to prepare? Okay, if this scenario happens, our businesses are going to be the least of our worries. Rule #1 on each of these scenarios: focus on and prioritize things you can impact.

See the following source for more information about the issues raised in this section:

- Ends of the Earth (National Geographic Channel) `http://channel.nation-algeographic.com/channel/ends-of-the-earth`

Situation Nine: Cyber-Hypothermia, Cyber-Heat-Stroke, Utility Terrorism

I hesitate to put this in the "things that could happen" section of the book because there is speculation that this either has happened or nearly happened already. Attacks on utility company networks and systems could cause brownouts or blackouts. Attacks such as these happening during a heat wave, disabling air conditioning systems, could (and likely would) cause fatalities, especially for the elderly or infirm.

These days, every utility problem, blackout or otherwise, is blamed on hackers . . . usually of the Chinese variety. Is there any merit to these claims? The *National Journal* on May 31, 2008 reported[5] that hackers may have been responsible for both the 2003 northeastern blackout and the February 2008 Florida blackout. Their story, entitled "China's Cyber-Militia," says Chinese hackers pose a clear and present danger to U.S. government and private-sector computer networks and may be responsible for two major U.S. power blackouts. The reporter cites computer security professionals, who in turn cite unnamed U.S. intelligence officials, who say that China's People's Liberation Army may have cracked the computers controlling the U.S. power grid to trigger the cascading 2003 blackout that cut off electricity to 50 million people in eight states and a Canadian province.

The Northeast Blackout of 2003 was a extensive power outage that occurred throughout parts of the Northeastern and Midwestern United States and Ontario, Canada on Thursday, August 14, 2003, at approximately 4:15 p.m. EDT (see Figure 9-14). At the time, it was the second most widespread electrical blackout in history (the first being the 1999 Southern Brazil blackout). The blackout affected about 55 million people total between the United States and Canada.

Figure 9-14

Source: `http://en.wikipedia.org/wiki/File:Map_of_North_America,_blackout_2003.svg` Image by Lokal_Profil

In February 2004, the U.S.-Canada Power System Outage Task Force presented their final report, identifying as the main cause of the blackout FirstEnergy Corporation's failure to trim trees in part of its Ohio service area. The report states that a generating plant in Eastlake, Ohio (near Cleveland), went offline amid high electrical demand, putting a strain on high-voltage power lines (located in a remote rural setting), which later went out of service when they came in contact with "overgrown trees." The cascading effect that resulted forced the shutdown of more than 100 power plants. Apparently when power plants sense severe volatility in the lines, they go into "safe mode," which effectively shuts them down to avoid overload. This is because electricity is used within a second or so of being produced. There is no method or capacity for large-scale storage, therefore shutdown is the only alternative.

Some speculate that the unseasonably hot day (about 88°F across many affected regions) resulted in higher than expected energy demand from air conditioning systems, which caused power lines to sag as higher currents heated the lines. These sagging lines came in contact with the overgrown trees in rural Ohio. Simultaneous to this was a computer "bug" that caused FirstEnergy's primary and backup systems to fail, and in all the chaos FirstEnergy failed to sever the connection to the larger regional power grid, sending erratic data showing false line conditions and effectively shutting down about 100 other power plants.

Some speculate a more sinister cause. Some might ask, why would hackers be interested in compromising the power grid and causing an outage? Military tacticians will tell you that any time you can create fear, panic, and chaos in war, it gives you an enormous advantage. So what causes fear, panic, and chaos? Usually those things that disrupt society, such as critical services, water, sewers, transportation, communication, can create a situation where social order can break down.

The northeast power outage hampered most essential services. Backup generation for many areas did not work as expected or capacity was too low. Water pressure in many areas was limited or nonexistent because of inoperable electric pumps. In some areas, this allowed sewage to creep into the water lines, forcing some to boil water to drink.

Communications remained operational in most areas; however, the increased demand overloaded the circuits, making it difficult for most to make calls . . . including emergency service calls. Mobile phone networks experienced significant service disruptions from overload because of the increased volume of calls.

In large cities, electrified commuter railways are often used and during this outage those were not in service, nor was the interstate passenger rail transport North-East Corridor service. Some cities were able to make some diesel-powered alternatives available within 48 hours. There was also an impact on air transport. Even the effects on the financial markets were widespread.

The blackout contributed to at least 11 fatalities. Some fatalities were a result of fires caused by candles. One man had a heart attack after having to climb 17 flights of stairs. In one interesting case, a guy was using the blackout opportunity to loot. During his attempt to break into a shoe store from the roof, he fell off and did not survive the impact. While no one died from heat stroke in the 2003 incident, imagine if that had happened in Phoenix rather than the northeast.

So how difficult is it to execute an attack compromising the U.S. power grid or other vital infrastructure? What is the likelihood of this occurring?

A survey of 100 information security experts at U.S. energy companies found that the majority believe that the standards set forth by the North American Electric Reliability Corp (NERC) are not adequate to protect the country's electric power grid.[6] More than half of those responding to the survey said that they must address at least 150 serious attacks each and every week. Two-thirds of respondents said they deal with at least 75 intrusions every week.

The Associated Press reported spies hacking into the U.S. power grid and installing malware that would allow them to disrupt service. The discovery of the intrusion came as a result of a government audit. The audit was triggered as a result of the March 2007 video released from the Idaho National Laboratory demonstrating what damage hackers could do if they seized control of a critical part of the electric grid. The video showed a power turbine spinning out of control, smoking, shaking, and shutting down.

The Wall Street Journal, which also reported this incident, noted that officials believe that the spies have not yet sought to do any damage to the national electric grid, but that they likely would in the case of war or another crisis. As you can imagine, governments, including the Chinese and Soviets, have denied any involvement in hacks on the U.S. systems.

The heart of the vulnerabilities lies in the technologies these utility companies use to manage, and especially remotely control, these systems and facilities. Some are even connected to the Internet. Employees who work remotely can cause major problems for any organization, but for utilities, it can be catastrophic. If the remote computer is compromised (such as a home computer or laptop) malware can spread to systems at the utility company. While sophisticated "spear phishing" attacks (targeted phishing attacks) have primarily been directed toward financial institutions and high net worth individuals, workers at utility companies may already be the next target of choice for hackers.

At a utility conference a few years ago, CIA analyst Tom Donahue told engineers about incidents in other countries where hackers had compromised electric utilities and then demanded payments in exchange for not disrupting power. According to Donahue, in one case the hackers did turn off the lights in multiple cities. He confirmed a SANS (SysAdmin, Audit, Network, Security Institute) public report. "There were apparently a couple of incidents where extortionists cut off power to several cities using some sort of attack on the power grid, and it does not appear to be a physical attack," he said.

The power grid is becoming a bigger target for hackers as more pieces of it are connected to each other or, in some cases, to the Internet. According to Tom Kellermann, vice president of security awareness of Core Security, "Most of the critical infrastructure of the U.S. has been penetrated to the root by state actors." Most experts agree that the fundamental problem is that we're paying more attention to the cyber-security of Facebook than to critical utilities.

Soon, it will be even more difficult to protect utilities against attack. Smart grid technology promises better efficiency by saving resources and being better to the environment. In order to fully utilize these smart grids, smart meters must be installed at homes and businesses. These devices essentially act as a node on the network. These meters are designed with wireless technology so the utility companies can read the meter, make changes, and get other information remotely. Will this make it possible for a hacker to turn off the power to your home? What kind of creative attacks could be performed with all these "smart" endpoints on the network? Could these endpoints be used to drill deeper into the utility network?

CNN has reported[7] that hackers have embedded malware in the nation's electricity grid. The two former federal officials who came forward also said that malware has been found in computer systems of oil and gas distributors as well. Although this was several years ago (2006), it has actually gotten easier over the years for hackers to compromise internal systems. CNN also reported malware found in telecommunications companies and financial services industries.

Let's be real. Malware is *everywhere*. There are so many different variants of "malicious software" (which can be anything) out there that of course every industry, every company, and most systems out there are infected with it. The question is whether these systems have a common command and control system with one group at the wheel. For the most part, I don't believe this is the case today, but I believe this is likely to change in the next 10 years. A day will come when embedded remote control software at most if not all critical infrastructure networks is controlled by a single group. They are likely on their way to that goal today. Then, when they want, in conjunction with their agenda, motives, and plan, they will hit us (and by us I mean the U.S.) where it will hurt the most. If they are smart they will wait for a large scale natural disaster, physical terrorist attack on American soil, or other phenomenon to piggyback on. This will create an even greater disruption and take significantly longer to recover from.

Will this be the work of governments? Probably. Will this be the Chinese or Russians? Probably. Other groups, too? Yes. Could it be independent groups with political or other agendas? Yes. Could there be religious, financial, or social motivations behind these groups? Yes. There does not have to be a single occupying force with cyber-warfare and cyber-espionage. A single system may have multiple groups or individuals that control it . . . perhaps without even knowing the other is there. One network often has hundreds or thousands of systems and each could be controlled by someone else. It would be like a successful siege on a castle, except the occupying forces all live within the walls and share resources. One just happens to live in the armory, the other in the kitchen, another in the dungeon, and one swimming in the moat.

There are several scenarios that come from this holistic critical infrastructure infestation. You will likely see the first officially reported human death from a hacker. Perhaps this will be a power outage where the cold or heat is too much for the infirm. Likely we will see the takedown of U.S. utilities as one of the weapons unfriendly nation states use against us in the coming years.

Situation Ten: The Pundit Hack

While cyber-criminals largely use their skills for the purpose of monetary gain, there is still a place in their hearts for getting recognition for hacking. In years gone by, hackers would post their pictures or political statements on compromised servers or desktop wallpaper with a clear indication of who the hacker was (or at least their alias or moniker). The hacker ego can only be satisfied by money to a certain point.

Cyber-criminals are also often in deep competition with others for similar services. Because hackers today and in the future will be "specialists," they often find themselves being outbid for common services by other hackers. So how do you set yourself apart from the sea of hacker junkies? What can give a hacker's digital resume and reputation the boost it needs?

Hackers have to also ask the question, "Why would other cyber-criminals want to work with me?" Hackers are usually specialists and no longer "one man bands"; they must work closely with others online (while maintaining anonymity of course) to facilitate their business requirements. Sometimes this is to rent a botnet, sometimes it is to acquire some 0-day code, or perhaps it is to sell compromised credit card data for cash or trade. Because criminals have to establish relationships with each other, hackers are always looking over their proverbial shoulders because they know that many federal agents are masquerading as hackers in an attempt to catch them. So how does an up-and-coming hacker establish his legitimacy, prove his skills, and get the attention of the right people? How better than a highly publicized compromise?

One way notoriety could be achieved in a large measure may be through picking out a particular pundit and hacking them. (What exactly is a pundit? According to the Merriam-Webster online dictionary, it's "a person who gives opinions in an authoritative manner usually through the mass media.") One reason this would be effective is because pundits are "news hackers" in a sense. They are in constant competition with each other. They steal stories from each other and they attack each other whenever they get a chance . . . sometimes in a more professional manner than at other times.

When a pundit is involved in a scandal, you hear about it on every other news outlet as they try to draw negative attention in the hopes of luring the devoted crowd away from that news person to their show. Pundits need ratings to stay in business. They need fresh relevant stories and to constantly figure out how to hold or increase market share.

Take for example, Bill O'Reilly and his sex scandal that was in the news beginning October 2004. Every other pundit made a point to focus on that story far longer than similar stories involving nonpundits. Pundits are circling sharks, always trying to find blood in the water that will lead to the next big story. When that blood is from one of their own, they do what they do best . . . capitalize. *The O'Reilly Factor* went from 3.1 million viewers to 2.5 million is just one year. Losing about 20 percent of your viewers in one year can be pretty devastating as the size of the audience drives commercial time, sponsors, and everything else. It is the lifeblood of any television program.

Bill O'Reilly is far from the only example. In fact, it is difficult to go a month without seeing at least one new story like this. Whether it be Rush Limbaugh, Mark Foley, or Matt Drudge, there is always a pundit that seems to be involved in hypocritical behavior, and there is nothing that other pundits love to expose and exploit more than their competitors' hypocrisy.

So with all these pundit sharks circling in the tank, what the little sharks want most is when one of the big sharks begin bleeding. One of the largest sharks out there currently is Glenn Beck. Glenn is a media mogul who has the attention of millions in the United States and around the world. His ultra-conservative and emotional approach is often attacked by others. His opinions are embraced by as many as despise him.

Pundits use online media tools such as Facebook and Twitter to promote themselves. Glenn Beck, for example, has over three million unique visitors to his website each month. A hacker who wants to make a political, social, or religious statement and gain notoriety at the same time could deface a popular website such as `glennbeck.com`. But why `glennbeck.com` specifically, when there are many other websites that have far more visitors? Defacing a prominent pundit's website means other pundits will pounce on the information and broadcast the story on every major newswire for several days (see Figures 9-15, 9-16, and 9-17), especially if the defacement is creative in ways that make it newsworthy. The hacker receives instant credibility and popularity. What could be a better resume builder than that?

Figure 9-15

Another reason to pick Glenn Beck is because he is already the punching bag for so many other pundits. Glenn can't do anything without people such as John Stewart of *The Daily Show*, Steven Colbert from *The Colbert Report*, and Keith Olbermann from *Countdown with Keith Olbermann* taking him to task. I can hear Steven Colbert now saying:

"It's Tip of the Hat/Wag of the Finger. I give a wag of my finger to Soviet hacker Dark Strider, who today took control of Glenn Beck's website and posted video of Glenn crying about his love for gold. What is that Jimmy? That is what his website has every other day? Oh. I'm sorry. A wag of my finger to Soviet hacker Dark Strider for taking control of Glenn Beck's website and posting "Glenn Beck is a cry baby, gold grubbing [censored]." Which is why I need to give a tip of my hat to Glenn for keeping his chin up. In a response from Glenn regarding his website defacement he said, 'The vulnerability that led to the defacement of the glennbeck .com website has been fixed [sniff sniff].' Hackers are terrorizing the digital world as we know it, which brings us to tonight's Word . . ."

Figure 9-16

Figure 9-17

Cascading media exposure would be relatively simple for a hacker to receive if they operate the way these media pundits operate. That is, it isn't about the news but about how the news is spun. The context and the story around the news event is what people want to hear about. What may happen in the future is that bored or motivated hackers looking for notoriety will creatively use pundits to achieve their goals.

Obviously, any pundit could be used for this purpose. A hacker would likely use any opportunity they find, large or small. The hack could be based on a website vulnerability, Facebook, email, or Twitter account compromise, or any other online media. Any breach large or small could be exploited and would likely have a domino effect on the other media outlets for high exposure.

Situation Eleven: Stock Manipulation

In Chapter 2, we discussed a real incident where United Airlines stock plummeted due to a series of unfortunate events which to this day cannot be linked to malicious intent. This scenario is meant to look at how someone could use similar and other tactics to artificially create the same outcome.

For years criminals have used "pump and dump" schemes to temporarily inflate the price of a particular stock. They do this by buying large quantities of the stock of a company when it is low. Often they use unknown penny stocks that trade for less than $1/share. They then send out an email to millions of mailboxes. These email lists are available online at little or no cost (usually cyber-criminals get them free). These emails vary in their styles and messages, but usually they tell the recipient about this stock that is about to explode. If they buy the stock now, they will be able to "ride the wave." Often they give a brief background on the company with some (usually phony) explanation as to why the stock is going to rapidly increase. "ABC Gold has just acquired a new mine that is going to produce 26 times the gold they mined last year and they will be announcing the acquisition on Thursday."

Many people buy into these schemes and buy the stock, and of course it begins to go up. They get excited and often buy more shares. Others hear about the opportunity a day or so later and see that the stock is rising, which gives legitimacy to the claims of the email. They buy in as well. The criminals who bought in first then sell once the stock reaches a target level. The stock begins to decline. Everyone attempts to sell off rapidly and most people end up losing money.

When it comes to stock manipulation, a criminal can either attempt to inflate or deflate the price of a stock depending upon their goals. Obviously, if someone wants to inflate the stock, they need to get others to purchase shares. If they want to deflate the stock value, they want to get people to sell shares of stock. In both cases, timing is critical because both scenarios rely upon deception, which will not last long (hours or at most days, depending upon the popularity of the stock).

In the next decade, we will likely see several scenarios that involve this type of fraud using a variety of methods. Chapter 2 described a seemingly innocent, perhaps even accidental, series of events that led to the collapse of United Airlines stock. This scenario took advantage of a legitimate story on a legitimate website that didn't have the proper date associated with it. That, combined with an unusual number of page hits on this bankruptcy story from several years earlier, brought the story to the forefront of the website. Google then indexed it and somehow a current date was posted with it. Then a Bloomberg analyst, without fact checking, posted the story on the stockbrokers' real-time news wire. That propagation led to a major sell off of "UAUA."

Rather than a legitimate story being rehashed, what if a hacker compromised a legitimate news agency website and injected a news article? The news article could be about a company filing for bankruptcy. It could be about SEC violations. It could report on executive fraud, insider trading, merger and acquisition announcements, or a host of other things. Most legitimate news websites are spidered and indexed several times a day, so it would not be difficult to get the timing right. Manipulating the media, or media hacking, is what we have been calling "macking." Let's hope that someone will do the fact checking before it goes on a major stock newswire, but like last time, they may not.

The same type of article or story could be used on other sites to get the same result. What if a hacker compromised the website of a Fortune 500 company? On the home page a news article or formal announcement is made about the acquisition of another company. The purported acquisition target could be the one that fraudsters are trying to pump and dump. Other announcements could be made from the official website of Fortune 1000 companies that could drive the price of the company's stock (or other companies' stock) up or down.

In another scenario, a hacker compromises a system at the very company they are trying to exploit the stock value of. Data security breaches are well known to cause a major drop in the stock value of a company. Look at TJMaxx, Heartland, and several others. Once the data breach is reported, within hours the stock has taken a major hit. The hacker captures or extracts some sensitive information. This is optional, but a great drop in stock price will result if personal or sensitive data is exposed or compromised. Normally with a data security breach, a hacker wants to stay under the radar as long as possible. This gives them the opportunity to extract more information, infect other systems, burrow in deeper, in an attempt to find other information that has value. But why go to all this effort when you could make far more money manipulating the stock?

Often it takes months and sometimes years before a company will announce a data breach. When they announce a breach it is on their terms, their timeframe, and they have time to control the media. Look at Heartland, for example. Their breach (which to date is the largest in U.S. history) happened over many months. They made the announcement of the data breach on January 20, 2009 during the presidential inauguration of Barak Obama.

A hacker (post-breach) could publicly announce the breach themselves. Building legitimacy of the breach they could post online the very sensitive and non-public information they extracted from the company. Offering no warning to the company, it would be difficult to handle "damage control." The stock price would likely drop significantly, especially if the breach was widely publicized. A hacker would make far more from shorting the stock than through selling the sensitive information online.

While there are many ways to create a situation where a company's stock price would fall rapidly, there are also several ways to create "pump and dump" scenarios as well. As I mentioned before, fraudsters have been doing this for years using penny stocks and spam email blast techniques. We will likely continue to see these in the future as well. People do not trust email like they once did. Email now and in the future will lack the legitimacy that is needed for a very successful pump and dump scheme. Criminals will turn to other online methods to do this.

Facebook, Twitter, and other social media outlets are very popular today and will likely continue to grow in popularity for the foreseeable future. Studies have shown that messages with instructions sent through non-email communication methods have at least a 10 times greater chance of being followed. In other words, if someone gets a message via Facebook, Twitter, instant messaging, SMS text messaging, or any other non-SMTP (Simple Mail Transport Protocol . . . i.e., regular email), they are far more likely to do what it says. This could include clicking links that can infect their systems or getting the inside tip on the next big stock explosion. Social networking and other non-SMTP communication methods are often trusted by the recipient because there is a sense of "network" or "friends" that you have previously authorized to communicate with you.

Cyber-criminals will utilize these other communication pathways to perform stock manipulation. The problem for criminals today is that there are some natural limitations in the method and volume one can send using these media. Hackers are very creative and over time, they will develop ways whereby they can subvert these limitations to send massive amounts of messages to these "closed" or "private" communities. Then, rather than all their pump and dump emails going into the spam folder, they will be read and followed by those who feel they got the message from a legitimate source.

Another method hackers could use is a "follow the leader" technique. Normally, when a well known stock investor or portfolio manager invests in a new company, others follow suit. This is certainly true with the king of all stock investors, Warren Buffett. Many individuals, portfolio managers and other brokers attempt to ride the coattails of Warren Buffett. While the success and failure rate is mixed for those who follow Mr. Buffett, there will always be those who do follow. Therefore, if we wanted to create a perception of legitimacy and excitement around a particular stock, who better to get behind it than Warren Buffett?

This scenario would work through the compromise of websites of well known stockbrokers, investors, and brokerages. Imagine if a hacker compromised Warren Buffett's company's official website, www.berkshirehathaway.com, and posted false information such as an announcement of a major shift in investment toward a particular company. If this information was made public through various news outlets prior to being uncovered as fraudulent, it might give a hacker exactly the bump in a particular stock that they were looking for.

Wherever there is a tremendous amount of money trading hands, criminals will work diligently to take a piece of it. While these attack scenarios are more difficult than others to pull off successfully, it only takes one success to make a tremendous amount of money.

Notes

1. "One Wilshire Telco Hotel Central" (The Center for Land Use Interpretation) http://www.clui.org/clui_4_1/pro_pro/exhibits/onewilshire.html#

2. For more information about Qwest Communications International, see http://www.fundinguniverse.com/company-histories/Qwest-Communications-International-Inc-Company-History.html

3. "First Wi-Fi pacemaker in U.S. gives patient freedom" (Reuters) http://www.reuters.com/article/idUSTRE5790AK20090811

4. Implantable Medical Devices: Security and Privacy for Pervasive, Wireless Healthcare (Dartmouth College Institute for Security, Technology, and Society) http://www.ists.dartmouth.edu/events/abstract-kevinfu.html

5. "China's Cyber Militia" (National Journal) http://www.nationaljournal.com/njmagazine/cs_20080531_6948.php

6. "Energy companies say NERC standards inadequate" (SC Magazine) http://www.scmagazineus.com/Energy-companies-say-NERC-standards-inadequate/article/141224/?DCMP=EMC-SCUS_Newswire

7. "Hackers reportedly have embedded code in power grid" (CNN.com) http://www.cnn.com/2009/TECH/04/08/grid.threat/index.html

Conclusion

Have you ever thought about how feasible the television shows are that you watch? Consider for a moment, the television series *Star Trek*, which is, in our opinion, more than a little unrealistic. Not because they were flying around space, going light speed, or finding alien life forms. No, those things are much more plausible than one key element. The future (according to the show and later the movies) is one where there was no money or compensation of any kind for your job. People do their jobs every day because it is what they should do and what they had trained for. Everyone in the Federation is honest and hard working. *Star Trek* envisions an entire society of people where there isn't any selfish ambition or motivation. This, of course, couldn't be further from the reality of our society (unfortunately). It was, in a sense, the ultimate goal in communism.

Think about it, if something like the "holodeck" actually existed, there would be a line all the way around the Enterprise with people waiting to get in *all the time*! No one would be doing their job. If any food you wanted popped out of a machine upon request, they would have to make the hallways much larger for our increased girth. Sure, being Captain is a great honor. Even being on the bridge would be great in just about any capacity. But what about the guy that has to repair the sewage system? I don't think that was his idea of a lifetime ambition without compensation (unless it allows him to skip to the front of the holodeck line).

Greed, selfishness, pride, lust, anger, wrath, apathy, gluttony, envy, and a host of other attributes is one side of the human coin. It is the side that drives some people to commit crimes. These are the realities of the world we live in. In a digital age, those crimes are often committed digitally. The further you can be from the actual crime scene, the greater chance you have of not getting caught. With the Internet, people can commit crimes from the other side of the world. While these attributes and people exist in our society, there will always be an ever-expanding information security problem. We must be ready to respond to these ever-changing, creative threats whenever and wherever they rear their ugly heads. Getting in front of that curve by understanding the evolution of threats and attacks helps us be better prepared to stop them.

2020

Predicting what the information security landscape will be like in the year 2020 is nearly impossible, and we won't know how accurate we have been until we get there. We have taken the best predictor of the future (the past) and applied modern techniques and technologies to create the best picture that we can. That being said, had we gone through this exercise in the year 2000, realistically we would have missed the mark on many points. For example, in 2000 we likely would have imagined a very secure PC, network, and Internet through the worldwide adoption and assimilation of public key infrastructure (PKI) or similar technology. What was once thought to be the silver bullet of authentication has turned out to be used in limited applications at best. Authentication, which is the linchpin of security, continues to be one of the biggest problems in information security, but is far from the only problem.

   What we have provided in this book are some thoughts and realistic predictions based on what we have seen over our careers, and we have allowed input from many experts for whom we have a great deal of respect. In some cases, we provided thoughts rather than specific predictions or guidance, as we felt that each person's unique environment, risk tolerance, and experiences were best served by simply adding our experiences to yours.

Information Asymmetry

The information security market was created in chaos and has become even more dysfunctional over the years. Because no single vendor offers a product that eliminates all of your information security threats, there are gaps. The few vendors that attempt to offer full suites don't properly tie them together and often fall very short within each of their component products as compared to best-in-breed vendors. Also complicating the industry are vendors that (unfortunately) act as the primary educators for organizations on information security threats and solutions. This creates natural "blind spots" for several reasons. First, vendors do not know and understand all the security threats out there. They also usually don't know enough about the organization's business, systems, network, third parties, customers, and employees to understand their specific threats. This means that the vendor only has solutions for some of the threats that they are aware of. Of those solutions, only some of them are considered "strong" or "market leading." As a result, the organization that is relying upon this vendor for information security awareness and education only gets a small slice of what they need.

So if an organization has 100 threats, they would likely look to information security vendors to help identify, understand, and mitigate these threats. At any given time, even the best security vendors understand less than half of the threats out there. They miss most of them because they don't know the threat exists or don't know enough about the client's organization to know whether the threat is legitimate for them. The vendor has solutions for only a fraction of those threats, and obviously doesn't explain their product or service limitations to the client. They explain only the threats for which they have strong, market-leading solutions. Furthermore, the vendor knows that the customer isn't going to buy all of their solutions, so they will usually educate the customer about three threats for which they have the greatest chance of closing business. The companies believe that these three threats are the biggest threats to their organization and represent the largest security gaps in their information security program when in reality there are usually much larger gaps and much more critical threats to identify and mitigate. Thus, the real critical threats, maybe those uniquely impactful to the specific enterprise, are often neglected, leading to catastrophic information security disasters.

But the reality is actually even worse than this. We have 15 to 20 years of compounded single point security solutions deployed in our companies. Organizations don't stop and look at their overall security threats, what they are trying to protect, and how effective their current solutions are. They hear about a new threat, usually in the media or from a security vendor, and then decide if they want to purchase a solution that mitigates that specific threat. Then, every few years, a security vendor will release a product that mitigates several threats, allowing customers to replace several systems and devices with one.

So, for example, an organization over the years purchased a firewall, an intrusion detection and prevention system, a web content filter, a spam filter, a virtual private network appliance, and gateway antivirus solutions. Then came the advent of the Unified Threat Management (UTM) appliance that had all of these solutions built into one single device. Most organizations have now traded out their single point solutions for these "all-in-one" devices. In the meantime, the threats have largely evolved, making these traditional security solutions far less effective than they once were. However, vendors that sell these devices don't often talk with customers about the changing risks and threats until they have a market-leading solution to help combat it. These same vendors then often have to walk on eggshells because they can't say anything that will erode their established business with the traditional security solutions while trying to sell the new solution. In other words, vendors will *always* give you a biased answer and recommendation regarding your information security needs. Self-serving behavior is human nature . . . it pays the bills for those of us in the IT security product and services industry. In reality, it happens in every industry; it's just easier to call "BS" in a less complex, slower-evolving industry.

Over the next 10 years, there will be more radical changes in the information security industry than we saw this past decade. The IT security problem that was created, then evolved, has now exploded, and continues to get worse; it is now so big that it will take major disruption, education, time, and money to fix. It is a confluence of economic, social, technological, and regulatory issues that are each coming very close to a tipping point that make for troubling times ahead. We say this not to create fear, uncertainty, and doubt, but rather to state the obvious from our vantage point and experience.

Tipping Point #1: Compliance Overload

The cost and complexity of information security best practices and compliance is very near a tipping point. CEOs, chief information security officers, compliance mangers, and others are saying "Enough is enough!" Organizations are on regulatory compliance overload. It used to be that each organization had to worry about a single regulation or compliance requirement. Banks only had to worry about GLBA (Gramm-Leach-Bliley Act). Healthcare only had to worry about HIPAA (Health Insurance Portability and Accountability Act). Today, there are so many compliance overlays that it is nearly impossible for organizations to keep up with them, in terms of both manpower and budgets. A healthcare organization today must adhere to HIPAA, HITECH (Health Information Technology for Economic and Clinical Health), PCI-DSS (PCI Data Security Standard), as well as a host of state and local data privacy and breach notification laws. There are federal rules of civil procedures regarding eDiscovery. If the company is public there is also SOX (Sarbanes–Oxley Act). Then, there are things like the Red Flags Rule and a host of others coming down the pike. This doesn't even take into account the multiple regulations that come into play if you operate in other countries, each regulation with its own set of requirements and demands, each with different auditing and enforcement standards, each demanding more and more of the IT budget. And at the end of the day, they are all basically trying to do the same thing: protect employees, customers, and shareholders from fraud and identity theft. Budgets have been stretched as far as they can and yet more and more compliance requirements are being loaded on organizations.

Organizations have been stretched to the breaking point, primarily because of a phenomenon commonly referred to as "information asymmetry." Information asymmetry is basically when one party is privy to more information than another party. The delta of knowledge between these two parties often leads to outcomes that put one party at a distinct disadvantage: a disadvantage that often leads to abuse. For a simple example, Alice decides to sell her used car. Brian is interested in buying the car, but he has only a fraction of the knowledge that Alice does about her car. If Brian had all the information Alice did, he may not want the car and certainly would have a more precise idea of what he should pay.

Information security is not any different. Information security experts, security vendors, and others are very knowledgeable concerning the broad and complex threat landscape. Organizations rely on these individuals to understand what they need. The gap in knowledge between these two groups has led to severe abuse, especially over the past decade. This is compounded when you add regulatory compliance. Most regulations are loosely defined. The interpretation by those vendors and "security experts" (whom we treat as authority figures) is believed to be exactly what we have to adhere to, in order to conform with various laws. This leads to an organization purchasing equipment and solutions that perhaps it didn't need or where perhaps a different solution would have been more appropriate. This lack of intellectual honesty has led the entire industry a long way off course.

Tipping Point #2: Data Breach Laws

Worse yet, most of the incidents of identity theft and fraud that occur are not correlated to incidents of information security breaches at all. Recently there has been a lot of push back on data breach disclosure laws. Organizations that reside in countries that have data breach disclosure laws spend twice as much on a data breach as those in countries that do not. While perhaps some of this is valid, like the cost of offering credit monitoring for victims, in most cases it simply opens the door for class-action lawsuits. Many of these cases do not even include victims as the plaintiff. Even in cases where the victims filed the suit, most never experienced any negative impact. No fraud occurred. No incidents of identity theft were reported. Still, companies must pay millions to settle these suits.

This is forcing companies to feel like they cannot or should not disclose a breach. So we are beginning to move backward in what those original data breach notification laws were really trying to accomplish. When California put together SB1386 (the first state-passed data breach notification law) did they really want this? Did they want incidents like the Veterans Administration, where a laptop is stolen that has sensitive information and the "victims" win a class-action lawsuit for 20 million dollars? Especially when the laptop is recovered within days and they are able to determine that the data was never accessed and in the years since there has not been a single incident of identity theft as a result?

Only a small percentage of identity theft is sourced from information security breaches. Most are your usual suspects of friends, family members, stolen wallets and purses, and so on. Changes are likely in store for this type of legislation as we move closer to this tipping point.

Tipping Point #3: Liability

The tipping point that we are racing toward at amazing speed is that of liability. When a credit card is stolen, who should be liable? When a data breach occurs, who should be left holding the bill? To date, this has often *not* been the person or organization that was negligent, careless, or whose actions ultimately led to the compromise. For years, if a customer of a bank (either personal or commercial) were to have a breach of their account, the bank would promptly take care of it regardless of where or how the breach happened. However, in a stunning change in policy some banks are now fighting back, especially because the losses are often significant.

Take the incident of PlainsCapital bank and its customer Hillary Machinery Inc. of Plano Texas. In late 2009, cyber-criminals from Romania and Italy wire transferred over $800,000 from Hillary Machinery's account to foreign accounts. Hillary sued the bank citing "inadequate security measures," and wanted the money restored. PlainsCapital filed a lawsuit in the U.S. District Court asking the court to certify that its security procedures were "commercially reasonable." The bank had sought to absolve itself from blame in the heist by stating that the unauthorized wire transfer orders had been placed by someone using valid Internet banking credentials belonging to Hillary Machinery.

Was this a move by PlainsCapital bank to simply "save face," to assure their other customers that they had safe and sound policies and procedures, or was this the first subtle step for banks to push back on customers regarding liability? The credentials used to log in and request the wire transfers were those of Hillary Machinery Inc. Did an insider at Hillary get malware installed on some system that led to the capture of the online banking credentials?

More banks are pushing back as well. Royal Bank of Scotland is now holding consumers to a higher level of liability if fraudulent transactions occur, especially in cases where system login credentials were compromised. With identity theft and fraud sharply rising, as well as the costs to deal with them, banks are finding themselves less and less willing to absorb all of these losses.

Industry solutions are keeping the proverbial liability "hot potato" going. Many merchants are beginning to upgrade to systems such as "Verified by Visa" and "MasterCard SecureCode." These systems include processes that are designed to have fewer chargebacks for merchants because of greater security when individuals make purchases. This allows merchants and banks the opportunity to push liability back on the consumer directly.

Banks, credit card processors, and others can certainly do a better job in attempting to detect and stop fraudulent behavior. There are many solutions available that are being deployed by these organizations to do just that. However, until the consumers become more aware and responsible for their own actions and their own system security, we will likely continue to see liability for breaches and losses pushed further toward the party closest to where the compromise occurred, which is usually the consumer.

Tipping Point #4: From Outsiders to Insiders

When asked, most compliance officers, IT administrators, and executives will say that insiders pose a greater threat to the organization than outsiders do. We agree. Yet for nearly all companies, far more is spent on technology and solutions to help mitigate external threats than on solutions to reduce exposure to insider threats. The old saying that we have a hardened perimeter but a soft and mushy core is true for most enterprises. Great effort and energy can be spent to penetrate an organization's security perimeter, but it only takes a little effort to create great havoc from within. There has been much speculation and debate around this topic over the years. From several studies that have been done it does appear that insiders truly are the greatest threat to an organization. So why do organizations not invest in ways to reduce this risk? There are several reasons for this. First, the smaller the organization, the more likely the company's owners and executives are to trust their employees and contractors. Second, for years there has been little in the way of effective tools and solutions to help reduce the risk from insiders, outside of surveillance cameras. Lastly, internal security typically has been difficult to implement without impacting the user experience, although that has improved over the past few years.

A new movement began a few years ago around this topic. Today more organizations have become aware of the serious threats that exist to their business from insiders. There are several insider threats that organizations need to be aware of, including fraud or other malicious activity, liability, productivity, and even carelessness. As a result, technology solutions are now available to help organizations deal with these serious issues.

Take for example the solution set offered by Awareness Technologies (ATI), a firm based in Los Angeles, California. Their solution consists of a software agent that is loaded on each system that reports back to a central SaaS-based management and monitoring system. The agent can perform several functions to help reduce risk from insiders. First, it performs web filtering so that you can monitor what employees are doing on the Internet. Monitoring the productivity of employees is simple with a solution like this, which goes beyond traditional web content filtering solutions. This actually shows you what the user did at the site, how long they were there, and more. It provides a contextual view of the user's web experience rather than a line in a report saying which website they went to. For example, this agent will record what the user types into search engines. Wouldn't you want to know if your user is typing things like "how to sue your employer" or "how to find a new job"?

It also has the ability to record everything the user is doing on the computer by taking screen shots every few seconds, which can be played back like a video. Not that most companies will spend all day watching video footage of what their employees are doing, but this is an invaluable tool when a company is suspicious of an employee's behavior or after an incident occurs. It acts as a forensic tool to help to determine what happened and who is at fault.

The ATI agent also has a data loss prevention feature that can detect and prevent employees from sending out sensitive information. A good portion of data breaches are caused when employees either inadvertently or maliciously send data out of the organization. Data breaches can be catastrophic to an organization. With so many breaches being caused by insiders, it is no wonder that software that can detect and stop data leakage is becoming a top priority for organizations.

Another key element for solutions that attempt to protect companies from insider threats is the ability to manage remote employees, such as travelers and telecommuters. One of the top causes of data breaches is lost and stolen laptops. Software solutions (including the ATI agent) can allow organizations to remotely "wipe" the laptop clean of any sensitive information. This can happen after the laptop is lost or stolen. It can also be used to track the laptop down to recover it. A huge portion of all data breaches could be avoided if all organizations used software solutions like these on their remote employee's laptops.

Companies are becoming more and more aware of the threats posed by their insiders. In the coming decade, we will reach a tipping point where information security spending goes from being almost entirely on solutions to mitigate the external risk to a more balanced approach between internal and external threats. As a result, we will see more and more companies developing solutions to deal with insider threats.

Tipping Point #5: From Network to Endpoint

Another tipping point we will see prior to the year 2020 is a rapid shift from network-based information security solutions to endpoint solutions. At this point, it should not come as a surprise to anyone that this will occur. Both insider and outsider threats attack the endpoints. That is where the attacks occur, therefore, that is where the detection and mitigation needs to occur. It is, of course, easier to deploy solutions that sit at gateway points and monitor the traffic to and from different areas (for example, between the Internet and your corporate network), but the reality today makes this difficult. Most attacks go directly after the endpoint. Once compromised, encryption and other obfuscation techniques are used that completely render these "edge-based" security solutions useless (for these types of attacks).

Securing the endpoint is no small challenge. The reason that edge-based solutions have been used since the dawn of the Internet is because managing endpoints is difficult. How do you ensure that the endpoint software is loaded on all systems? What about remote users such as travelers and telecommuters? What about updates? How do you manage them? How do you monitor them? What endpoint security solution providers will begin to offer is a hybrid solution that puts agent software on the endpoint, but has everything centrally managed from an SaaS or a cloud-based management and monitoring platform. This model of putting agent software on the endpoint and managing it centrally in the cloud is going to be the standard for all good, effective endpoint security solutions.

Tipping Point #6: Cloud Computing

As we discussed in a previous chapter, cloud computing is really making a splash. In reality, today there are only a few types of businesses that are realizing all the true benefits of cloud computing. Online gaming companies that need to offer low-cost, highly scalable and flexible systems are one example. Another example is a new company called Varolo. Varolo is a service that allows people to get a free membership and then watch ads in exchange for jackpots and prizes. Additionally, user's can invite their friends and build a "village" (as they call it) and earn money each time their friends watch ads. The earning extends to the user's entire social network up to four degrees of separation. So the user can earn money on her friends through the friends of her friends' friends' friends. The interesting thing about Varolo is they built their infrastructure entirely in the cloud. Each virtual machine instance in the cloud can support some number of simultaneous users. When the system detects that they are above 70 percent utilization, it automatically launches or "spins up" another virtual machine instance supporting more users. As utilization decreases (at night for example), the virtual machines are "spun down." Because cloud computing providers charge by the hour, Varolo only pays for the systems and bandwidth it needs in real time. Varolo was also able to launch the company without ever buying Internet bandwidth or a single piece of hardware and they can support nearly an unlimited number of users on their service. Cloud computing makes it possible for many companies to launch more quickly, grow faster, be more dynamic, and control costs more effectively.

There will be a tipping point in the next 10 years as cloud computing services become more secure and widely used. At that point, we will see a mass migration toward these solutions for their cost savings and scalability. What will drive this to reality is security and compliance. There is a fear regarding the lack of security in cloud-based services. Cloud-based services by their very nature are shared infrastructures. Sharing requires tight security controls and solutions. Because cloud computing is so new, security solutions are sparse and immature at best. These will improve over time. With better security (and a good track record), auditors and regulators will feel comfortable having organizations use cloud-based systems. Adoption will quickly occur as more and more companies realize the benefits of cloud computing.

Beyond Tipping Points

This book has spent considerable time on events that will define what information security will look like in the year 2020. Soon we will learn what part cyber-terrorism, the economy, politics, media pundits, technology, technology vendors, and many other factors will play in defining the future of information security. In the year 2020, when we look back on the previous decade, we will likely realize that we created as many new problems as we have solved. We will see that we have made a lot of progress in some areas, while digging ourselves into deeper holes in others.

Information security by its very nature is fluid and dynamic. That is what makes it both challenging and exciting for so many people in the industry. That is what makes it frustrating and difficult for those outside the industry. Each month, week, and sometimes each day, there is something new to combat.

If you had to write the newspaper headlines (although there probably won't be any newspapers) for the top 10 information security news events that would happen over the next 10 years, you would probably do pretty well. You wouldn't know the names of the companies. You wouldn't have the exact number of records compromised. You wouldn't know exactly the method of fraud or identity theft committed. You wouldn't know the dates. You wouldn't have the exact amount of money lost. But generally you could probably come up with headlines that will happen.

This would probably work because most information security events are predictable. We have tried to show in this book some of the more unusual things that may be in our future as well as the natural evolution of those techniques we see today. But there will undoubtedly be some surprises along the way as well.

As long as greed, selfishness, pride, lust, anger, wrath, apathy, gluttony, envy, and other such human traits exist, there will be criminals trying to take advantage of others. There will also be information security experts there to stop them . . . unless we invent the holodeck, in which case we'll all be in there.

Contributing Author Biographies

Steve Addison, Vice President Business Development, Cosaint

Steve Addison has over 20 years of project management, development, marketing, and operations management experience in engineering, software, and e-learning companies. He started his career as a project manager with British Aerospace in Stevenage, UK working on the development of guided missile systems. After studying for his doctorate, he returned to industry as an engineering design consultant with Frazer-Nash Consultancy before joining Flomerics, a CAE software vendor. As western region manager and later CIO and director of marketing at Flomerics, Steve was based in San Jose, California, and Boston, Massachusetts, where—among his other duties—he managed the customer training program, and developed the company's Internet strategy, including public and intranet websites, and SaaS tools for mechanical engineers.

   In 1999, Steve left Flomerics and joined Knowledge Impact—an e-learning company specializing in custom learning and change management solutions for CRM/ERP implementations—as a practice director and then vice president of consulting services. In 2000, Steve joined SecurityPortal to lead their product development programs, including the development of Information Security University (web-based training for security professionals), SecuriStat (an online security benchmarking application), and a security knowledge center. He co-founded Cosaint in 2001 and has been active in product development and consulting, as well as leading the company's business development efforts.

Steve has an MA and a PhD in Engineering from King's College, Cambridge. He was a member of the teaching faculty at City University, where he taught and developed curriculum for both the classroom and distance learning programs within the Computer Science program. He has also taught Technical Communications and Operations Management for Henry Cogswell College in Everett, Washington.

He has authored classroom and WBT courses on topics as diverse as information security, privacy, intellectual property law, mechanical engineering, operations management, technical communications, and computer programming. Steve is also an active blogger on the Security Awareness Training blog, and teaches a workshop on "Building a Practical Security Awareness Training Program," which has been presented in locations across the United States including Seattle, Portland; Salem, Oregon; Anchorage, Alaska; and Washington, DC to organizations including Alaska Air, Nordstrom, State of Washington, State of Oregon, King County, Frontier Bank, T-Mobile, the Department of Veterans Affairs, DHHS, Safeco, Nautilus, and the City of Portland.

Steve's comments appear at the end of the "Social Networking Threats" section of Chapter 4, and after the "Evolving Purpose into Action" section in Chapter 7.

S. Dirk Anderson, CISA, CPISM, QSA, Managing Director, Coalfire Systems

S. Dirk Anderson is a leader in the field of information security with nearly 20 years of experience encompassing network security and assessment, information protection, IT compliance, physical security, and risk management. His resume includes positions as principal consultant at Leviathan Security, senior manager of global network security for Global Crossing, chief security architect for Conqwest (now Towerwall), and manager of information security for Confertech International. He now leads the governance, risk, and compliance delivery practice for Coalfire Systems out of their headquarters office in Colorado.

His broad range of experience, from the management of multimillion-dollar budgets to highly technical roles, has provided him with a unique perspective on the successful integration of business and technology. Mr. Anderson's breadth of experience also extends to the sizes and types of industries with which he has worked. Past clients have included multinational retailers, banking, telecommunications, investment, energy, manufacturing, and governmental organizations.

Mr. Anderson is also a requested speaker and trainer who has served as a visiting lecturer for Regis University's Master's in Information Assurance program, and as an instructor to the National Credit Union Administration (NCUA) auditors. He has presented to numerous state governments and organizations and professional bodies, including ISACA, ISSA, and at AFCEA's Technet on topics ranging from e-commerce security to information assurance and critical infrastructure protection (IA/CIP). He also writes on the topic of information security and has contributed to works such as the SANS "Incident Handling–Step by Step" guide.

Dirk's comments appear at the end of the "Testing Your Information Protection: Penetration Test/Vulnerability Test/Risk Assessments" section in Chapter 6.

Douglas W. Barbin, CPA, CISSP, CFE, GCFA, PCI-QSA, Director, Assurance and Compliance Services, SAS 70 Solutions, Inc.

Doug Barbin is a director at SAS 70 Solutions, a company that provides technology assurance and compliance services with an emphasis on SAS 70/SSAE 16 audits, PCI validation, and ISO 27001/2 compliance. He oversees complex engagements that touch multiple compliance requirements and is also responsible for firm-wide marketing, for which he moderates the SAS 70 Solutions-sponsored blog, The Pragmatic Auditor (`www.thepragmaticauditor.com`).

After starting his career as a forensic accountant with a "Big 4" global accounting firm, Doug has spent the last 10 years working in the trenches of a wide variety of information security topics from breach investigation and audits to product management and marketing. As a result, he understands the perspective of both the security consultant and the managed services/SaaS provider. Prior to joining SAS 70 Solutions, Doug was director of product management for VeriSign's Managed Security Services business, where he was responsible for the MSS "SaaS" platform architecture and compliance. Prior to that, Doug led VeriSign's western U.S. security consulting practice, where among other projects, he led some of the prototype PCI assessments under Visa's CISP program.

Doug maintains a number of accreditations, including certified public accountant (CPA), certified information systems security professional (CISSP), certified fraud examiner (CFE), PCI qualified security assessor (QSA), and GIAC certified forensic analyst (GCFA), an accreditation he helped create. He is also an active member of CloudAudit (`www.cloudaudit.org`) and has spoken at a variety of conferences related to cloud computing. He graduated cum laude with BS degrees in accounting and criminal justice from Penn State University and has an MBA from Pepperdine University.

Doug's comments appear at the end of the "The Path to 2020" section in Chapter 2, and after the "SaaS and Cloud Computing" section of Chapter 6.

Tim Belcher, Chief Technology Officer, NetWitness

As chief technology officer for NetWitness, Tim Belcher is responsible for the company's overall product vision, development, and technology roadmap. Previously, Mr. Belcher co-founded Riptech where he served as CTO. At Riptech, Mr. Belcher was the visionary behind Caltarian, the award-winning and break-through security event correlation technology that was the foundation for

Riptech's security monitoring services. Ernst & Young recognized Mr. Belcher for his success with the "Entrepreneur of the Year" award in 2001.

Tim's comments appear at the end of the "The Malware Problem" section in Chapter 3, and after the "Botnets" section of Chapter 4.

Rob Bolton, Author, *Lose the Pressure . . . Win the Deals*

Rob Bolton is a dynamic sales leader with a successful track record of consistently delivering strong and sustainable market and revenue growth, developing and executing strategic business plans, and building highly focused and effective sales organizations. Bolton is a regular contributor on the topics of sales and technology. His first book, *Lose the Pressure . . . Win the Deals,* is set to be released in August 2010, and he publishes a sales blog at `www.salesshot.blogspot.com`.

Rob has spent the last 19 years working for some of the most respected companies in business. He started his career as a regional salesperson working for a technology division of GE Capital, climbing the corporate ladder with companies like Lucent Technologies, BT, and Perimeter eSecurity. With an affinity toward the design and execution of sales strategies, Rob most recently joined 1901 Group to help fortify their mission, vision, and global acquisition of enterprise customers (`www.1901group.com`).

Throughout his IT career, Rob has witnessed firsthand the challenges that customers face with traditional technology deployments and management models, and is an evangelist on the financial and operational benefits of "cloud-based" offerings.

Rob's comments appear at the end of the "The Impact on Journalism" section in Chapter 2, and after the "Botnets" section of Chapter 4.

Counse Broders, Industry Analyst

Counse Broders is an industry analyst who is an independent consultant and was, prior to that, senior research director for telecom services at Current Analysis for 8 years. Counse has written for and been quoted in a variety of magazines and newspapers, including *The Telephony, CIO, The Washington Business Journal, The Washington Post,* and a variety of other publications and specialty journals. He has also spoken on and moderated panels at industry trade shows, such as VON (Voice On Net), Streaming Media East, and Comptel. He has been a keynote speaker at industry events, including the Global Carrier Security Summit (sponsored by IBM ISS) and the Atlanta Telecom Professionals banquet. Counse holds a MBA in Telecommunications from University of Dallas and a BBA in Engineering Management & Finance from University of Texas at Austin.

Counse's comments appear at the end of the "Security in 20/20 Hindsight" section in Chapter 6.

Niall Browne, CISA, CCSP, CISSP, CCSI, CISO & VP Information Security, LiveOps

Niall Browne is the CISO of LiveOps, where he is responsible for defining and managing the Enterprise Security, Audit, Risk, and IT Regulatory Compliance programs. LiveOps offers two solutions for Enterprises: Contact Center in the Cloud, a SaaS technology platform for managing global contact centers, and Workforce in the Cloud, an on-demand workforce for outsourcing call center calls with over 20,000 independent agents.

Niall has been co-chair of the BITS Shared Assessments development committee for the past 4 years. This audit program was created by the U.S. Financial Services Roundtable BITS, the Big 4 accounting firms, and the leading U.S. financial institutions for the purpose of evaluating the controls of service providers in the United States and internationally. As a service provider, he has also led IT security assessments, including PCI-DSS level-1, ISO 27002, SysTrust, SAS 70 Type II, BITS Agreed Upon Procedures (AUP) and FFIEC examinations. In addition to the above, he is also chair of the BITS Shared Assessments Cloud Committee, and is on the steering committee of Cloud Security Alliance (CSA) Controls Matrix.

Prior to LiveOps, Niall was responsible for information security at Yodlee, a financial services SaaS provider that manages three trillion dollars in assets, and has over 20 million consumers.

In 2004 Niall was the lead security architect for the European Union presidency.

Niall's comments appear at the end of the "2020: Remote Access Continues to Be a Problem" section in Chapter 3.

Dipto Chakravarty, General Manager Cloud Security and CISO, Novell

Dipto Chakravarty is the general manager of Cloud Security at Novell, Inc. He also serves as the CISO and vice president of worldwide engineering and provides strategic direction and execution leadership for building Novell's security and identity products. Prior to Novell, Chakravarty led the company turnaround for e-Security, Inc., leading to its $72M acquisition by Novell. He has been a serial entrepreneur with a number of venture-backed startups, including Artesia, a firm he founded with a management buyout from the Thomson Corporation in 1999, using $25 million Series A funding from Warburg Pincus to build software for managing rich media. Prior to serving as the CTO and founder of Artesia, Chakravarty was a director at Thomson's consulting practice for financial and publishing markets, where he undertook a corporate venture of starting a software division with $10 million in funding to build digital asset management software in 1996. Earlier, he held a variety of engineering positions at IBM's AIX kernel and VLSI groups, at A&T's Unix monitoring products group, and at Bell Lab's device drivers group.

In addition to being a 25-year industry veteran, Chakravarty is the author of two bestselling computer books from McGraw-Hill on the topics of Unix/AIX operating system architecture and PowerPC architecture, which have been translated into five languages, has published over 45 technical papers in refereed journals, and holds several patents. Chakravarty holds a BS and MS in Computer Science and Electrical Engineering from University of Maryland, an EMP from Wharton Business School, and a GMP from Harvard Business School.

It is hard to compress a quarter of a century's professional experiences into a three-paragraph biography, but suffice it to say that the best parts of Chakravarty's career have been shaped by opportunities and advice from his mentors. Having worked with some of the true intellects and living legends of the computer industry, his career has always been so much fun that it has never felt like work, rather it was everyday learning from the best and the brightest.

Chakravarty's comments appear at the end of the "The Movement Toward National Identity Management" section in Chapter 3.

Eddie Chau, Chairman, Firmus Security Ltd

Before founding Firmus together with Alan See (CEO) and Eric Yeow (VP), Eddie Chau was the founder and CEO of e-Cop Pte Ltd, which grew to become a market leader in the information security industry. He pioneered the first 24/7 Managed Security Services in the world with e-Cop, which was acquired in 2007 by a wholly owned subsidiary of Temasek Holdings Pte Ltd. Previously, Eddie had held senior management positions at IBM and Computer Associates Inc. Drawing on his vast experience, he has also been interviewed on CNBC Asia, Channel NewsAsia, Intelligent Enterprise, MIS Asia, and Network Computing Asia, among others. Eddie holds an MSc in Communication Engineering from Imperial College, London.

Eddie's comments appear at the end of the "The Security Software Vendor" section in Chapter 3.

Dale Cline, President and Chief Executive Officer, netForensics

Dale Cline serves as President and Chief Executive Officer of netForensics, Inc., where he is responsible for setting the company's strategic direction and for leading its growth as a global provider of enterprise-security information management solutions. Prior to joining netForensics, Dale was president of Knowledge Products, a division of Global Knowledge, where he managed the growth and expansion of Knowledge Products's flagship product, and prior to that, served as president and chief operating officer for InfoRay Inc., a provider of cross-enterprise supply chain event management solutions.

Earlier in his career, Dale worked for Network Associates, where he served in various roles, including vice president of worldwide channels and president of the Americas Organization; as president of MediaPath Technologies, a software company based in Israel; and in software and sales management at Microsoft Corp.

Dale holds a bachelor's degree from Rutgers University and a master's degree from the New Jersey Institute of Technology.

Dale's comments appear at the end of the "Personal Information and Data Correlation" section in Chapter 3.

Suzi Connor, Director Information Technology Infrastructure and Operations, U.S. Department of Health and Human Services

Suzi Connor serves as the Department of Health and Human Services (HHS), director of information technology infrastructure and operations (ITIO) to provide administrative and technical supervision for ITIO's cross-cutting information technology (IT) service delivery team. In this role, she provides expert consultation and advice on the development and implementation of IT strategic plans and policies, information assurance and network operations, IT modernization, enterprise architecture, data quality, and business requirements activities.

Ms. Connor has more than 14 years experience in the IT field with a unique combination of business skills, program management expertise, and IT technical knowledge blending both private and public sector experience. She has a proven track record encompassing federal and DoD programs along with lifecycle management, strategic planning, business and technical operations, business development, and financial management.

Ms. Connor has successfully used her technology background and strong analytical and decision-making skills to strategically build and manage consulting and service delivery practices. Her portfolio of skills includes strategic and organization planning; financial modeling and development of corporate budgets; strategic sourcing and acquisition support; contract management and administration; client service delivery; performance management, consulting services; IT security systems; and development and implementation of marketing programs.

Ms. Connor possesses a bachelor's degree in finance and accounting from Indiana University of Pennsylvania and has advanced studies towards a master's degree in information technology from John's Hopkins University, and is a graduate of Harvard's Kennedy School of Government, Senior Executive Fellows Program.

Suzi's comments appear at the end of the "Hindsight is NOT 20/20" section in Chapter 1.

Mike Cote, Chief Executive Officer, SecureWorks

Mike Cote became chairman and CEO of SecureWorks in February of 2002. Under his leadership, the firm has grown to become one of the leading security services firms. Prior to joining SecureWorks, Cote held executive positions with Talus Solutions, a pricing and revenue management software firm acquired by Manugistics in 2000. Cote joined Talus from MSI Solutions, a web application development and systems integration company, where he was chief operating officer. In addition to other technology executive roles, Cote's early career included international assignments with KPMG. Cote's leadership style is punctuated by open communication, high integrity, and a client-centric philosophy. Cote is a certified public accountant and a member of Business Executives for National Security. He is a graduate of Boston College with a double major in computer science and accounting.

Mike's comments appear at the end of the "The Security Culture" section in Chapter 2.

David Cowan, Partner, Bessemer Venture Partners

Since joining Bessemer Venture Partners in 1992, David has invested in more than 20 startups that have since gone public. The first Forbes *Midas List* ranked David among the world's top 10 venture investors.

David has invested in network technology (Ciena, P-Com), Internet services (PSI-Net, Keynote, Flycast, Netli), and consumer Internet (Hotjobs, Blue Nile). In 1995 he cofounded Verisign as a Bessemer-funded spinout of RSA and served as VeriSign's initial Chairman; his other data security investments have included Counterpane (acquired by BT), Cyota (acquired by RSA), ON (acquired by Symantec), Postini (acquired by Google), Qualys, Tripwire, Tumbleweed, Valicert and Worldtalk. (Tumbleweed acquired Valicert and Worldtalk after they went public). David's current portoflio includes Billshrink, Delivery Agent, GetInsured, Lifelock, LinkedIn, MashLogic, Nominum, Playdom, Reputation Defender, Smule, and Zoosk.

David received both his A.B. in math and computer science and his M.B.A. degrees from Harvard University. Follow David on Twitter, read his blog *WhoHasTimeForThis?,* including the "Startup Stuff for Entrepreneurs," post, or his posts on Bessemer Investments.

David's comments appear in at the end of the "Venture Capital and Investment into IT Security" section in Chapter 7.

Don DeBolt, Director of Threat Research, CA Internet Security Business Unit

Don DeBolt is the director of threat research for the CA-ISBU. Over the last 12 years, he has led Threat Research teams and security operations on the quest to identify new security breaches while protecting against the latest malware threats. From 1996 to 2000, Don learned the art of penetration testing while consulting for both Ernst & Young and Deloitte. In 2000, Don took a position with one of the first managed security services providers, Counterpane Internet Security, and soon moved into the position of SOC manager. While at Counterpane, he helped establish key efficiencies through the use of advanced correlation logic. In 2004, Don moved to CA and has been working to ensure a strong foundation in anti-malware research. Don is helping evolve research operations and research technology in line with the growth of malware today. Don leverages a global team of researchers and advanced Crawler and Honey-Client technologies to proactively acquire malware samples and intelligence. Don is an avid cyclist and enjoys commuting to work by bicycle.

Don's comments appear at the end of the "Security: An Industry or a Feature of IT?" section in Chapter 7.

Dennis Devlin, CISO, Brandeis University

Dennis Devlin is chief information security officer for Brandeis University. Over the past 4 decades, Dennis has established and led enterprise-class programs in information security, digital privacy, identity management, networking, electronic messaging, business continuity, emergency notification, and server and network operations in higher education and industry.

Prior to his current role, Dennis was vice president and chief security officer for The Thomson Corporation (now Thomson-Reuters) and a member of the senior IT leadership team at Harvard University; he began his career in IT at American Hoechst Corporation (now Aventis).

Dennis is a graduate of the University of Pennsylvania and has completed extensive continuing education in IT leadership. He has been featured in many articles on security and written for *CSO Magazine* and *SC Magazine*. He has also served on CSO advisory boards for RSA Security, Qualys, Verdasys, GeoTrust, ChosenSecurity, LogMatrix, and the CSO Editorial Advisory Board for *SC Magazine*, and he is a faculty member of the Institute for Applied Network Security (IANS).

Dennis's comments appear at the end of the "The Security Culture" section in Chapter 2.

Tom Dring, Director of Enterprise Infrastructure, Noble Energy

Currently director of enterprise infrastructure for Noble Energy, Tom Dring has over 25 years of experience in information technology management, infrastructure deployment, business system delivery, and program management. He has leveraged his experience in the energy, professional services, banking, and aerospace industries. Prior positions include VP of business systems and divisional CIO at UK-based Intertek Group, and management positions at The Concours Group, Red Sky Interactive, Shell, Chevron, and JPMorgan Chase. He was educated at Texas A&M University, where he obtained a bachelor of science degree in computer science.

Tom's comments appear at the end of the "Email, Instant Messaging, and SMS" section in Chapter 5.

Thomas Dunbar, SVP, Global IT Chief Security Officer, XL Global Services, a member of XL Group plc

As global IT chief security officer, Tom Dunbar holds global responsibility for XL Group's overall Information Risk Management program. This includes the company's information security strategy, tactics, planning, governance, architecture, and operations. Mr. Dunbar is responsible for the company's security policies and standards, including Information Risk Management. He oversees the company's IT forensics and eDiscovery efforts. Additionally, he leads XL's IT compliance program, which includes responsibility for Sarbanes-Oxley and other regulatory requirements. Mr. Dunbar is a member of the IT Leadership team, the Operations Risk Committee, and the Privacy Council. He joined XL in 2002 as their first global IT CSO.

Mr. Dunbar has 12 years experience in information security. He holds both the CISSP and CISM certifications. Prior to joining XL, he was director of information security programs at Citigroup, where he was responsible for the management of information security officers through the Citigroup global network, and the direction of information security programs including policy, standards, training, awareness, metrics, and financials.

Mr. Dunbar holds a bachelor of arts degree in mathematics from the College of the Holy Cross in Worcester, Massachusetts. Mr. Dunbar is a co-inventor of record on two patented information security effectiveness/measurement tools: Citigroup Information Security Evaluation Model (Citi-ISEM) and the Information Security Metrics Program.

Mr. Dunbar is the recipient of the 2006 SC Magazine Award CSO of the Year.

Thomas's comments appear at the end of the "Information Security Drivers" section in Chapter 2, and after the "Buying Security: Defining the Value" section of Chapter 7.

Mike Ferrari, Senior Director of Services, Allied Telesis

As a senior director of services, Mike Ferrari leads the Professional Services and Support organizations for Allied Telesis. Over a 20+ year career in telecommunications, Mr. Ferrari has specialized in local, access, and backbone network design, engineering, integration, and operations. This includes extensive experience with a variety of enabling technologies, including IP, ATM, DSL, wireless, WAN, VoIP, and network management systems. Throughout his career, he has held a variety of diverse positions in management, engineering, product and project management, and consulting. Michael has a MSEE degree from George Mason University and BSEE degree from N.C. State University.

Mike's comments appear at the end of the "Voice over IP" section in Chapter 5.

Luis E. Fiallo, Managing Director, China Telecom Americas

Luis E. Fiallo brings to the table a wealth of executive-level operations experience that enables him to build, transform, and bring profitability to technology companies operating in North America, Asia (China), Europe, and South America. With a reputation for being a leader in the technology field, he was appointed by George W. Bush to the President's Information Technology Advisory Committee (PITAC) and by Timothy Kaine to the Commonwealth of Virginia Governor's Broadband Roundtable.

In his most recent position as managing director of China Telecom Americas, Fiallo led the development and structuring of the largest independent international operating subsidiary of China Telecom Corporation—where he grew market share from 2 percent to 40 percent and doubled business margins in just 5 years.

Prior to joining China Telecom, Luis was president and founder of Fiallo & Associates, a management consultancy and capital formation organization. During that time, he served as interim COO to lead the corporate turnaround of iLearning, a distance learning company owned by Sylvan Learning Systems and later sold to Educational Testing Services (ETS).

Before iLearning, Mr. Fiallo was vice president of eBusiness Solutions for BCE Teleglobe, where he built and managed one of the world's largest integrated hosting and communication services, and he was vice president of Data Services and Web Hosting for Applied Theory Corporation—a national ISP—where he served on the management team that took the company public.

Luis has held senior roles at IBM, Sprint, and Cable & Wireless, where he started his career in data networking and computing solutions. Since then, he has been called on time and time again to lead new initiatives and early-stage ventures with market expansion and business development responsibilities.

Fiallo is a frequent speaker around the world on topics related to next-generation networking, content distribution services, and the evolution of China's and Asia's Information and Communication Technology (ICT) market. He has also co-authored multiple federal- and state-level reports related to cyber-security, use of IT in healthcare, supercomputing, and broadband development.

Luis is an active member of the business community and currently serves on the board of advisors for Mochila Inc., Lore Systems, and Opus 8. He is involved in local community affairs, serving on the board of directors for the Business Alliance of George Mason University in Fairfax, Virginia, and the Luther Rice Society Council of George Washington University in Washington, DC. He also serves on the board of directors for Net Giver Foundation, a nonprofit community development organization.

Mr. Fiallo received a bachelor's degree in business administration in international business from George Washington University, and a master's degree in information systems from The American University.

Luis's comments appear at the end of the "IT Security Revolution" section in Chapter 6.

Suprotik Ghose, Head of Networks & Information Security at a leading financial service firm

Suprotik Ghose is the head of Networks & Information Security at a leading financial services firm. In this role, Suprotik is responsible for infrastructure security of systems, databases, and networks, as well as application security and compliance.

Previously, he founded a software company and raised multiple rounds of venture funding to build a software security management product that allowed efficiencies in provisioning costs, accelerated revenue recognition, and increased consumer satisfaction. Prior to that, Suprotik was the vice president for wireless products at Inciscent, senior consulting manager at AT&T's Security team, and vice president at Citigroup in Citibank's Information Security group.

Suprotik is certified as a CISA, CISM, and CISSP and holds an MBA from University of Illinois at Urbana-Champaign, a graduate management degree from the Indian Institute of Management, Calcutta (IIM-C), and an undergraduate electrical engineering degree from Birla Institute of Technology, India.

Suprotik's comments appear at the end of the "The Portable Media Debacle, A.K.A. Mobility" section in Chapter 3.

Don Gray, Chief Security Strategist, Solutionary

A veteran of technology applications development since 1991, Don Gray brings "in-the-trenches" information security experience to his role as Solutionary's chief security strategist. In his role, Don leads the Solutionary Engineering and Research Team (SERT) and is directly involved with researching new threats and overall information security trends. Gray is regularly quoted in the media as an information security expert and is a frequent speaker at industry events, including Gartner Security Summit, Forrester Security Forum, CSO Breakfast Club series, and key channel partner events.

Don joined Solutionary through its acquisition of VigilantMinds, where he was a co-founder and chief technology officer. Prior to that, he was a technologist for companies like marchFIRST, Idea Integration, and Mellon Bank. Don received a BS in Computer-Based Systems Management from California University of Pennsylvania.

Don's comments appear at the end of the "Intrusion Detection Systems, Intrusion Protection Systems, and Data Loss Prevention in 20/20 Hindsight" section in Chapter 6.

Andy Greenawalt, Founder and CTO, Continuity Control

Andy Greenawalt is the founder/CEO of Continuity Control, an award-winning company simplifying compliance for the financial services industry. Prior to founding Continuity Control, Andy had founded, served as CTO, and was on the board of Perimeter eSecurity. Perimeter eSecurity pioneered the security as a service industry and has been one of the fastest-growing companies in the country with over a dozen awards to its credit. Andy also is the president of Gnostic Ventures, speaks on SaaS and the creation of value, is the entrepreneur partner at CTech, and serves on the boards of the Connecticut Technology Council and the Yale Entrepreneurial Institute. He studied philosophy and linguistics at UMass Amherst.

Andy's comments appear at the end of the "GRC" section in Chapter 2.

Justin Greene, Chief Technology Officer, SECCAS

Justin Greene was a founder of SECCAS LLC, an application service provider that delivers messaging compliance technologies to regulated industries and processes millions of transactions each day. At SECCAS, Justin led the development of all software applications and the build out and management of all services and infrastructure. After 5 years of revenue growth and 4 years of profitability, SECCAS was successfully sold to Perimeter Internetworking in 2007. Prior to SECCAS, Justin was a founder and CTO of ClicVU, Inc. an Internet technology company that produced advertising and messaging technology products including the Spamex Disposable Email Address Service, which is still in operation today. Additionally, Justin served as chief software architect for SixDegrees.com, a groundbreaking social networking site, which was launched in 1997 and sold to Youthstream networks in 1999 for $129 million. The intellectual property originating with SixDegrees.com was licensed by LinkedIn.com for their current business networking website. Justin attended University of Colorado at Boulder, where he studied aerospace engineering.

Justin's comments appear at the end of the "Storage and Retention of User-Generated Content" section in Chapter 5.

Ray Harris, President & Chief Executive Officer, WebCast Group

Ray Harris is the vice president of sales and marketing and CEO of the Webcast Group, Incorporated. He is a leading technologist in the fields of video compression and video networking as well as a marketing person who understands the mechanics of sales channels and the importance of branding.

Mr. Harris has been involved in digital compression technology since 1992 when he was the President of Optibase, Inc. While at Optibase, he was responsible for developing the world's first commercially available MPEG1 encoder, the first MPEG digital ad insertion decoder for CATV, and one of the first MPEG 2 DVD encoders. He was instrumental in the growth and success that led to Optibase going public.

Prior to Optibase, Mr. Harris was under exclusive contract with NTT Electronics, where he consulted on technology including MPEG2 over ATM, MPEG2 multicasting, MPEG4, and home DVD recording systems.

Ray's comments appear at the end of the "Online Webinars and Collaboration Tools" section in Chapter 5.

Gus Harsfai, President and CEO, Ceryx

Gus Harsfai is one of the leading experts on Microsoft Exchange in North America and has provided messaging expertise and counsel to Fortune 500 companies for over 20 years. Gus founded the company that eventually became Ceryx (`www.ceryx.com`) in 1990 and oversaw messaging deployments and migrations for the government of Canada, Unilever, Baker and McKenzie, Pharma Plus,

Magna Entertainment, Yellow Pages, and other companies throughout Canada, the United States, and South America.

Gus's efforts earned the company the distinction of being the primary source for email-related services throughout the Fortune 500 community. He is regularly quoted in the media on topics related to messaging, Microsoft Exchange, and Ceryx's effective approach to spam management and messaging security.

Gus's comments appear at the end of the "Spam" section in Chapter 4.

Christopher Hart, CISSP, Chief Information Security Officer (CISO), Life Technologies

Chris Hart is currently the CISO for Life Technologies, a global leader in biotechnology tools and genetic technology development. Along with responsibility for information security, Chris also leads the Compliance organization as well as the Disaster Recovery program. He brings more than 15 years of information security, compliance, and risk management experience to the table.

Prior to Life Technologies, Chris held the position of CISO with the Invitrogen Corporation, which became Life Technologies after acquiring Applied Biosystems in 2008. During this time, Chris lead the integration of the Information Security and Compliance programs of these two multibillion-dollar corporations in only 10 months.

From 2000 to 2006, Chris was the CISO of Hughes Network Systems, which later became Hughes Communications. Hughes is a global leader in the satellite communications space.

Prior to 2000, Chris co-founded a consulting and training company called Boson Communications, where he was the principal for information security consulting. Boson provided a broad spectrum of IT services but focused on information security, risk management, and technology training. While the company no longer offers the consulting practice, it was re-incorporated into Boson Software, LLC in 1999 and is a leader in the technical training and testing space. (www.boson.com)

Chris's comments appear at the end of the "The Impact on Journalism" and "The Social Engineer" sections in Chapter 2, and after the "Mobility Threats" section of Chapter 4.

Rick Howard, Director of Intelligence, iDefense, a business unit of Verisign

Rick Howard is responsible for the day-to-day intelligence-gathering and distribution efforts at iDefense and is charged with developing strategic and tactical plans for the department. He is an experienced computer security professional with proven success in the use of network intelligence for network defense. Prior to joining iDefense, Rick led the intelligence gathering activities at Counterpane Internet Security and ran Counterpane's global network of Security Operations

Centers. He served in the U.S. Army for 23 years in various command and staff positions involving information technology and computer security. He retired as a lieutenant colonel in 2004. He spent the last 2 years of his career as the U.S. Army's Computer Emergency Response Team (ACERT) chief, where he coordinated network defense, network intelligence, and network attack operations for the Army's global network. Mr. Howard holds a master of computer science degree from the Naval Postgraduate School and an engineering degree from the U.S. Military Academy, where he also taught computer science later in his military career. He has published many academic papers on technology and security and most recently contributed as an executive editor to the first book published by Verisign/iDefense: *Cyber Fraud: Tactics, Techniques and Procedures.*

Rick's comments appear at the end of the "World Events" section in Chapter 2, and at the end of the introductory section in Chapter 5.

Mike Hrabik, President and Chief Technology Officer, Solutionary, Inc.

Mike Hrabik, a founding partner and chief technology officer of Solutionary, is the principal architect for Solutionary's patented ActiveGuard software and Security Operations Centers (SOCs). He is charged with establishing strategy and direction for the company's IT functions, and is the corporate advocate for information security and business continuance best practices. He is also responsible for outlining the company's technology vision, including technological planning, strategic initiatives, development, and future growth.

Mike has more than 25 years of high-level experience in technology services organizations, where diversity and complexity require the integration of people, process, and technology. Prior to joining Solutionary, Mike was a partner at ITI Marketing Services, Inc., where he served as director of systems and operations.

After his tenure at ITI, Mike served as the vice president of technology for NetCount Price Waterhouse, LLC, a Los Angeles-based third-party web-measurement and analysis company. Following NetCount's sale, Mike spent 2 years consulting with multiple companies in the Internet and wireless fields.

Mike is a member at large of the Omaha Chapter of the FBI's InfraGard program, regularly speaks at influential industry events and is frequently quoted in the media as a security expert. He received his BS in Computer Science from the University of Nebraska at Omaha.

Mike's comments appear at the end of the "Advanced Persistent Threat in 2020" section in Chapter 3.

Mark Iwanowski, Managing Director, Trident Capital

Mark Iwanowski joined Trident Capital in 2005 as a Venture Partner and will be a managing director in Fund VII, focusing primarily on CleanTech and Business Process Outsourcing. Mark has 25 years of experience successfully leading multiple global businesses in the high-tech industry for both commercial and government customers. Mark was most recently senior vice president global IT for Oracle Corporation. Prior to Oracle, Mark managed a systems integration, ASP, and outsourcing business for SAIC.

Mark was previously president of the R&D Division of Quantum Magnetics, an industry leader in explosive and illegal drug detection technology. Mark has also held executive positions with Raytheon and Honeywell.

Early in his career, Mark worked for Bechtel, involved in project engineering of large-scale power plants, and while working at the Jet Propulsion Lab was involved in various solar energy R&D projects for both terrestrial and space applications. Mark was also involved in pioneering use of high-energy fuel cell and energy storage systems used in long-range underwater systems at his first start up company, Applied Remote Technology.

Mark currently serves on the board of directors of several Trident portfolio companies, including Neohapsis, MegaPath Networks, RoyaltyShare, and Xunlight. He also serves on the board of advisors for TriCipher and formerly served on the board of advisors of Webify (acquired by IBM). He is also on the board of advisors of LignUp and MaxSP.

Mark holds a BS in engineering/business from the University of Pennsylvania, a master's degree in engineering from California Institute of Technology, and an MBA from National University. Mark has received multiple management excellence awards throughout his career.

Mark's comments appear at the end of the "The Impact of Virtualization" section in Chapter 3.

Mark Kaish, SVP Technology Operations, Cox Communications

Mark Kaish is the senior vice president of technology operations for Cox Communications. He is responsible for the lifecycle support of all Cox products, national voice and data networks, internal and customer-facing applications, billing operations, information security, and PC and LAN support. He also leads improvement and cost reduction initiatives in support of field IT and network groups.

Prior to being promoted to his current position, he was the vice president of voice development and support. In that role, he provided leadership for the future development, deployment, and support of Cox Digital Telephone initiatives. He worked with engineering, marketing, and operations to oversee the company's overall voice strategy and the integration of voice product features across all Cox products.

Prior to joining Cox, Kaish served as vice president of next generation solutions for BellSouth Corp. Previously, he served as executive vice president of hosting services and sales support for Savvis Communications.

Kaish holds bachelor's degrees in economics and public policy studies from Duke University and an MBA from the University of Virginia. Before entering the communications industry, Kaish served four years as a supply officer in the U.S. Navy.

Mark's comments appear at the end of the "Voice over IP" section in Chapter 5.

Rob Kraus, Senior Security Consultant, Solutionary

Rob Kraus is a senior security consultant for Solutionary, Inc. Rob, a Certified Information Systems Security Professional (CISSP), is responsible for organizing customer requirements, on-site project management, and client support, while ensuring quality and timeliness of Solutionary's products and services.

Rob was previously a remote security services supervisor with Digital Defense, Inc., where he performed offensive-based security assessments consisting of penetration testing, vulnerability assessment, social engineering, wireless and VoIP penetration testing, web application penetration tests, and vulnerability research. As a supervisor, Rob was also responsible for leading and managing a team of penetration testers who performed assessment services for Digital Defense's customers.

Rob's background also includes contracting as a security analyst for AT&T during the early stages of the AT&T U-verse service as well as provisioning, optimizing, and testing OC-192 fiber-optic networks while employed with Nortel Networks.

Rob speaks at information security conferences and universities in an effort to keep the information security community informed of current security trends and attack methodologies.

Rob's comments appear at the end of the "Star Wars" section in Chapter 4.

Maria Lewis Kussmaul, Co-Founder and Partner, America's Growth Capital

Maria is a co-founder and partner in the investment banking group at America's Growth Capital, focusing on the IT security, data center and communications sectors. Prior to AGC, Maria was co-founder and general and venture partner of Castile Ventures—a seed and early-stage venture capital firm. Maria's Wall Street career spanned three firms: Smith Barney, Shearson Lehman, and Cowen & Co. At Cowen & Co., Maria served as Global Head of Data Networks & Internet Investment Banking Activities. Previously, Maria was named to the Institutional Investor All-American Research Team for 13 consecutive years. Maria is a Chartered Financial Analyst. She received her B.A. in Economics from Rutgers University, and her M.B.A. from the Wharton School of Business.

Maria's comments appear in at the end of the "Consolidation of the IT Security Industry" section in Chapter 7.

Mark D. McLaughlin, President and CEO, VeriSign

Mark D. McLaughlin has served as president and chief executive officer, and as a director of VeriSign since August 2009. Prior to being named CEO in August 2009, McLaughlin served as president and chief operating officer from January

2009 to August 2009. Previously, Mr. McLaughlin held a number of key positions at VeriSign from 2000 to 2007, including serving as executive vice president of products and marketing. Mr. McLaughlin's other contributions include having run the company's Naming Services business, where he led the successful negotiation of the current agreements for the management of the .com and .net registries. Before leading the Naming Services business, he served as vice president of corporate business development, as well as general manager of the VeriSign Payment Services business.

Prior to VeriSign, Mr. McLaughlin was the vice president of sales and business development for Signio, a leading Internet payment company, and was instrumental in the negotiation and acquisition of Signio by VeriSign in 1999. Before joining Signio, Mr. McLaughlin was the vice president of business development for Gemplus, the world's leading smart-card company. And prior to Gemplus, he also served as general counsel of Caere Corporation and practiced law as an attorney with Cooley Godward Kronish LLP.

Mr. McLaughlin received his JD degree, magna cum laude, from Seattle University School of Law and his BS degree from the United States Military Academy at West Point. Mr. McLaughlin served as an attack helicopter pilot in the U.S. Army and earned an Army Commendation Medal and Airborne Wings.

Mark's comments appear at the end of the "Consolidation of the IT Security Industry" section in Chapter 7.

Nick Mehta, Chief Executive Office (CEO), LiveOffice

As CEO, Nick Mehta's focus is on continuing to grow LiveOffice's market leadership in the software-as-a-service messaging industry. Serving in senior operating roles for public and private companies in the enterprise and consumer technology markets for much of his career, Nick has built a well-respected reputation in the email and messaging industry. He spent more than 5 years at Symantec Corporation and Veritas Software Corporation (acquired by Symantec in 2005), where he served as vice president and general manager of the Enterprise Vault (formerly KVS) information archiving and discovery software business from its acquisition in 2004 until 2007. During this time, the business grew from $23 million in annual sales in 2004 to more than $200 million in 2007 and received recognition from ESG, Gartner, Forrester, IDC, and Radicati as being the leading product in the "on-premise" email archiving market. Nick has also held other roles leading product management for all email-related businesses at Symantec and previously for CommandCentral, a suite of storage management solutions.

Prior to Veritas, Nick ran product management at XDegrees, a venture-funded storage software startup which was acquired by Microsoft. Before that, Nick co-founded his first business during college in the mid-1990s, a venture-funded online golf retailer called Chipshot.com that became one of the top 20 online retailers of its time. Most recently, Nick served as an entrepreneur-in-residence at venture capital firm Trinity Ventures.

Nick holds a bachelor's degree in biochemical sciences and a master's degree in computer science from Harvard University.

Nick's comments appear at the end of the "Storage and Retention of User-Generated Content" section in Chapter 5.

David Meizlik, Director of Product Marketing and Communications, Websense

David Meizlik is the director of product marketing and communications at Websense. He oversees product marketing for all Websense products, including Websense TRITON, Web security, data security, and email security solutions, as well as corporate marketing communications. Meizlik joined Websense in early 2005 and has had responsibilities covering channel marketing, emerging business opportunities, product marketing, and marketing communications. He is responsible for leading product marketing, go-to-market strategy, and outbound marketing for Websense content security solutions.

Meizlik has a master's degree in communication management from the University of Southern California and a bachelor of science in business administration from the Marshall School of Business.

David's comments appear at the end of the "Breach Impact on Public Companies" section in Chapter 2, and after the "Security: an Industry or a Feature of IT?" section of Chapter 7.

Richard P. Nespola, Chairman of the Board & CEO, TMNG

Richard P. Nespola is the founder, chairman, and CEO of The Management Network Group, Inc., the leading provider of strategy, management, operational, and technology consulting services to the global telecommunications, media, and entertainment industries. TMNG Global and its operating divisions, Cambridge Strategic Management Group (CSMG) and Cartesian, have performed services for more than 1200 clients worldwide. With some 600 consultants, the firm is headquartered in Overland Park, Kansas, and has offices in Boston, Chicago, London, New Jersey, New York, Shanghai, and Washington, DC.

During Rich's diversified career in telecommunications, he has acquired extensive experience in developing strategic and tactical plans across a broad range of areas. He has spearheaded assignments and assisted clients with their transformation to new business models, infrastructure, and the processes and systems required to meet the needs of a dynamic marketplace.

TMNG Global worked with a partner to develop an advanced Wireless Technology Lab in San Diego, California—the first of its kind in the nation, providing a vendor- and technology-neutral environment for the testing and showcasing of emerging advanced wireless technologies, infrastructure, applications, and operations.

Prior to founding The Management Network Group in 1990, Rich held executive positions with MCI and Sprint. Rich serves on several corporate boards, is a member of the Executive Council of the International Engineering Consortium, and was named by *Phone+* magazine in 1997 and in 1998 as one of the indus-try's 25 most influential people. He received the Ernst & Young Entrepreneur of the Year Master Award, making him a national finalist and winner of the midwestern region award. Rich previously served as a director and chairman of the Association of Telecommunications Financial Managers.

Rich also served as co-chairman of the Kansas City New Economy Council and as director of the Technology Advisory Board of United Missouri Bank. In addition, he was part of the adjunct faculty in the College of Management, of Long Island University. He is currently a trustee of Long Island University, the sixteenth largest private university in America. Rich received a BA and an MBA from Long Island University.

He is the recipient of the Distinguished Alumnus Award and also received the President's Volunteer Service Award for civic participation from President Bush. Rich has been published in various industry journals, has made pre-sentations at numerous industry forums, and is often quoted by the press on industry trends.

Rich's comments appear at the end of the "Budgets and Prioritizations" section in Chapter 7.

Steve O'Brien, Senior Vice President, Managed Messaging Services, USA.NET

As vice president of managed messaging services at USA.NET, Steve O'Brien is responsible for the strategy, development, and execution of the company's suite of on-demand services. Prior to this role, O'Brien spent 6 years as the senior director of operations responsible for all operational aspects of USA .NET-hosted exchange, network infrastructure, and security. Prior to USA.NET, O'Brien worked at Qwest Communications where he served as senior manager of production services, senior manager of distributed computing, and manager of enterprise services support team. O'Brien is an active member of Microsoft's Technology Adoption Program (TAP); holds Microsoft, Cisco, and CheckPoint certifications; and has over 15 years of experience managing and architecting large scale information technology solutions.

Steve's comments appear at the end of the "UCC and UCC Compliance Requirements over the Next Decade" section in Chapter 5.

Michael Rasmussen, J.D., OCEG Fellow, CCEP, Risk & Compliance Lecturer, Writer, & Advisor

Michael Rasmussen is the authority in understanding governance, risk, and compliance (GRC) processes. He is a sought-after keynote speaker, author, and advisor on risk and compliance issues around the world and is noted for being the first analyst to define and model the GRC market for professional services and technology.

With more than 15 years of experience, Michael's objective is to assist organizations in defining GRC processes that are efficient, agile, effective, accountable, and transparent.

A leader in understanding risk and compliance standards, frameworks, regulations, and legislation, Michael aims to improve corporate integrity through advancing GRC initiatives. He has served in leading roles in public policy contributions to U.S. Congressional reports and committees, and currently serves on the Leadership Council and Steering Committee of the Open Compliance and Ethics Group. Michael has been quoted extensively in the press and is respected for his commentary on broadcast news channels.

In June 2007, Treasury & Risk recognized Michael as one of the 100 most influential people in finance with specific accolades noting his work in "Governance and Compliance: Saving the Planet and the Corporation." Most recently, in October 2008, he was recognized as a "Rising Star in Rocky Times: Corporate America's Outstanding Executives Under the Age of 40."

During his career, Michael has worked in the market analyst, consulting, and enterprise sectors. Prior to founding Corporate Integrity, Michael was a vice president and "top analyst" at Forrester Research, Inc. Before Forrester, he led the risk consulting practice at a professional services firm in the Midwest. Earlier, his career included industry experience in healthcare as well as manufacturing.

Michael's educational experience consists of a juris doctorate from the Oakbrook College of Law & Government Policy and a bachelor of science degree in business from the University of Phoenix. Michael is currently in the master of divinity program at Trinity Evangelical Divinity School.

Michael's comments appear at the end of the "GRC" section in Chapter 2.

Chris Richter, CISM, CISSP, Vice President and General Manager of Security Products and Services, Savvis

Chris Richter is VP and general manager of security products and services at Savvis, a leading cloud hosting, network, and security services provider, where he is responsible for the managed-security line of business, engineering, strategy, and product portfolio. Chris has assisted many enterprises in adapting their premise-based infrastructure risk management programs and security controls to Savvis's outsourced virtualized and shared-infrastructure services. As a Savvis representative to the PCI Security Standards Council, Chris is a contributor to the organization's Special Interest Group for Virtualization and Cloud Computing. Chris is a member of ISSA and ISACA, and for more than 20 years has held various security and IT services management and consulting positions at companies such as Digital Equipment Corporation, Compaq Global Services, 3Com, Cable & Wireless, and Sterling Software. He is a Certified Information

Systems Security Professional (CISSP) and a Certified Information Security Manager (CISM), and has served as a technical advisor and board member of several Silicon Valley-based IT product and services companies.

Chris's comments appear at the end of the "SaaS and Cloud Computing" section in Chapter 6.

Frank J. Ricotta Jr., Chief Technology Officer, Enterprise Information Management, Inc.

Frank J. Ricotta brings over 26 years of experience as EIM's CTO, a startup CEO, strategic consultant, IT executive, and engineer. Mr. Ricotta is recognized as one of the industry's leading experts on advanced applications and information technologies. Throughout his career, he has led re-engineering efforts focusing on using advanced technologies to achieve a competitive position in the marketplace. These projects, international in scope, focus both on critical cost-saving strategies and on building corporate revenues.

Prior to becoming the CTO for EIM, Inc., Mr. Ricotta founded and ran several companies including Innerwall, Inc., a cyber-security software and services company, and Noochee Solutions, a software company focused on developing next-generation telecommunication operational support systems. Prior to Noochee, Mr. Ricotta was the managing partner of the DMW Group, LLC, an international network consultancy. Mr. Ricotta began his career in the United States Air Force where he served as an officer.

Mr. Ricotta is the coauthor of *Computing Strategies for Re-Engineering Your Organization*, published by Prima in December 1993, as well as numerous articles appearing in technical and management journals.

He also holds several patents: Computational System for Operating on Externally-Defined Data Based on Client Defined Rules, and patents pending for Systems and Methods for Enterprise Security with Collaborative Peer to Peer Architecture; System and Method of Non-Centralized Zero Knowledge Authentication a Computer Network; Zero-touch Enterprise Access (ZEAP); and Virtual Security Fences.

Frank holds an MBA in International Finance from St Mary's University and a BS in Computer Science from the United States Air Force Academy.

Frank's comments appear at the end of the "The Impact of Politics" section in Chapter 2, and after the "Internet Protocol in 2020" section of Chapter 3.

Zachary Scott, Chief Executive Officer (CEO) of Ironlike Security Consulting

With 10+ years experience in the information technology sales and consulting space, Zachary Scott has become intensely passionate about helping organizations identify ways to manage risk, reduce costs, and increase revenue by aligning IT spending with strategic intent. Before founding Ironlike Security Consulting in 2010, Mr. Scott served in both principal consultant and executive leadership roles at some of the most prestigious specialized IT security firms including: director of North America channel sales at TriGeo Network Security, regional vice-president at Perimeter eSecurity, and director of sales for Red Cliff Solutions.

Zachary's comments appear at the end of the "The Emotions" section in Chapter 2, and after the "Doppelganger Attacks" section of Chapter 4.

John Shaw, Chief Operating Officer, VBrick Systems

John Shaw brings more than 25 years of experience building networking and software businesses. Prior to joining VBrick Systems, he was chief executive officer of Aptima, Inc., a major provider of predictive analytics and Web 2.0-related products and services. Previously, Mr. Shaw was with Cisco Systems for 7 years, where he held several senior marketing positions. He was a member of the leadership team that formulated and executed the company's voice over IP strategy, representing one of Cisco's fastest-growing product segments. Mr. Shaw joined Cisco via the 1998 acquisition of Summa Four, a leader in the programmable switching market, where he was vice president of marketing and business development. During Mr. Shaw's 7-year tenure, Summa Four's revenues grew fivefold and the company went public. He also spent 5 years with AT&T in several sales positions. Mr. Shaw holds a BA in Economics from Bowdoin College, and an MBA from Harvard Business School.

John's comments appear at the end of the "Video over IP" section in Chapter 5.

Eric Shepcaro, Chief Executive Officer and Director, Telx

Eric Shepcaro is responsible for leading and directing the strategy, growth, and operations of Telx. He joined the company with over 25 years of experience working in the network/IT industries in both public and startup companies. Most recently he worked for AT&T, where he served as senior vice president of business development and emerging services and chaired AT&T's Emerging Technology Customer Board. He has also held executive positions at Netelligence Technologies, Digital Island, which was sold to Cable & Wireless, and Sprint. Shepcaro holds a bachelor's degree and an MBA. He is a frequent speaker at leading industry events and has published several papers.

Eric's comments appear at the end of the "Breach Impact on Public Companies" section in Chapter 2, and after the "The Purpose of IT" section of Chapter 7.

Scott Simpson, Director of Security Consulting, Solutionary

Scott Simpson is director of security consulting services at Solutionary, Inc. Scott holds Certified Information Systems Security Professional (CISSP), Certified Information Security Manager (CISM), and Qualified Security Assessor (QSA) certifications. He is responsible for staffing and leading engagements, organizing customer requirements, on-site project management, and client support, while ensuring the quality and timeliness of Solutionary's products and services. Scott has a broad range of security skills and specializes in delivering high impact consulting engagements to his clients.

As director, Scott is responsible for continuous improvement of service offerings and supporting client needs from pre-sales support through delivery. He is an active engagement leader across the breadth of Solutionary consulting services. In this role, Scott has been an integral part of several successful compliance submissions, negotiated with the card brands and acquiring banks, and helped clients define compensating controls sufficient to meet the intent of the standard. Additional engagement-led activities include establishing detailed work plans for large enterprise security assessments, application security assessments, internal and external penetration assessments, security architectural reviews, wireless security assessments, and more.

Scott has over 12 years of experience in IT security and has held positions with Sunera, LLC, KMPG, LLP., Networks, Inc., and Broadslate Networks, Inc.

Scott's comments appear at the end of the "Website Middleware Threats" section in Chapter 4.

C.J. Spallitta, Executive Director, Global Product Marketing Security Solutions, Verizon

With more than 20 years in the field of technology, 15 of those in IT security, C.J. Spallitta runs Verizon Business Security Solutions's Global Product Marketing team. C.J. joined Verizon Business in 2007 as the result of the acquisition of Cybertrust, where he also ran Global Product Management. He is responsible for the complete product lifecycle of all managed security services, identity management products and solutions, and Verizon Business's compliance programs.

Mr. Spallitta has extensive experience in security product management, product marketing, business development, and consulting, while working for companies such as GTE Internetworking, PricewaterhouseCoopers, USInternetworking, Security Assurance Group, and Cybertrust.

He holds an MBA and a BBA in Business Administration and Information Systems from Loyola University Maryland.

C. J.'s comments appear at the end of the "The Path to 2020" section in Chapter 2, and after the "The Network Edge" section of Chapter 3.

Paul Stich, Chief Executive Officer, Dasient

Paul Stitch is a successful senior executive with 25-plus years of experience building great teams, developing innovative strategic plans, and executing to deliver outstanding results. Paul has 10 years of CEO experience working directly with the leading VCs and Private Equity Funds, including Accel, Behrman Capital, Bessemer, Doll Capital Management, Foundation Capital, Meritech, Morgan Stanley, Oak Investment Partners, and Venrock.

Previously, Paul held positions such as president and CEO of Autonomic Networks, president and CEO of Counterpane Internet Security (Acquired by British Telecom), president and CEO of Peak XV Networks, president and CEO of Groundswell, vice president of IBM Global Services, and Partner of KPMG Consulting. Paul also has been a speaker at many industry/technology conferences, including Gartner, Fortune, RSA, Infosec, Supercomm, and CTIA.

He is also an outside director for Esoterix, a leading laboratory services company, which was acquired by Laboratory Corporation of America in 2005.

Paul's comments appear at the end of the "Hindsight is NOT 20/20" section in Chapter 1.

Dan Summa, Chief Executive Officer, Kindling

Dan Summa is president of Kindling, a powerful idea management and collaboration solution for both big and small enterprises. Kindling allows companies to produce and track ideas from all areas of their business and to capture innovative solutions from their employees.

Prior to running Kindling, Mr. Summa was at SECCAS, a financial compliance service company, which he joined in 2006 as president. At SECCAS, Mr. Summa focused on customer service, product enhancements, and operations. These efforts resulted in significant revenue and corresponding profit increases. SECCAS was acquired in January 2008 by Perimeter Internetworking Corporation, a Goldman Sachs–backed company.

Prior to joining SECCAS, Mr. Summa was a partner at Genesys Partners, Inc., a merchant bank and venture capital firm focused on making investments in early stage high-tech companies. In this capacity, Mr. Summa was responsible for all financial aspects of those companies, including negotiating and securing financing, devising and implementing restructuring strategies, and working with management to design, establish, and manage their finances, internal controls, corporate policies, and procedures.

Mr. Summa graduated from the Wharton School of the University of Pennsylvania with a Bachelor of Science degree in economics. He currently sits on the Children's Press Line board of directors.

Dan's comments appear at the end of the "Online Webinars and Collaboration Tools" section in Chapter 5.

Michael Svihra, Deputy Director, Information Technology Infrastructure and Operations (ITIO), U.S. Department of Human and Health Services

Michael Svihra has over 20 years of technical and executive management experience in the IT industry. He possesses a unique and diverse skill set in establishing, managing, and providing technical and programmatic support to federal, commercial, and global managed IT services programs. Prior to joining his active position within the Department of Human Services, Mr. Svihra held senior leadership positions with firms such as The World Bank, UUNet Technologies, and Unisys Corporation.

Michael's portfolio of practiced skills includes building, revitalizing, and optimizing organizational infrastructure, products and services, processes, security solutions, and technology design to deliver expected results and facilitate growth. Michael Svihra possesses a bachelor's degree from West Virginia Wesleyan and holds multiple advanced technical certifications.

Michael's comments appear at the end of the "The Social Engineer" section in Chapter 2.

Jim Tiller, Vice President Security North America, BT

Jim Tiller is a dynamic information security executive with over 17 years of experience in the industry working with companies around the world to develop and implement business-aligned security strategies enabling organizations to achieve their business goals. Jim is a published author producing three books and a contributing author to more than nine others, including the *Official (ISC) Guide to the CBK* and the last six editions of the *Information Security Management Handbook*. Jim has contributed a great deal to the industry through producing several security patents, supporting RFC development, contributing to security standards, and collaborating on new technology solutions. For more insights to Jim's activities, publications, and industry involvement, please visit `www.realsecurity.us/weblog`.

Jim's comments appear at the end of the "The Missing Deterrent" section in Chapter 6.

Rob Ward, Managing Director, Meritech Capital

Rob Ward was a founder of Meritech in 1999 and focuses on investment opportunities in enterprise infrastructure and software, digital media, and medical technology companies. He has been directly involved with previous Meritech investments such as Acopia, IntraLase, MarketAxess, and TopSpin, and he led the firm's successful investments in Acclarent, Counterpane, Fortinet, Netezza, NetSuite, Quigo, and Reliant.

Rob joined Meritech from Montgomery Securities where he was a principal in the Private Equity Group, raising late-stage capital for private information technology, financial services, and medical technology companies. Prior to joining Montgomery, Rob was with Smith Barney, where he spent 5 years in the Corporate Finance department in New York and San Francisco.

Rob received a BA degree from Williams College and a MS degree from the Massachusetts Institute of Technology, and currently serves as tutor at Eastside College Preparatory School in East Palo Alto, California.

Rob's comments appear at the end of the "Venture Capital and Investment into IT Security" section in Chapter 7.

Irida Xheneti, Security Product Marketing Manager, Novell

Irida Xheneti is the security product marketing manager at Novell where she is responsible for developing the security go-to-market and positioning strategy. Prior to Novell, Irida was an industry analyst at IDC, covering the security services market. In this role, Irida provided market insight and competitive analysis, as well as positioning and go-to-market advice on the security services space, including consulting services, implementation services, and managed security services. Prior to joining the IDC Security Services and Identity Management team, Irida was a research analyst for the Worldwide IT Markets group in IDC's Global Research Organization. Irida holds a bachelor of arts degree in international relations and French from Wellesley College.

Irida's comments appear at the end of the "The Impact of Virtualization" section in Chapter 3.

Eric Yeow, Co-Founder and Vice President, Firmus Security

Eric Yeow co-founded Firmus Security in 2008 after more than 10 years of experience working in the information security industry. Firmus Security is a leader in the provision of specialized security testing services and solutions to help companies secure their IT infrastructure against security breaches and attacks.

Prior to founding Firmus Security, Eric was the Business Director of e-Cop Malaysia during his tenure there from 2001 -2008 and was responsible for the development of new businesses and leading the sales force of the company. Under his sales leadership, e-Cop's dominance in the Malaysian MSS market was unassailable and e-Cop was recognized as the de-facto MSS market leader in information security circles.

Married with one child, Eric holds a Degree in Business Administration from The University of Tasmania, Australia.

Eric's comments appear at the end of the "Vulnerability Exploits" section in Chapter 4.

Amit Yoran, Chief Executive Officer, NetWitness

Amit Yoran has been serving as CEO of NetWitness since November of 2006. Prior to NetWitness, he was appointed as director of the US-CERT and National Cyber Security Division of the Department of Homeland Security, and as CEO and advisor to In-Q-Tel, the venture capital arm of the CIA. Formerly, Mr. Yoran served as the vice president of Worldwide Managed Security Services at the Symantec Corporation. Mr. Yoran was the co-founder of Riptech, a market leading IT security company, and served as its CEO until the company was acquired by Symantec in 2002. He served as an officer in the United States Air Force in the Department of Defense's Computer Emergency Response Team. Mr. Yoran serves as a commissioner on the CSIS Commission on Cyber Security for the 44th Presidency and numerous other industry advisory bodies.

Amit's comments appear at the end of the introductory section in Chapter 5.

Index

CPSIA information can be obtained at www.ICGtesting.com
Printed in the USA
BVOW062059260911

272181BV00003B/133-168/P